Brad Miser

QUE®
800 East 96th Street,
Indianapolis, Indiana 46240 USA

CONTENTS

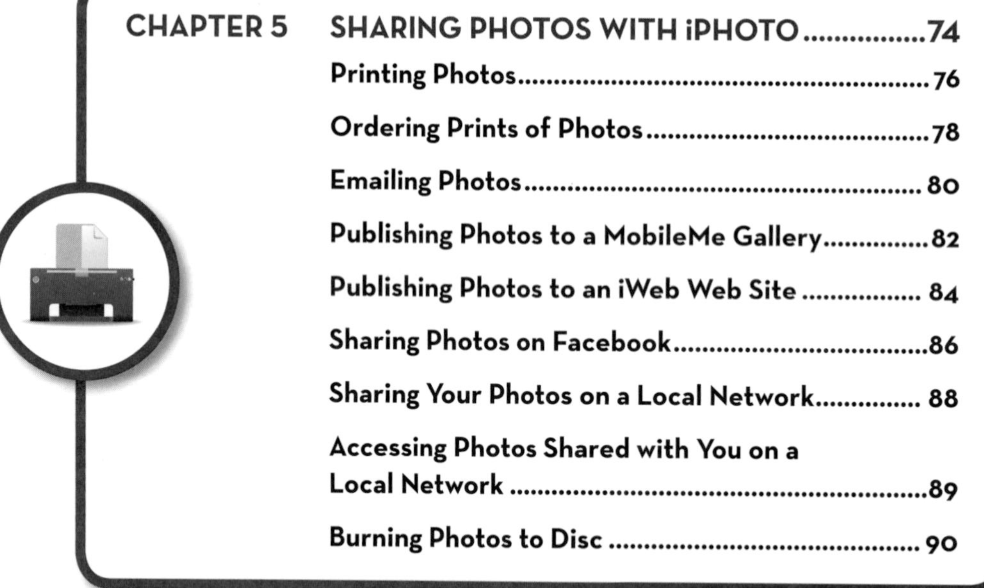

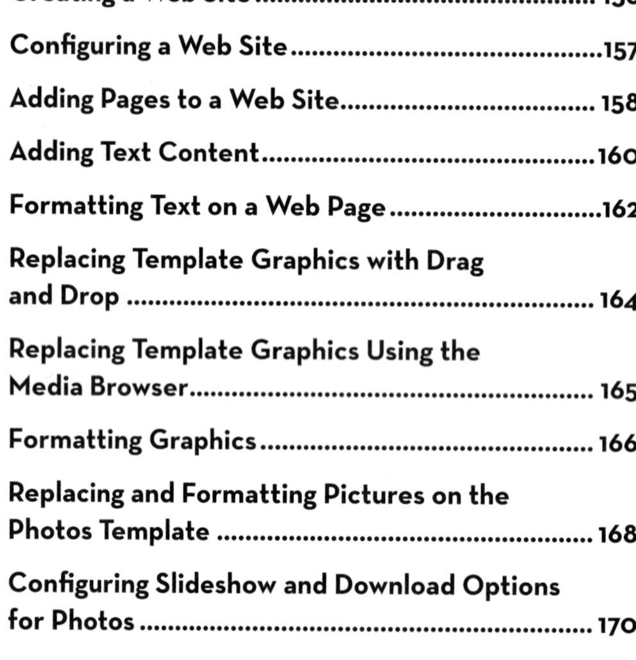

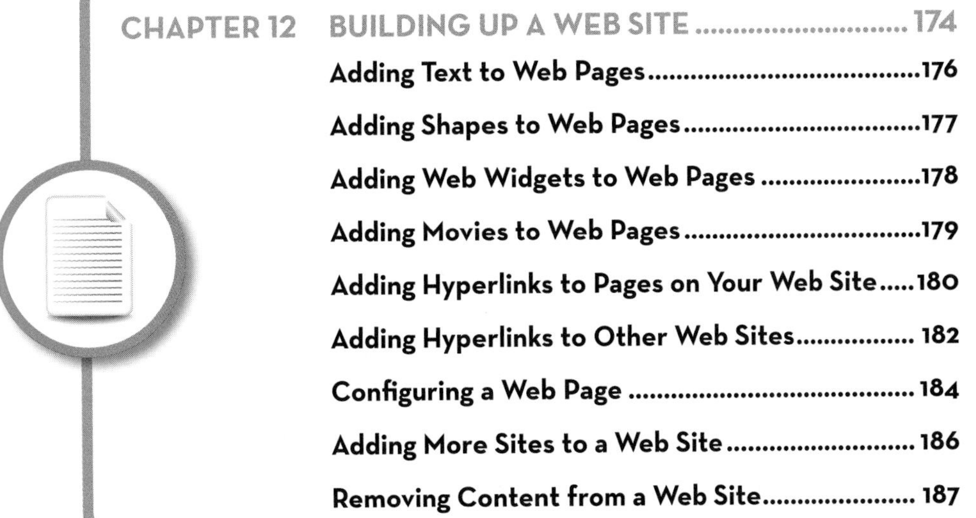

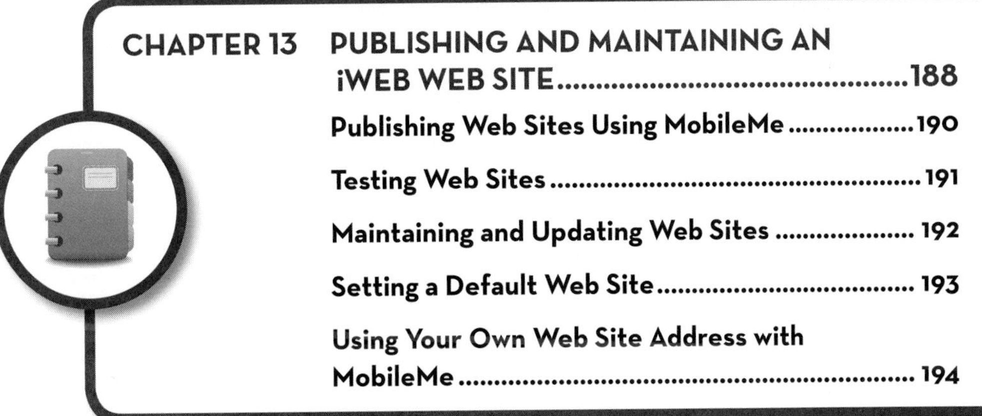

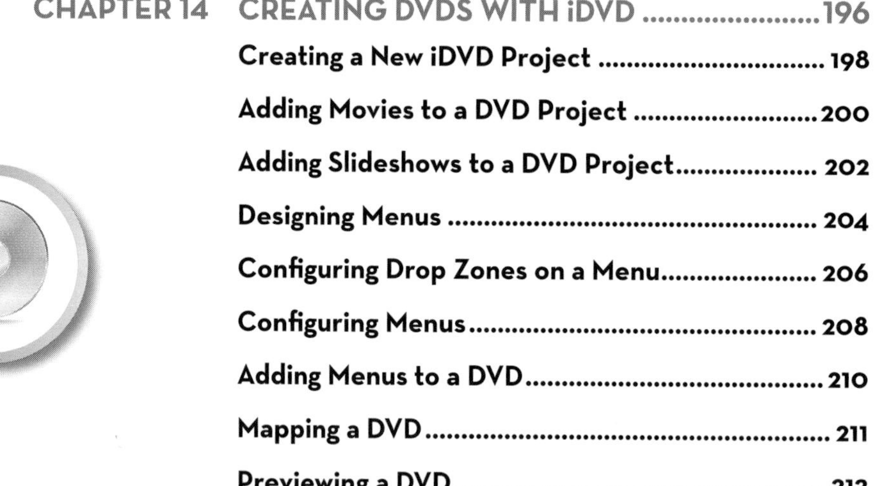

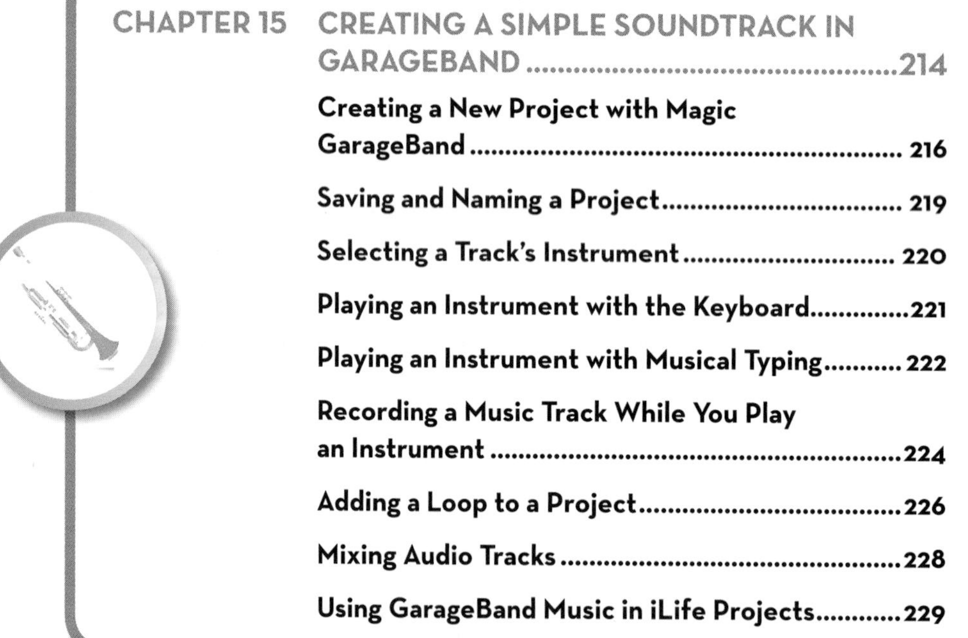

EASY iLIFE '09

ISBN-13: 978-0-7897-3978-0
ISBN-10: 0-7897-3978-X

Library of Congress Cataloging-in-Publication Data

Miser, Brad.
Easy iLife 09 / Brad Miser.
p. cm.
Includes index.
ISBN 978-0-7897-3975-9
1. Interactive multimedia. 2. iLife. 3. Macintosh (Computer) I. Title.
QA76.76.I59M586 2009
006.7--dc22
2009012019

Printed in the United States of America
First Printing: May 2009

TRADEMARKS

All terms mentioned in this book that are known to be trademarks or service marks have been appropriately capitalized. Que Publishing cannot attest to the accuracy of this information. Use of a term in this book should not be regarded as affecting the validity of any trademark or service mark.

WARNING AND DISCLAIMER

Every effort has been made to make this book as complete and as accurate as possible, but no warranty or fitness is implied. The information provided is on an "as is" basis. The author and the publisher shall have neither liability nor responsibility to any person or entity with respect to any loss or damages arising from the information contained in this book.

BULK SALES

Que Publishing offers excellent discounts on this book when ordered in quantity for bulk purchases or special sales. For more information, please contact

U.S. Corporate and Government Sales
1-800-382-3419
corpsales@pearsontechgroup.com

For sales outside of the U.S., please contact

International Sales
international@pearson.com

Associate Publisher
Greg Wiegand

Acquisitions Editor
Laura Norman

Development Editor
Todd Brakke

Managing Editor
Patrick Kanouse

Project Editor
Mandie Frank

Copy Editor
Keith Cline

Indexer
Tim Wright

Proofreader
Williams Woods Publishing

Technical Editor
Yvonne Johnson

Publishing Coordinator
Cindy Teeters

Designer
Anne Jones

Compositor
Bumpy Design

ABOUT THE AUTHOR

Brad Miser has written extensively about technology, with his favorite topics being anything whose name starts with i, such as iLife, iPhone, and iPod. In addition to *Easy iLife '09*, Brad has written more than 30 books, including *My iPhone*, *Absolute Beginner's Guide to iPod and iTunes*, *Special Edition Using Mac OS X Leopard*, *Teach Yourself Visually MacBook Air*, and *MacBook Pro Portable Genius*.

Brad is or has been a sales support specialist, the director of product and customer services, and the manager of education and support services for several software-development companies. Previously, he was the lead proposal specialist for an aircraft engine manufacturer, a development editor for a computer book publisher, and a civilian aviation test officer/engineer for the U.S. Army. Brad holds a bachelor of science degree in mechanical engineering from California Polytechnic State University at San Luis Obispo and has received advanced education in maintainability engineering, business, and other topics.

Brad would love to hear about your experiences with this book; you can write to him at bradmacosx@mac.com.

DEDICATION

To those who have given the last full measure of devotion so that the rest of us can be free.

ACKNOWLEDGMENTS

To the following people on the *Easy iLife '09* project team, my sincere appreciation for your hard work on this book:

Laura Norman, my acquisitions editor, who provided the opportunity for this book and brought it to fruition. Todd Brakke, my development editor, who helped guide the book to ensure that it would be useful to its readers. Mandie Frank, my project editor, who skillfully managed the hundreds of files that it took to make this book. Yvonne Johnson, my technical editor, who did a great job to ensure that the information in this book is both accurate and useful. Keith Cline, my copy editor, who corrected my many misspellings, poor grammar, and other problems. Marta Justak, my agent, for getting me signed up for this project. Que's production and sales team for printing the book and getting it into your hands

WE WANT TO HEAR FROM YOU!

As the reader of this book, you are our most important critic and commentator. We value your opinion and want to know what we're doing right, what we could do better, what areas you'd like to see us publish in, and any other words of wisdom you're willing to pass our way.

As an associate publisher for Que Publishing, I welcome your comments. You can email or write me directly to let me know what you did or didn't like about this book—as well as what we can do to make our books better.

Please note that I cannot help you with technical problems related to the topic of this book. We do have a User Services group, however, where I will forward specific technical questions related to the book.

When you write, please be sure to include this book's title and author as well as your name, email address, and phone number. I will carefully review your comments and share them with the author and editors who worked on the book.

Email: feedback@quepublishing.com

Mail: Greg Wiegand
Associate Publisher
Que Publishing
800 East 96th Street
Indianapolis, IN 46240 USA

READER SERVICES

Visit our Web site and register this book at www.informit.com/title/9780789739759 for convenient access to any updates, downloads, or errata that might be available for this book.

INTRODUCTION

The iLife suite might be one of the best things about having a Mac. It's called a suite because it includes the following applications:

- iPhoto
- iMovie
- iWeb
- iDVD
- GarageBand

Each of these applications empowers you to do amazing and creative things with digital photos, movies, and sound, and then you can publish what you create online and on DVD.

The iLife applications are great for several reasons. First, they are powerful and feature packed so that you have amazing toolkits available to you with almost no limits to what you can do. Second, they are well designed so that you can focus on your projects rather than the software. Third, they are designed to work together so that you can use the content in each application for projects in the other applications easily. For example, you can use photos in iPhoto or in iMovie projects or publish them in iWeb with just a couple of mouse clicks.

This book is designed to make your entry to the iLife, well, easy. (It's not hard to figure where we got the book's title, is it?) This book is designed to be as visually appealing and intuitive as the iLife software itself. As you flip through its pages, you will see lots of graphics and just a little text to guide you on your way. You will accomplish the tasks with a minimum of reading; steps are linked to the graphics to make it easy to follow along.

The book is organized into groups for each application. Within the groups, the chapters start at the beginning for that application and move toward the "end" in the same way you do projects. You can jump to any application's first chapter and get going without reading the chapters that came before (for example, move to Chapter 7 to get going with iMovie). You should definitely read Chapter 1 to get started because that chapter includes topics that apply to all the applications.

The best way to learn how to be creative with iLife is to use its applications to create your own projects. The steps in this book will get you going and help you combine your content and creativity with the amazing iLife tools with great results. So, grab your Mac, open this book where you want to start, and enjoy!

PREPARING iLIFE 09

iLife is an amazing suite of applications that enables you to do all sorts of amazing things. The suite consists of iPhoto, for working with digital photos and images; iMovie, for creating amazing movies; iWeb, which you can use to create and publish your own Web sites; iDVD, for building your own DVDs, complete with sophisticated menus and effects; and GarageBand, with which you can create and manage music and other audio.

In this chapter, you learn some key tasks that prepare the way for your use of iPhoto. This includes installing and updating iLife applications, obtaining and configuring a MobileMe account on your Mac, and protecting yourself against the loss of the great content you'll create with the iLife applications.

You'll see that this chapter is relatively short because you can quickly move through these tasks to get into the heart of the matter, using iLife applications for your own projects.

iPhoto

Store, organize, edit, and share your digital photos; then create amazing projects

iMovie

Make your own movie masterpieces with your video, music, audio, and other content

iWeb

Create and publish your own Web sites to show off the fruits of your iLife labors

iDVD

Put your iLife projects on custom DVDs so that you can enjoy them with a standard DVD player

GarageBand

Make your own music and mix audio for projects; it's an audio studio on your Mac

INSTALLING iLIFE 09

If you've purchased a Mac after January 2009, it already has iLife 09 installed, so you can move ahead to the next section. If you got your Mac before that, you need to install iLife 09 on your computer

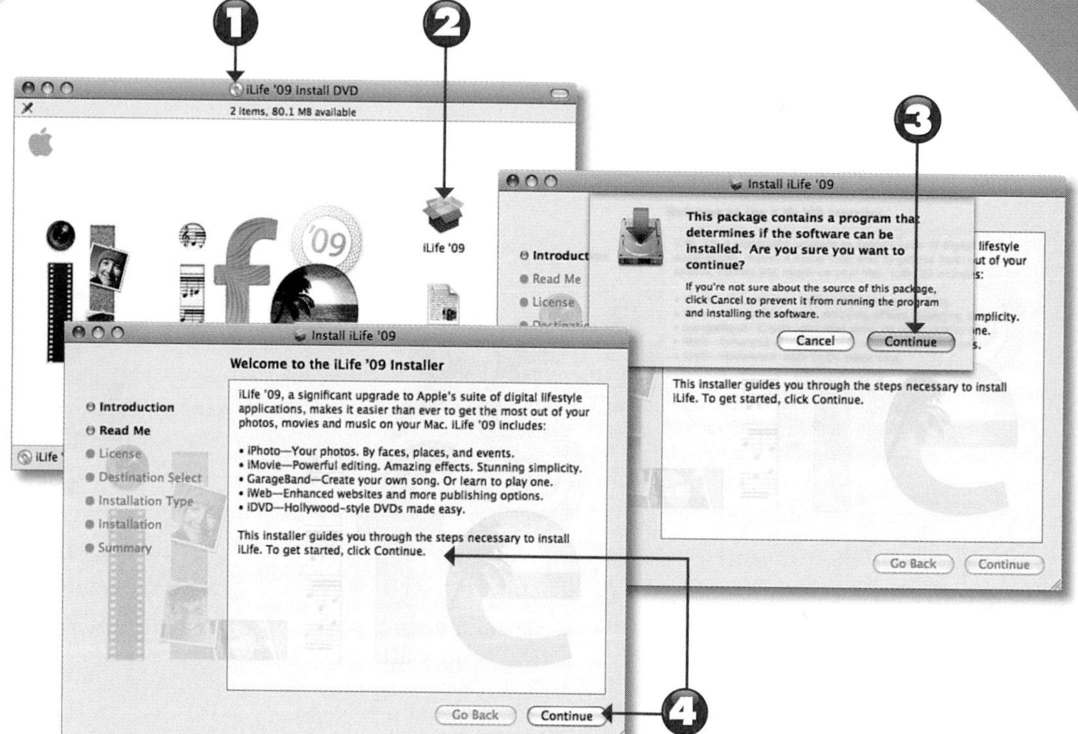

Start

1. Insert the iLife Installation disc into your Mac's drive.
2. Double-click the **iLife '09** installer.
3. Click **Continue**.
4. Follow the onscreen instructions to complete the installation.

End

NOTE

No DVD? If you are installing iLife on a Mac without an internal SuperDrive, iDVD might not install by default. To check this, when you get to the Standard Install screen, click the **Customize** button. Make sure the iDVD check box is checked. Check the check boxes for any of the other applications if they aren't checked either. Then click **Install**. ■

UPDATING iLIFE APPLICATIONS

Apple routinely updates the iLife applications to fix bugs or to introduce new capabilities. You should ensure that your iLife applications are current, and configure your Mac to keep them current automatically.

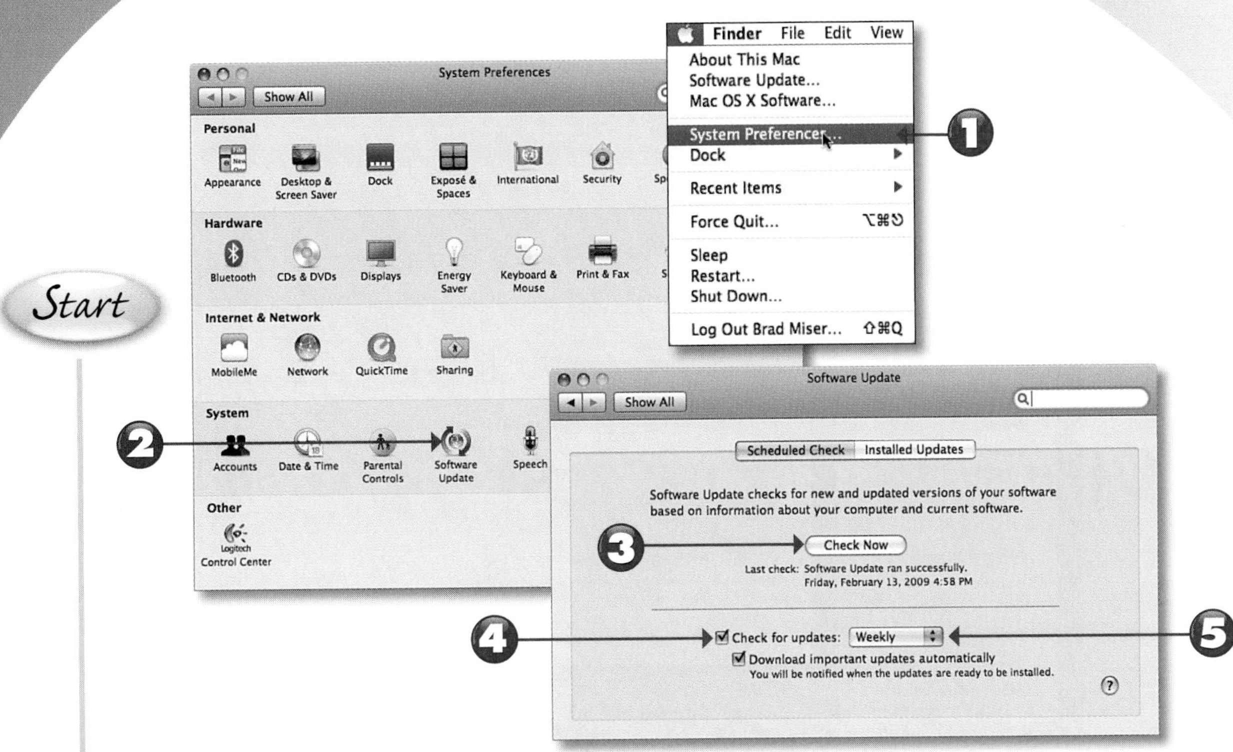

Start

1. Choose Apple menu, **System Preferences**.
2. Click the **Software Update** icon.
3. Click **Check Now**. If you are notified that updates are available, download and install them.
4. Enable the **Check for Updates** check box.
5. On the pop-up menu, choose **Weekly** or **Daily**.

End

NOTE

Keeping Current Your Mac checks for updates to all your Apple software, according to the frequency you set on the pop-up menu. ■

TIP

Download Automatically, Too If you check the **Download Important Updates Automatically** box, updates to Mac OS X and critical software are downloaded automatically. ■

OBTAINING AND CONFIGURING A MOBILEME ACCOUNT

MobileMe is a great partner for iLife because when you have a MobileMe account, you can easily share the results of your iLife work on the Web. In iPhoto, you can publish your photos to your Web gallery, where they can be viewed, downloaded, and enjoyed by anyone who visits your site. Using iWeb, you can create an entire Web site and then publish it using your MobileMe account with just a couple of mouse clicks. To prepare your MobileMe account, obtain it online and then configure its information in Mac OS X.

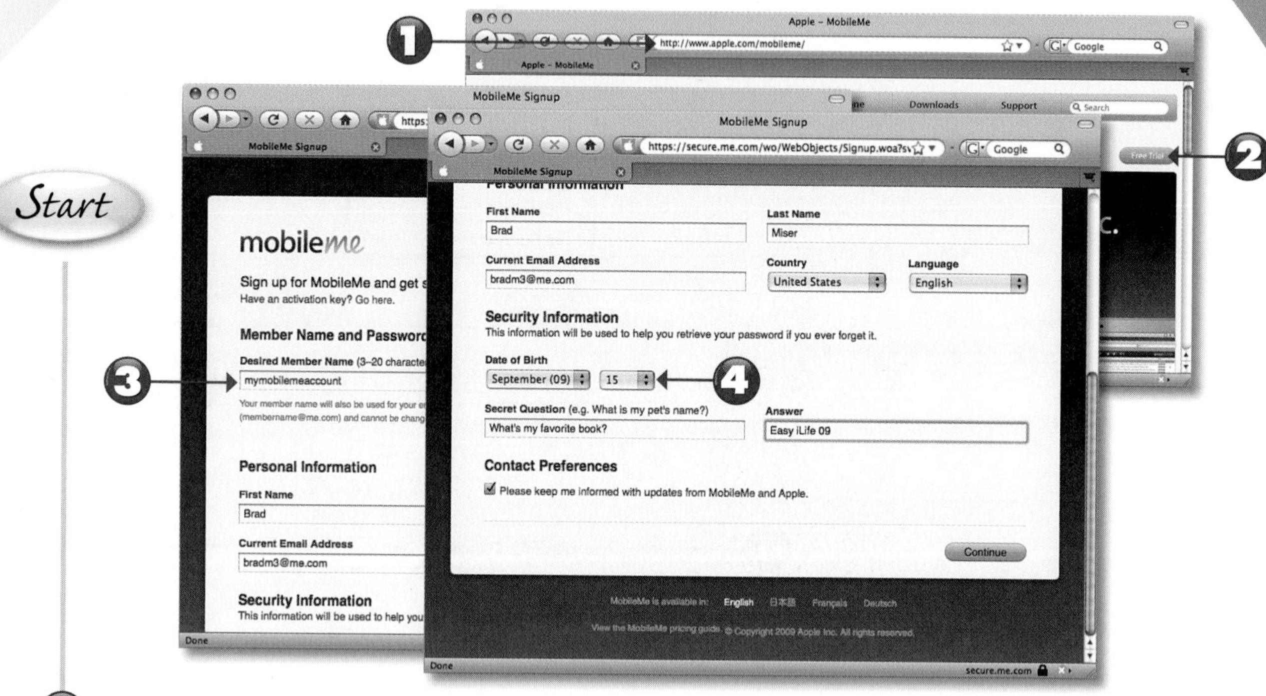

1. Use a Web browser to move to www.apple.com/mobileme/.

2. Click the **Free Trial** button.

3. Fill out the top part of the first page of the online form.

4. Complete the bottom part of the form and click **Continue**.

Continued

TIP

Member Names Are Important Be thoughtful about what you choose for your member name. This name is visible in several places, most notably your email address, which will be membername@me.com. ■

NOTE

Free for Now The free trial account is good for 60 days. After that time, the credit card you provide during the sign-up process is charged the $99 annual MobileMe fee. ■

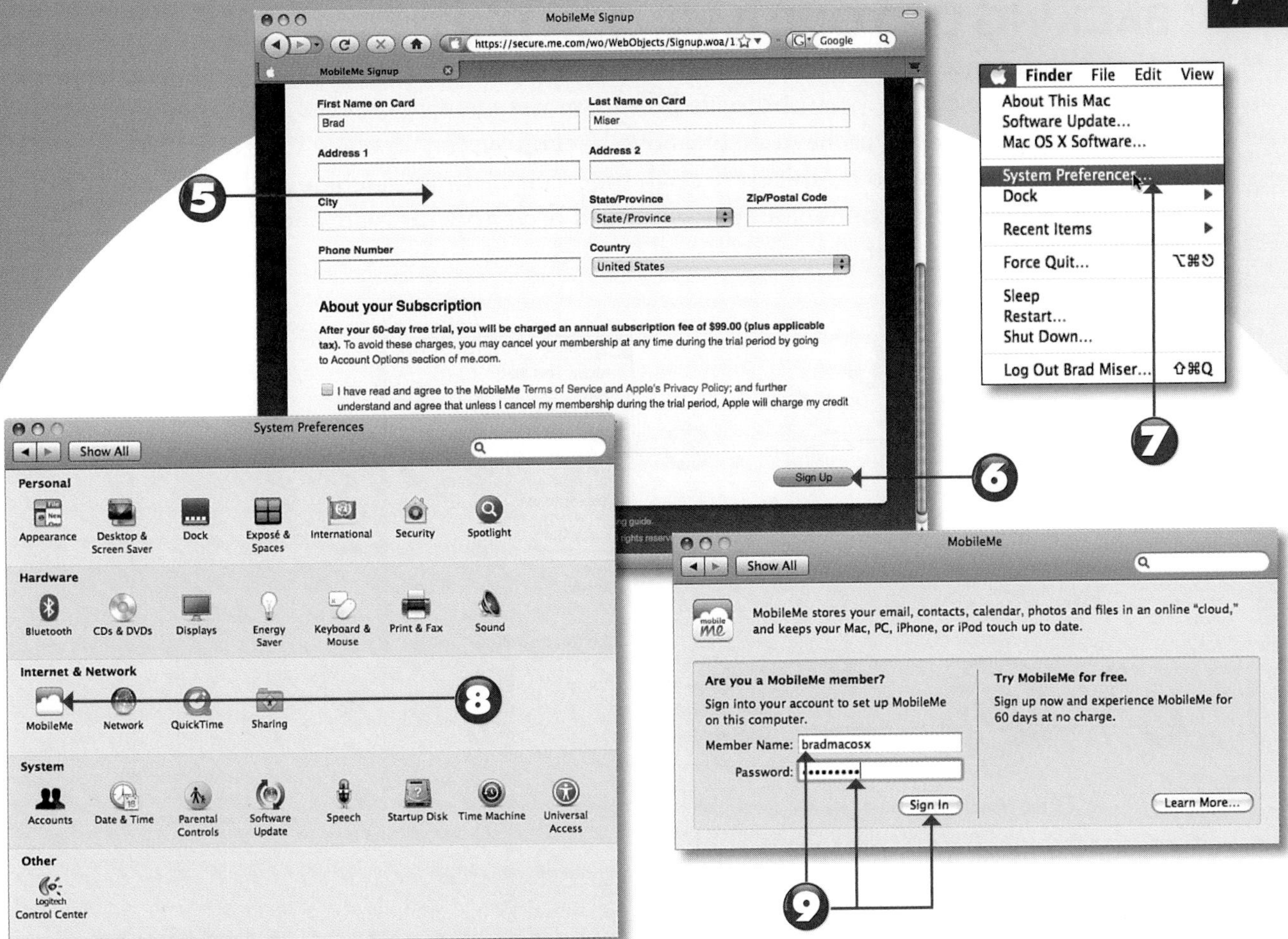

5. Complete the second page of the form.

6. Click **Sign Up**. Your account is created. You see your member name on the confirmation page.

7. Choose Apple menu, **System Preferences**.

8. Click the **MobileMe** icon.

9. Enter your member name and password, and then click **Sign In**.

End

NOTE

Only You Can Be You Your member name has to be unique. So if the first one you try isn't, you're prompted to try again. ■

NOTE

Share It You can also obtain a $150 Family Pack account that includes four additional MobileMe accounts. You can also upgrade your disk storage space with either type of account. ■

BACKING UP YOUR iLIFE CONTENT

Much of the content you create or use with iLife applications is literally irreplaceable at any price. This includes your photos in iPhoto, movies you've created in iMovie, and so on. You should make sure you have an effective backup system in place to protect this content. One of the best ways to do this is through Mac OS X's Time Machine feature. To use Time Machine, you need to connect an external hard drive to your Mac, and then configure Time Machine to back up to it.

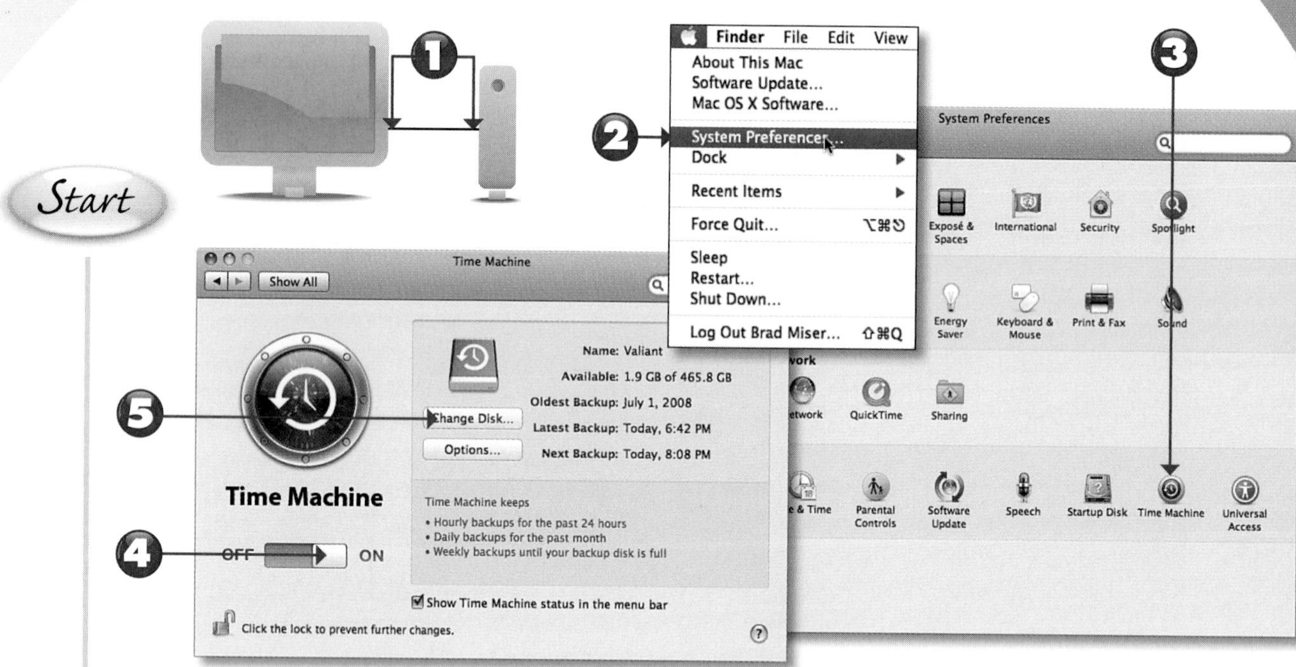

1. Connect a USB hard drive to your Mac.
2. Choose Apple menu, **System Preferences**.
3. Click the **Time Machine** icon.
4. Click **On**.
5. Click **Change Disk**.

Continued

NOTE

Automatic Backup Configuration When you connect an external hard drive to your Mac, you are prompted to configure Time Machine to use that drive as a backup. ■

NOTE

What Kind of Drive? You can use just about any kind of external USB hard drive as a backup drive. The most important factor is size of the drive. Get the largest drive you can afford. ■

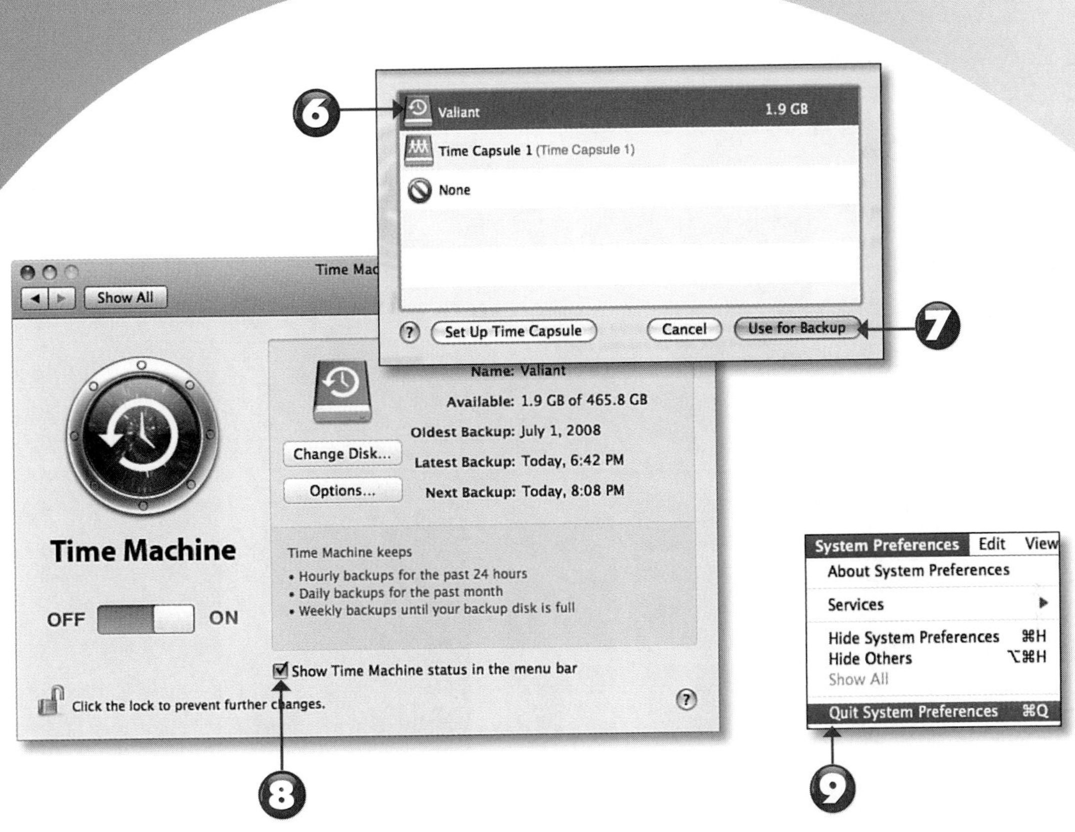

6 Select your backup disk.

7 Click **Use for Backup**.

8 Enable the **Show Time Machine Status in the Menu Bar** check box.

9 Choose **System Preferences**, **Quit**. Time Machine backs up your files onto the backup disk.

TIP

Take Up Less Room on Your Backup Disk To reduce the size of your backups so that you can back up files for a longer period of time, click the **Options** button, click the **Add** (+) button, choose files you don't need to back up (the System and Library folders are good choices), click **Exclude**, and click **Done**. ■

NOTE

Time Capsule Apple's Time Capsule is a useful device because it includes a hard drive along with an AirPort Extreme Base Station. This enables you to use Time Machine to back up wirelessly. ■

RESTORING YOUR iPHOTO PHOTOS

If the day arrives when you can't locate photos in your iPhoto Library, you'll be very glad you've taken my advice and backed up your photos using Time Machine, because recovering your photos is a snap.

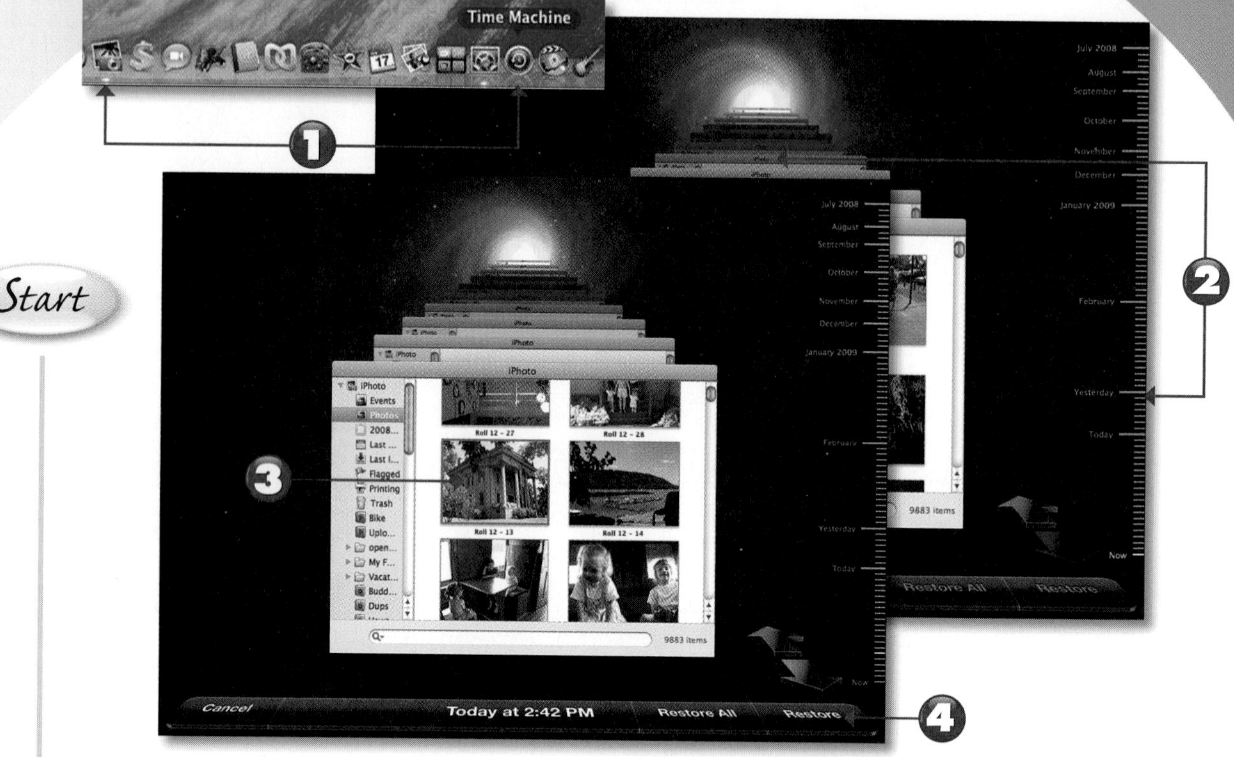

1. Open iPhoto and then click **Time Machine** from the Dock.
2. Click the windows "back in time" or click the timeline on the right side of the screen until you see the missing photos in your iPhoto library.
3. Select the photos you want to restore.
4. Click **Restore**. The photos are restored to their previous locations.

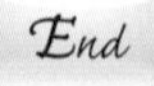

NOTE

Restore from Applications Currently, iPhoto is the only iLife application from which you can restore photos from within the application. ■

NOTE

What's This iPhoto You'll learn about iPhoto in Chapters 2 through 6. ■

RESTORING OTHER iLIFE CONTENT

Time Machine backs up your files, even those that aren't in iPhoto. So, if you find some content you've created, such as a movie, missing from your desktop, you can recover the missing files by going back in time to a point where the missing files still existed.

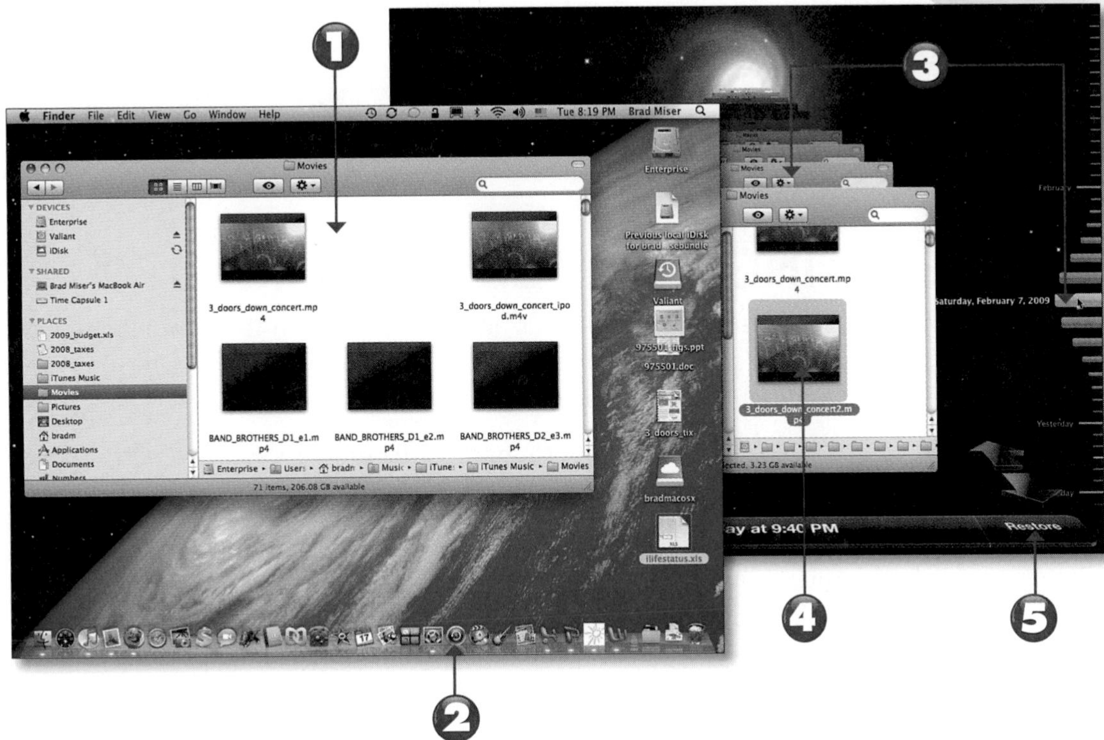

Start

1. Open a Finder window showing the location where the missing file was.
2. Click the **Time Machine** icon.
3. Click the Finder windows "back in time" or click the timeline on the right side of the screen until you see the missing files.
4. Select the missing file.
5. Click **Restore**. The file is restored to its previous location.

End

NOTE

No Backup Lasts Forever When your backup hard drive gets full, Time Machine automatically removes the oldest files from the backup to make more room on the drive. Therefore, you should also save important files in another format, such as on DVD, to create an archive that you keep forever. ■

GETTING STARTED WITH iPHOTO

iPhoto is the iLife application that's all about digital photos. You can use this great application to store, organize, and view your photos. This alone is valuable, but that's where iPhoto is just getting started.

You can use your photos to create many different kinds of projects. These include Web pages, Facebook photo albums, greeting cards, calendars, photo books, well, you get the idea.

In this chapter, you learn the core tasks that get you started down the iPhoto road. These include adding photos to your iPhoto library, viewing photos and slideshows, and getting information about your photos.

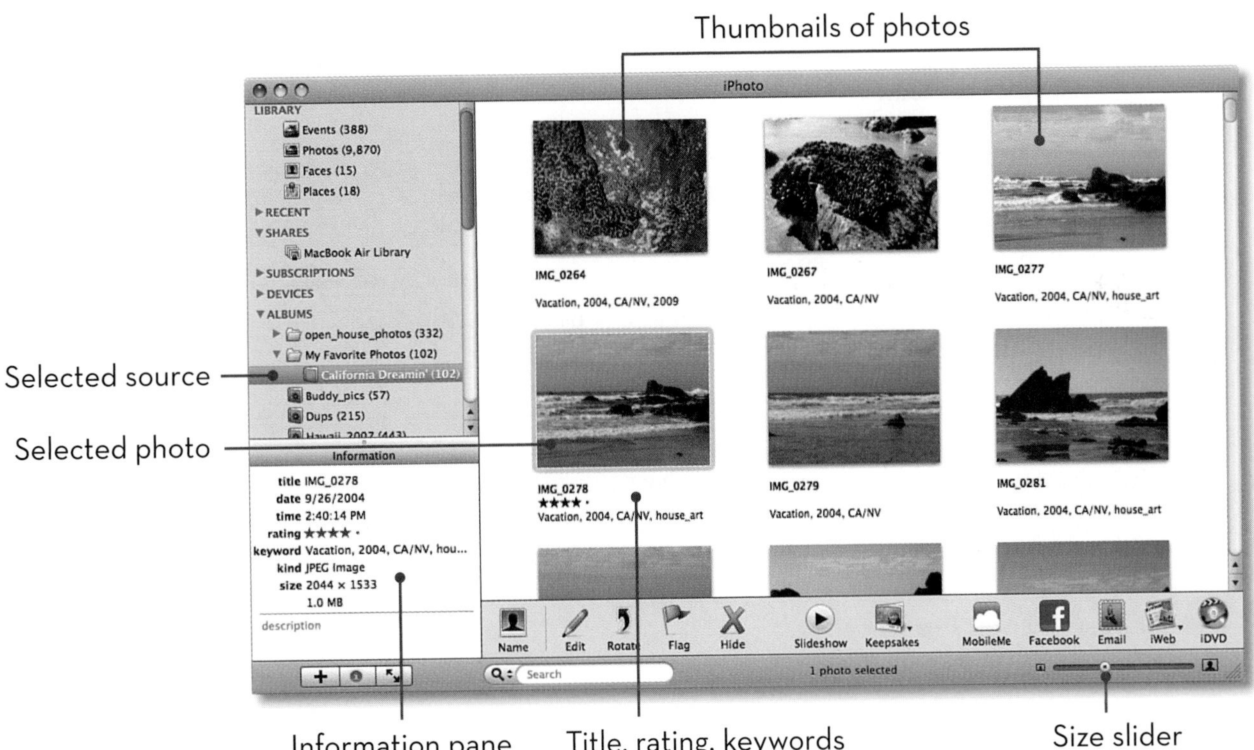
Thumbnails of photos
iPhoto
LIBRARY
Events (388)
Photos (9,870)
Faces (15)
Places (18)
RECENT
SHARES
MacBook Air Library
SUBSCRIPTIONS
DEVICES
ALBUMS
open_house_photos (332)
My Favorite Photos (102)
California Dreamin' (102)
Buddy_pics (57)
Dups (215)
Information
title IMG_0278
date 9/26/2004
time 2:40:14 PM
rating ★★★★
keyword Vacation, 2004, CA/NV, hou...
kind JPEG Image
size 2044 × 1533
1.0 MB
description
IMG_0264
Vacation, 2004, CA/NV, 2009
IMG_0267
Vacation, 2004, CA/NV
IMG_0277
Vacation, 2004, CA/NV, house_art
IMG_0278
★★★★
Vacation, 2004, CA/NV, house_art
IMG_0279
Vacation, 2004, CA/NV
IMG_0281
Vacation, 2004, CA/NV, house_art
Name
Edit
Rotate
Flag
Hide
Slideshow
Keepsakes
MobileMe
Facebook
Email
iWeb
iDVD
Search
1 photo selected
Selected source
Selected photo
Information pane
Title, rating, keywords
Size slider

PREPARING iPHOTO FOR IMPORTS

You'll want to add photos from a digital camera to your iPhoto library. You should configure iPhoto so that it opens automatically whenever you connect a camera to your Mac. This is the default setting, but you should know how and where to set it.

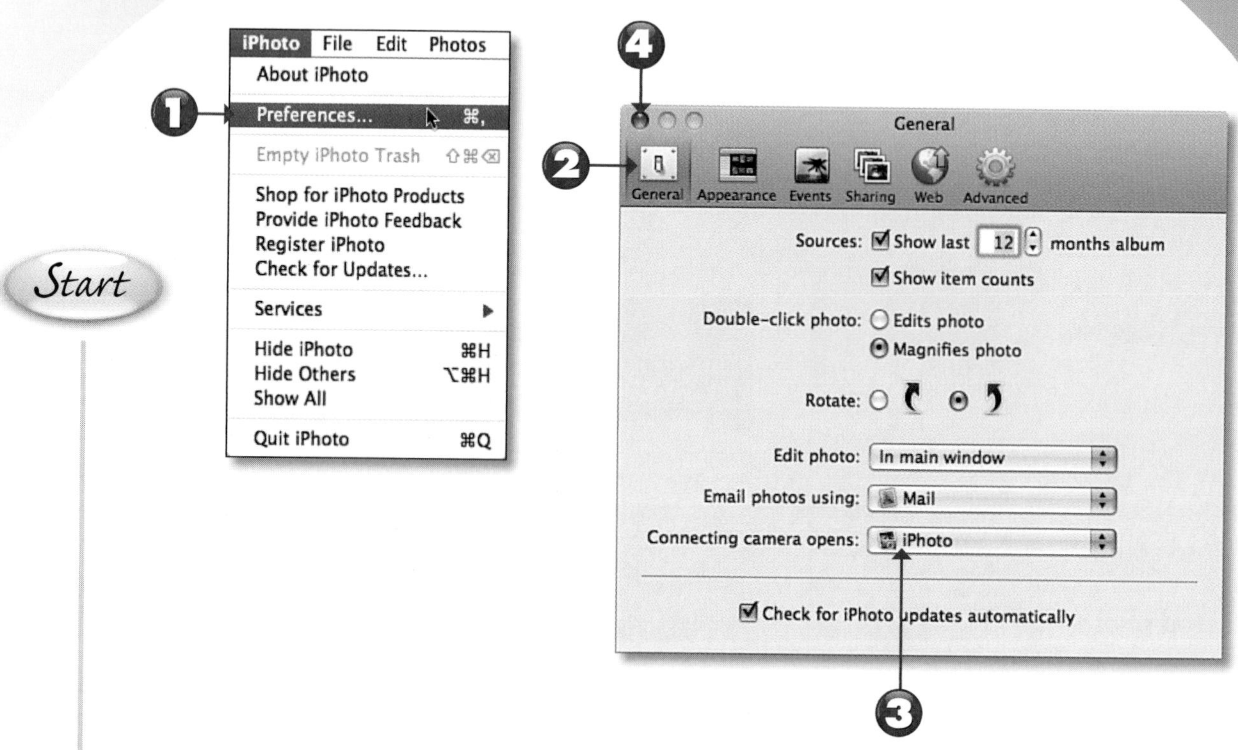

1. Choose **iPhoto**, **Preferences**.
2. Click the **General** tab.
3. On the Connecting camera opens pop-up menu, choose **iPhoto**.
4. Close the iPhoto Preferences dialog box.

End

NOTE

Compatible Camera? Most modern digital cameras are compatible with iPhoto, meaning that when you connect the camera to your Mac, iPhoto recognizes it as a camera and is able to import photos from the camera's memory card into your iPhoto library. ■

IMPORTING PHOTOS INTO THE PHOTO LIBRARY

To be able to work with photos in iPhoto, you import them into the iPhoto library. The most common source of photos is a digital camera. When you want to move photos from the camera to your library, connect the camera to your Mac and then import its photos.

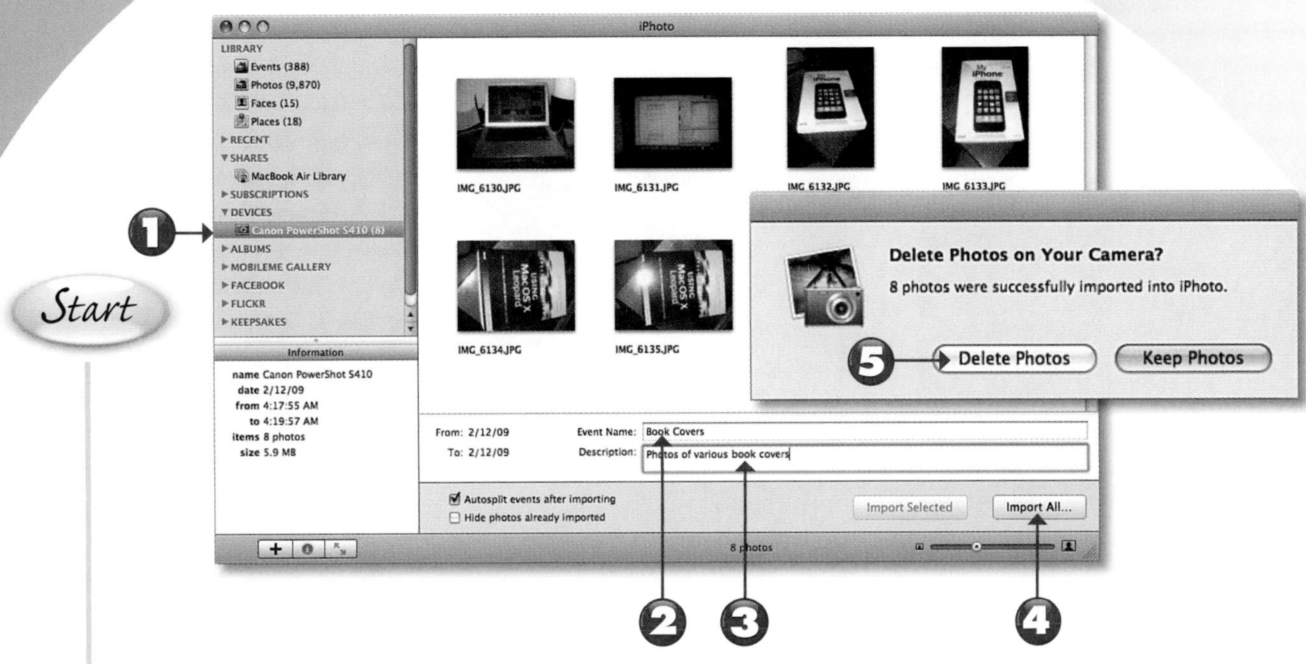

1. Connect the camera to a USB port on your Mac. iPhoto recognizes the camera, and it is selected on the Source list.
2. If the photos are all from the same event, enter an event name. By default, all the photos taken on the same day are in the same event.
3. Enter a description of the photos.
4. Click **Import All**.
5. To delete the photos you imported from the camera, click **Delete Photos**.

End

TIP

Be Selective If you don't want to import all the photos on the camera to your library, select the photos you do want to import and click **Import Selected**. ■

TIP

Import from Other Sources You can import photos from other sources by choosing **File, Import to Library**. Move to and select the source of photos you want to import. Then click **Import**. ■

VIEWING PHOTOS

The first step to view photos, and for most other iPhoto activities for that matter, is to select the source of photos you want to view. There are many sources available to you on the Source list in the left pane of the iPhoto window. When you select a source, the photos it contains appear in the Viewing pane, which is the large pane on the right side of the window.

Start

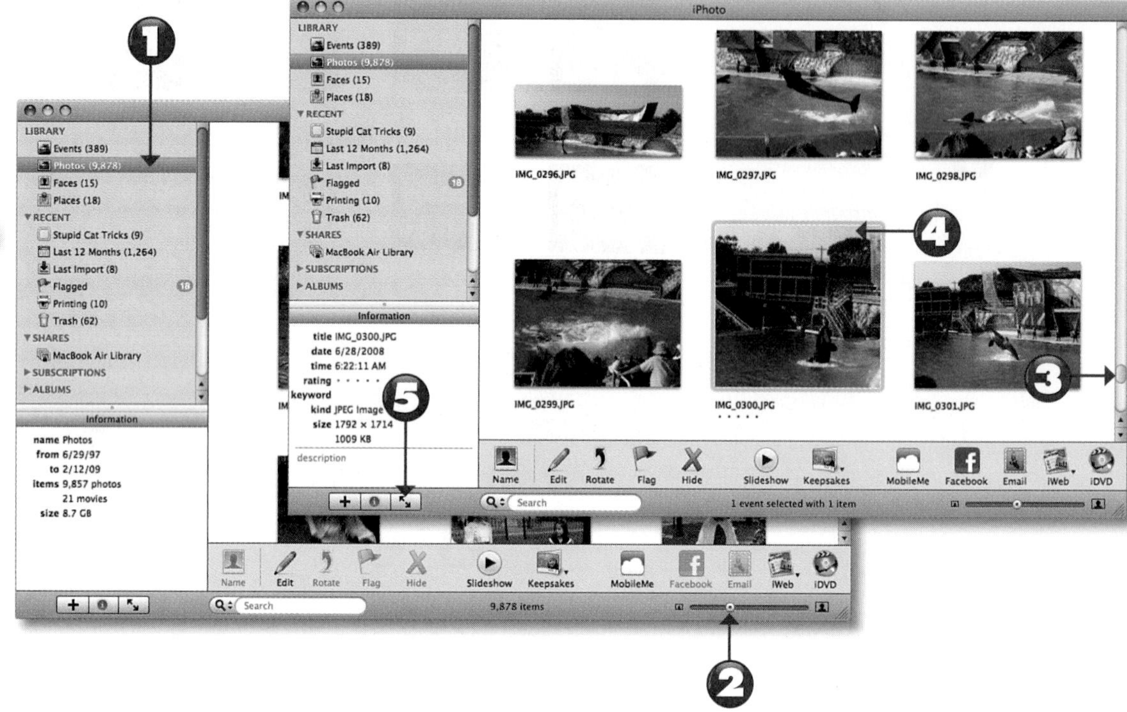

1. Select **Photos** to see all the photos in your library.

2. Drag the size slider to the left to increase the number of photos you see or to the right to decrease the number you see.

3. Drag the scrollbar up and down the window to browse all the photos in the source until you see thumbnails of photos you want to view.

4. Select a photo you want to view.

5. Click the **Full Screen** button.

Continued

TIP

Size with a Key Press To move the size slider to the leftmost position press **1**. To move it to the rightmost position so that the thumbnails are at their largest size, press **0**. ■

NOTE

Newest Photos in the Library The Last Import source in the Recent section contains the collection of photos you imported during your last import session. ■

6. View the photo.

7. Point the mouse cursor at the bottom of the screen. The toolbar appears.

8. Click the **Previous** or **Next** button to view the previous or next photo in the selected source.

9. Click the **Exit** button. You return to the iPhoto window.

End

TIP

Full Screen When you are viewing photos in Full-Screen mode, you can move to the previous or next photo in the source by pressing the left- or right-arrow key, respectively. ■

NOTE

Events, Faces, and Places, Oh My Some sources, including Events, Faces, and Places, organize photos into groups based on the information associated with those photos. You learn how to view photos in those groupings later in this chapter. ■

VIEWING PHOTOS IN EVENTS

Events are collections of photos taken or associated with a specific period of time. By default, when you import photos, all the photos associated with each day are collected into an event for those days. Events are useful because you can use them to view photos by the dates they were taken.

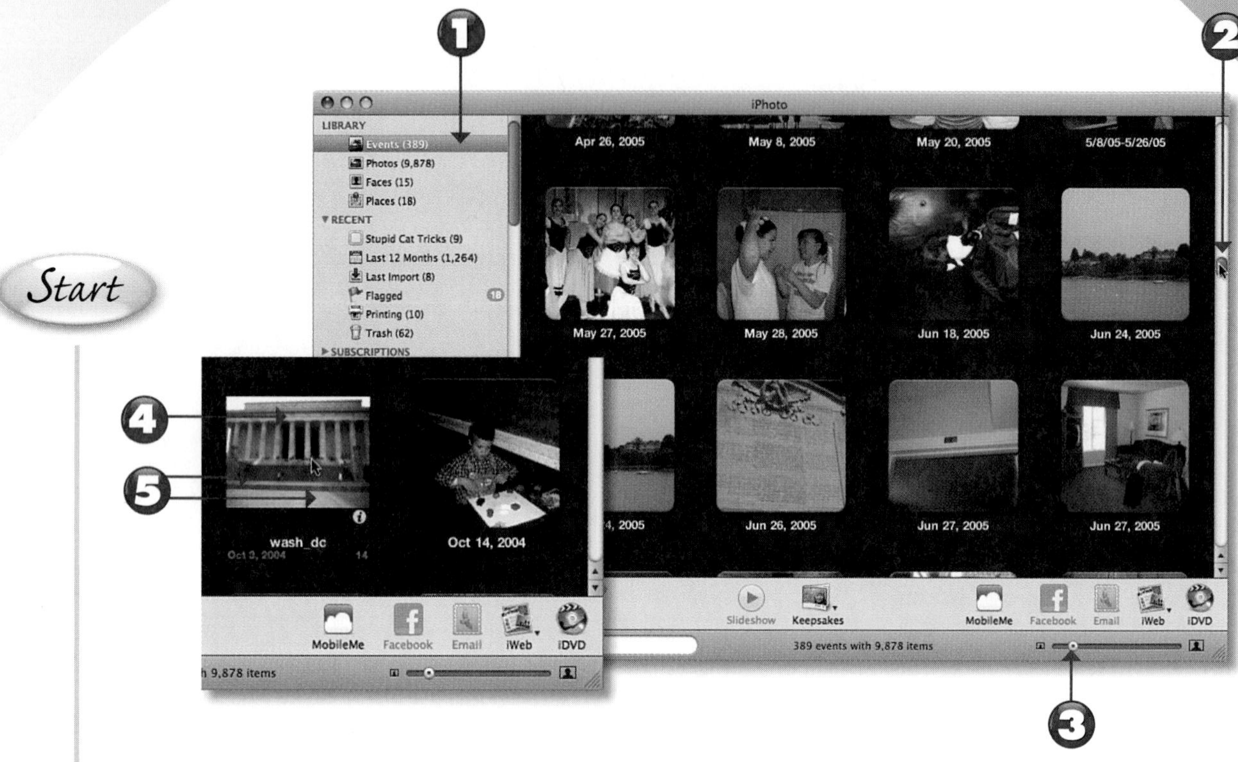

1. Select **Events** on the Source list. You see frames for the events in your library. At the bottom of the frames, you see the events' titles, if entered, or dates, if no title was entered.
2. Drag the scrollbar up or down to browse your events.
3. Drag the size slider to the left or right to change the size of the event frames.
4. Point to an event in which you are interested. The date appears under the title along with the number of photos it contains.
5. Drag across an event's frame. You preview its photos.

Continued

NOTE

What's in a Name? When you import photos, if you enter a name and description for an event, that information is applied to only one event. ■

NOTE

Changing Dates You can create or modify your own events, move photos between events, and perform other event actions. These topics are covered in Chapter 3. ■

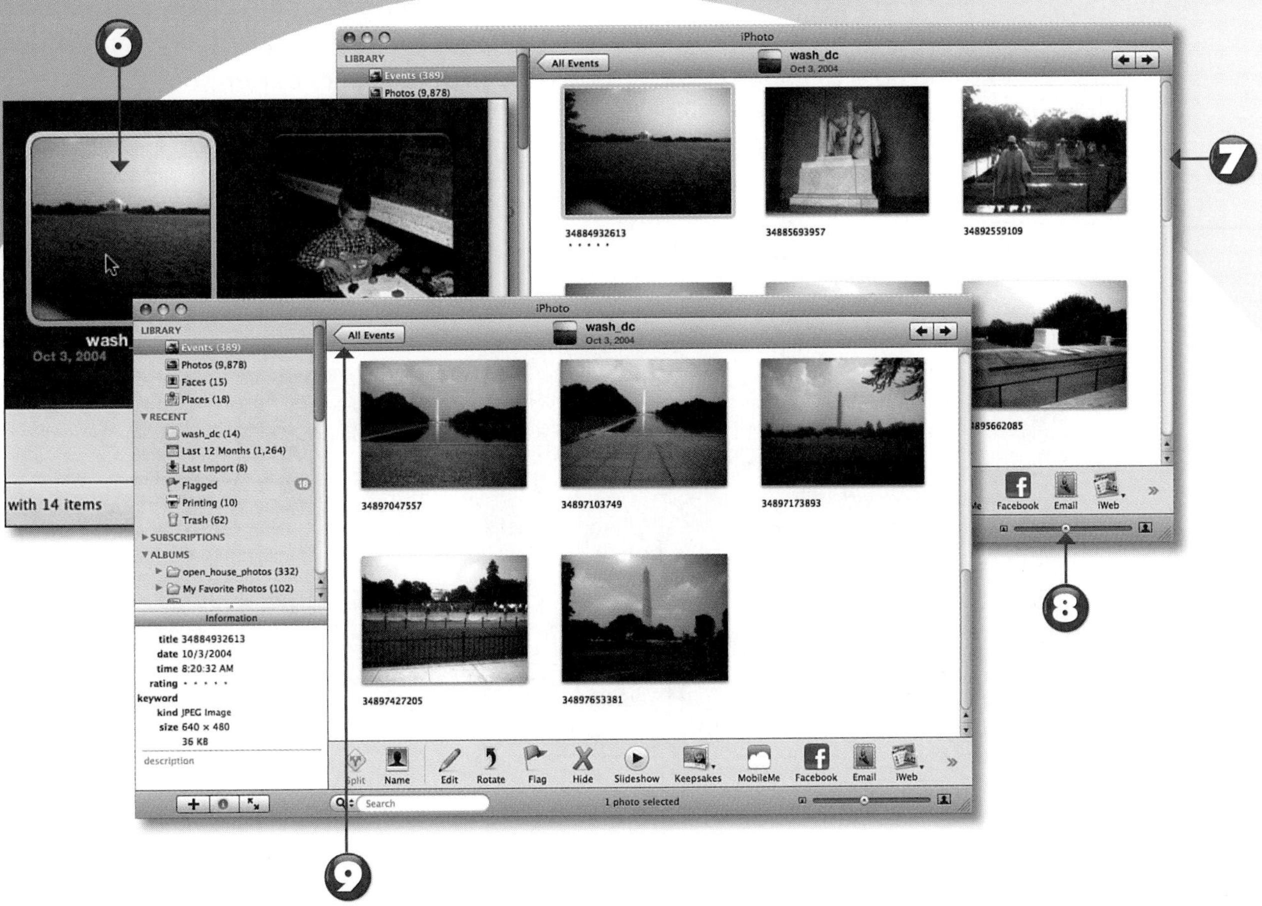

6 Double-click an event. You see its photos in the Viewing pane.

7 Drag the scrollbar to browse the photos in the event.

8 Use the Size slider to change the size of the photos in the Viewing pane.

9 Click **All Events** to move back and see the event frames again.

End

TIP

View in a Separate Window To view an event's photos in a separate window, **right-click** or **Control-click** the event's frame and choose **Open in Separate Window**. In the resulting window, you can browse the photos in the event. ■

TIP

Moving to More Photos When you are viewing an event's photos in the Viewing pane, you can view the previous or next event's photos by clicking the left- or right-arrow buttons at the top of the window. ■

IDENTIFYING FACES IN PHOTOS

iPhoto has a Face-Recognition tool that it uses to identify photos for you based on the faces of the people in those photos. This is a great way to view photos that include specific people and to be able to find photos for projects, such as a calendar or photo book. To use this feature, you associate names with the faces iPhoto identifies. As you train iPhoto to recognize specific faces, it gets better at identifying those faces in your photos.

Start

1. View photos showing people whose faces you want to identify.
2. Select a photo with faces you want to label with names.
3. Click the **Name** button.
4. Click **Unknown Face** under a face iPhoto has identified with a white box. The text becomes "Type Name."

Continued

TIP

Missing Faces If there are faces in a photo that iPhoto doesn't identify as a face (there's no box around it), you can add the face by clicking **Add Missing Face**, positioning and sizing the resulting box around the face, clicking **Done**, entering the person's name, and pressing **Return**. ■

5 Type the name of the person whose face is selected and press the Return key.

6 Click the right-facing arrow at the end of the name tag. iPhoto finds photos that the feature has identified as containing that face.

7 Click the **Confirm Name** button.

8 Click once on photos in which the person appears. The label becomes the person's name.

Continued

NOTE

Face Panes When you are in the Confirm Name mode, the Viewing pane always contains two panes. The top pane contains the photos in which the person's name has been confirmed, and the lower pane shows photos that may contain the person's face.

NOTE

A Learning Computer The more you train iPhoto to recognize a person's face, the more accurate it is at finding that person in your photos.

1. Click twice on photos that don't include the person's face. The label becomes "Not *the Person's Name*."
2. Scroll down the window to see the next set of photos.
3. Click once on the photos that include the person and click twice on the photos that don't include the person.
4. Repeat steps 10 and 11 until you've done all the photos, or at least a large number of them. Click **Done**.

End

NOTE

Finding Photos After you've finished confirming a face, iPhoto identifies more photos containing that face, and you can continue to confirm the face in the additional photos.

NOTE

Aging Faces iPhoto does an amazing job of identifying a person's face at a variety of ages. When you tag a face with a name, iPhoto can find photos of that person even when they span many years, including time periods where the person ages from a young child to an adult.

VIEWING PHOTOS BY FACES

After you have labeled faces, you can use the names and faces of people to view photos in which they appear. Each face you've named has its own frame. To view the photos containing that face, you open its frame.

Start

1. Click **Faces** on the Source list.
2. Browse the frames until you see the frame for the person whose photos you want to view.
3. Double-click the face frame.
4. Browse and view the person's photos.
5. Click **All Faces** to move back to your face frames.

End

TIP

Confirming Faces If Faces includes pictures for someone it shouldn't, click **Confirm Name** and double-click the photos that iPhoto thinks include the person, but don't. ■

NOTE

A Sideways Look iPhoto can only identify faces that are looking directly at, or nearly directly at, the camera. Add other faces with the Add Missing Face feature. ■

ASSOCIATING PHOTOS WITH KNOWN PLACES

Using iPhoto, you can tag photos by locations so that you can find and view photos based on where they were taken. Some cameras, notably the one in Apple iPhones, capture GPS information automatically so that when you import photos, they are associated with places automatically. If photos don't have place information, you can add it manually. One way is to locate places that are known to iPhoto based on Google Maps.

Start

1. Select the photo you want to associate with a place and click the **Info button** located in the lower-right corner of the photo's thumbnail.
2. Click **Enter photo location**.
3. Type the name of the place you want to associate with the photo.
4. When iPhoto identifies the place, select it and press the **Return** key. You see the location of the place on the map at the bottom of the window.

Continued

NOTE

Appearing Places After you've associated a place with a photo, that place appears on the map in the bottom of the Info window for that photo. ■

TIP

Discovering New Places If you can't find the place by typing its name, see the next section to locate and identify a new place. ■

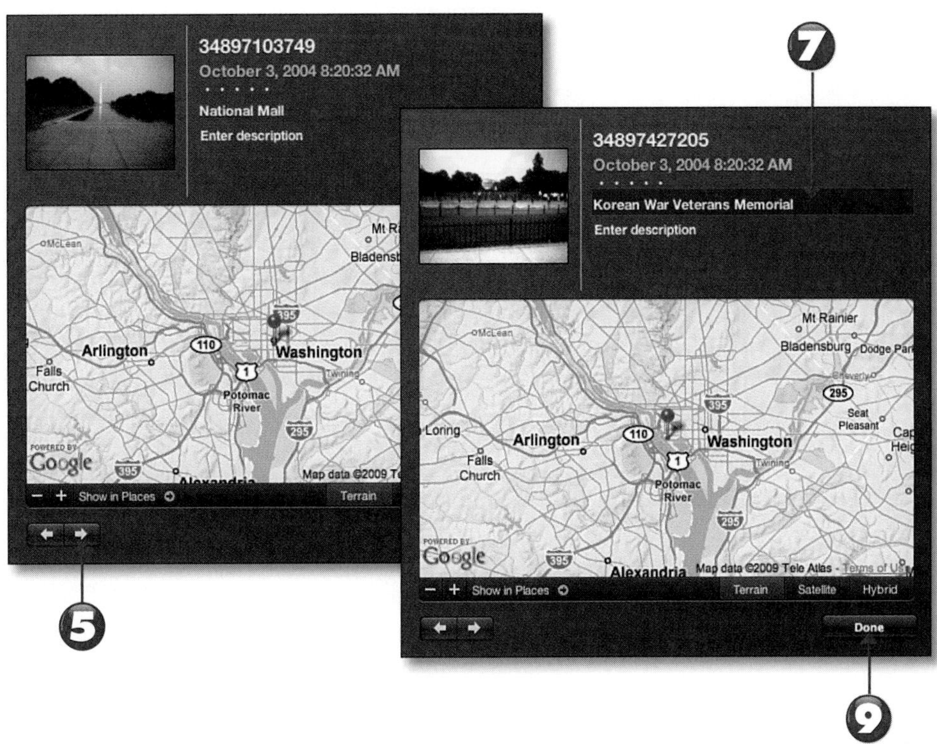

5. Click the right-facing arrow to move to the next picture.

6. Type the place name in the Enter Photo Location field.

7. When iPhoto displays the correct location on the list, select it and press the **Return** key.

8. Repeat steps 5 through 7 for each photo you want to associate with places.

9. Click **Done**.

End

TIP

Zooming Using the **Zoom Out (-)** and **Zoom In (+)** buttons located in the lower-left corner of the Info window, you can zoom in on the map. ■

TIP

Different Map Types Click the **Terrain**, **Satellite**, or **Hybrid** buttons to select the kind of map displayed. ■

ASSOCIATING PHOTOS WITH NEW PLACES

If Google Maps can't find a specific place, you can search for locations and save them so that you can easily add those places to a photo. For example, if you search for a location called My House, Google Maps probably won't find it. If you search for your address, however, you can save it as a place called My House. Then, you can easily associate photos with your house's location by selecting My House.

1. Choose **Window**, **Manage My Places**.
2. Click the **Google Search** tab.
3. Type an address for which you want to search and press the **Return** key.
4. Select the address.

Continued

TIP

Saving Places After you've saved a location, it appears when you search for a photo location in a photo's Info dialog box, just like other locations available via Google Maps. If you named a location My House, you can search for My House, and it will appear on the list of places. ■

TIP

Searching You can search for places by just about any criteria, such as attraction name, general location, and so on. ■

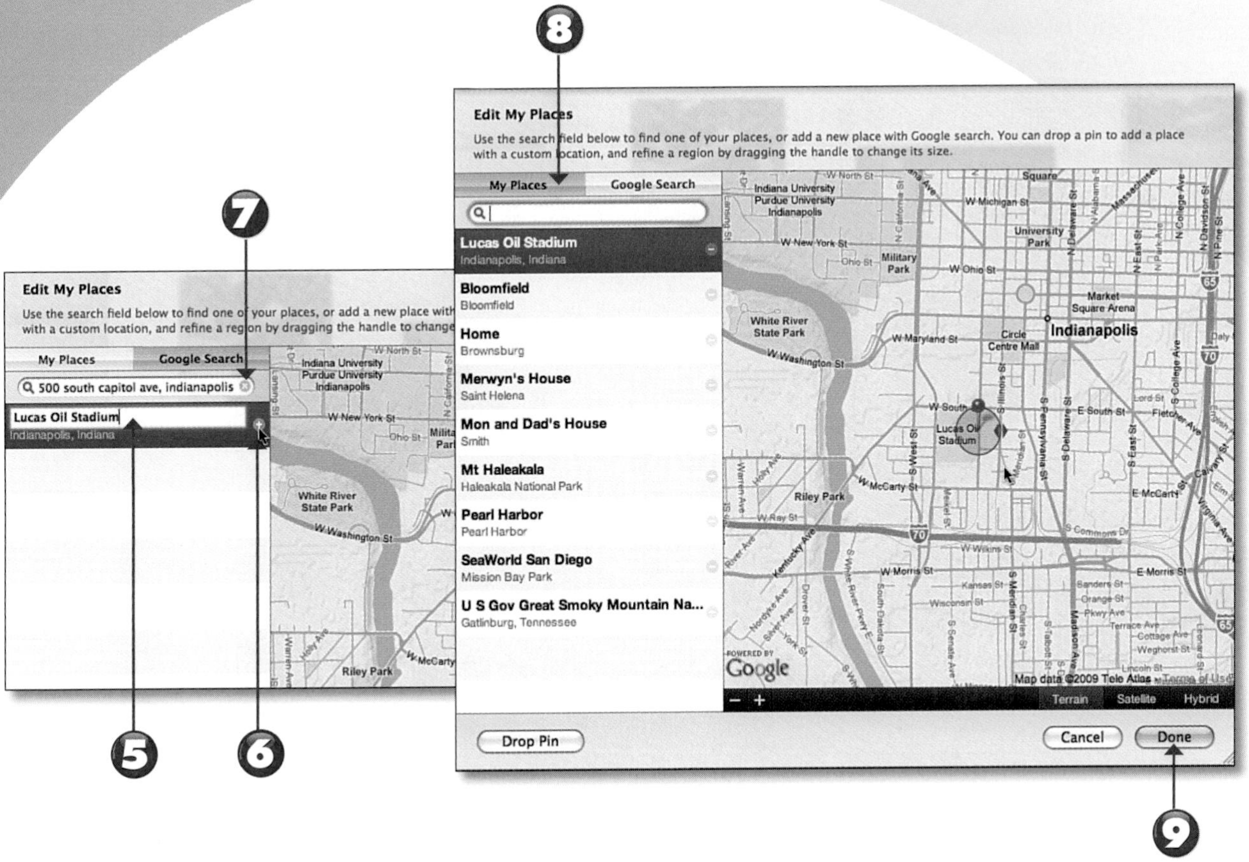

5 Type a label for the location.

6 Click the **Add** button. The location is added to your My Places list.

7 Click the **Clear** button. You see all the addresses you have saved and that are available for you to associate with photos.

8 Click **My Places**.

9 Click **Done**.

End

TIP

You Can't Go Back Again To delete places from your My Places list, click the **Remove** button (-) along the right side of the My Places tab.

TIP

Resizing Places To change the size of the area associated with a place, click the left- or right-facing arrows on the circle surrounding the location's pin on the map.

VIEWING PHOTOS BY PLACES USING THE MAP

When you have places associated with photos, you can use them to find photos. When you use the map, you see pins at each location where you have photos, making it simple to view photos associated with specific locations.

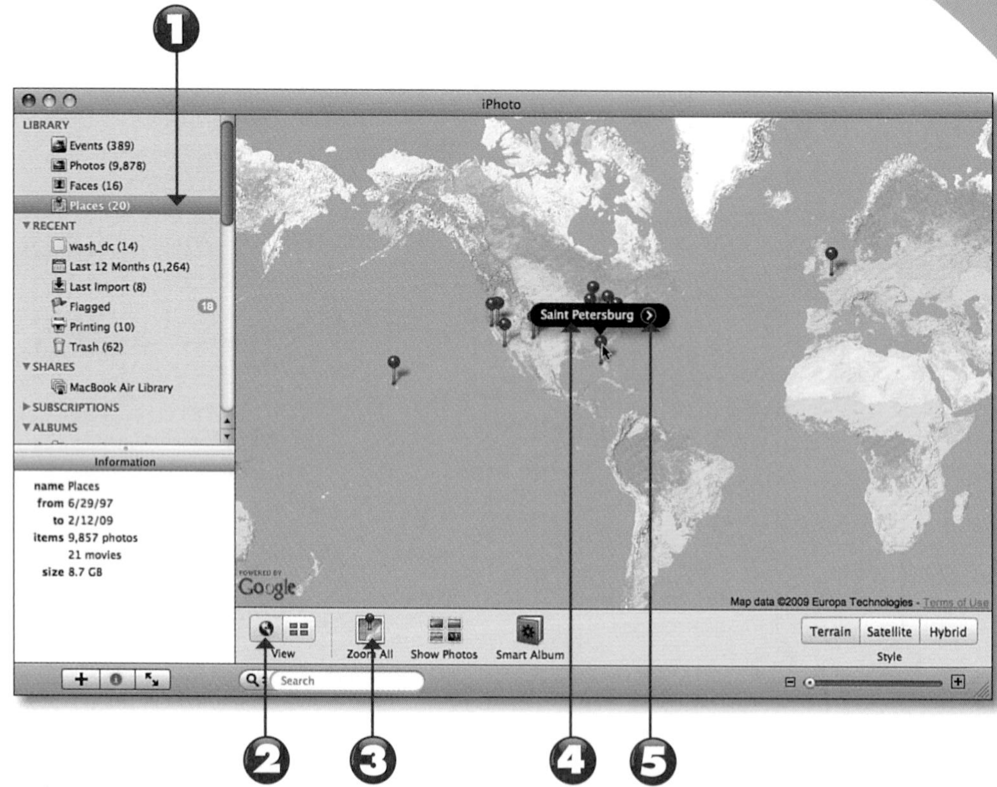

Start

1. Click **Places**.
2. Click the **Map** button.
3. Click **Zoom All**. This causes the map to show all the locations with which photos are associated.
4. Point to a location of interest to you. Its name appears above its pin on the map.
5. Click the right-facing arrow at the end of the location's name to view all photos associated with that place.

End

TIP

You Can Go Back Again To get back to the map, click **Map**. ■

TIP

More on Zooming You can zoom in or out of the map by using the size slider. You can move around the map by dragging it. ■

VIEWING PHOTOS BY PLACES USING THE LIST

You can also view photos by browsing the list of locations with which photos are associated. This more precise method lets you see the full names of the places you browse.

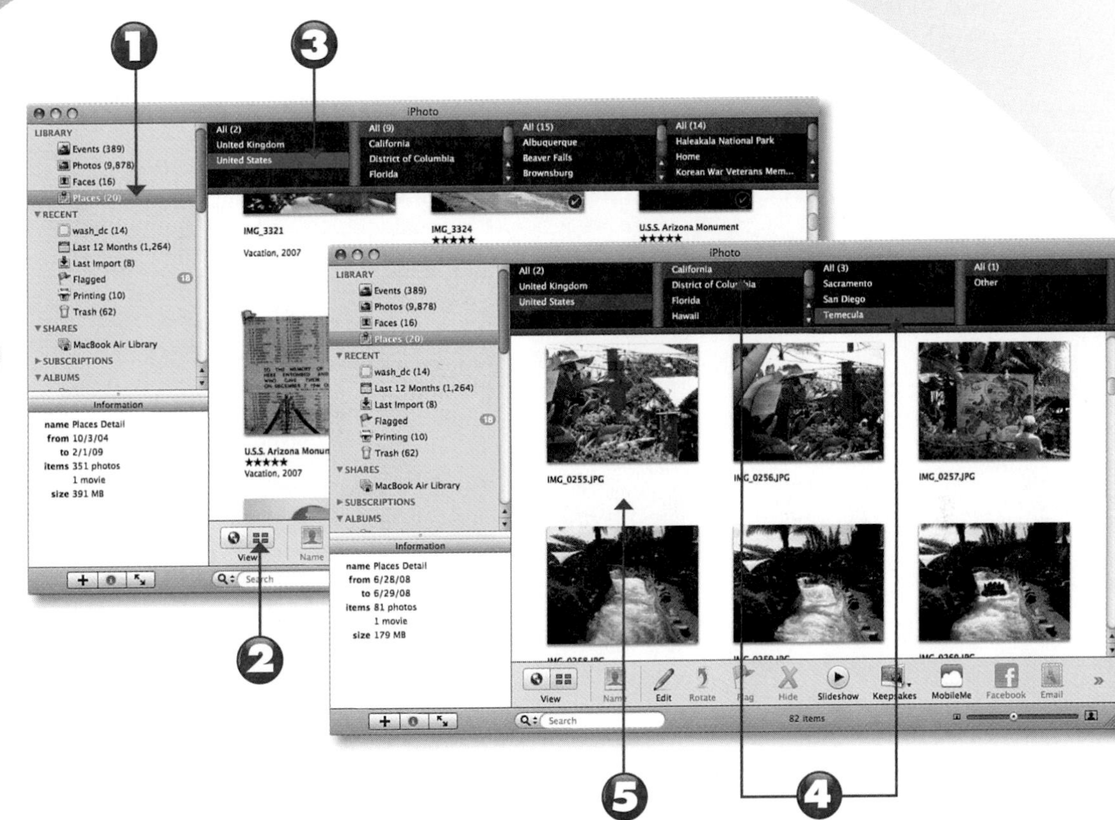

Start

1. Click **Places**.

2. Click the **List** button.

3. Click the first category associated with photos you want to view, which is country. Photos associated with that country appear in the bottom pane of the window.

4. Select the other categories that you want to see.

5. View the photos associated with the location you've selected on the list.

End

TIP

Seeing the Map If you click the **Map** button, you see the map zoomed so that you see the locations you have selected. ■

NOTE

Relative Categories The items you see in the various category columns depend on the locations associated with your photos. ■

VIEWING PHOTOS IN SLIDESHOWS

Looking at a group of photos in a slideshow is a great way to enjoy them as they fill the screen and iPhoto moves through the pictures automatically. You can choose options for a slideshow, such as how long each photo is onscreen and what music you want to play during the slideshow.

Start

1. Select the photos you want to see in a slideshow. You can select photos individually, choose a photo album, or choose any other source on the Source list.
2. Click the **Slideshow** button.
3. Click the theme you want to use for the slideshow.
4. Click the **Music** tab.
5. Select the source and music to which you want to listen while the slideshow plays.

Continued

NOTE

Slideshow Projects Viewing photos in Slideshow mode as described here isn't intended to create permanent slideshows that you save. When you want to save a slideshow so that you can watch it any time, you create a slideshow project as you learn in Chapter 6, "Creating Projects in iPhoto." ■

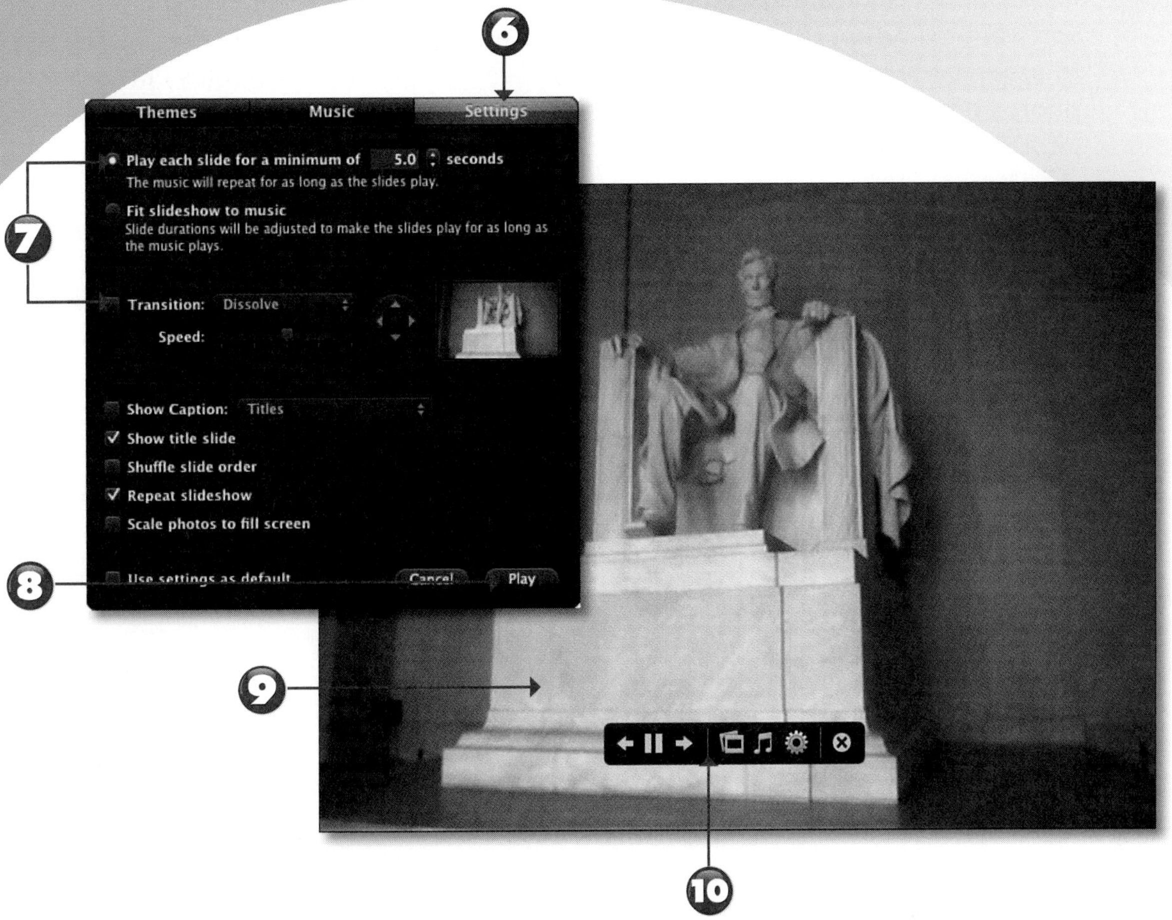

6. Click the **Settings** tab.

7. Select playback options, such as how long each slide appears on the screen and the transition effect between slides.

8. Click **Play**. The slideshow plays.

9. Move the pointer on the screen.

10. Use the controls on the toolbar to control the slideshow.

End

TIP

Controlling the Show To change the slideshow's settings, click the Gear icon on the slideshow toolbar. To exit a slideshow, press the Escape key. ■

NOTE

Retained Settings The slideshow settings are retained and used each time you select the same group of photos and play a slideshow, until you change them. ■

VIEWING PHOTO INFORMATION

Photos can include a lot of information, and that information is important, especially when you want to find specific photos for projects and other purposes. Earlier, you learned how to associate faces and places with photos; these are just two examples of how you can tag photos with different information. In this section, you learn a couple of ways to view the information tags for your photos.

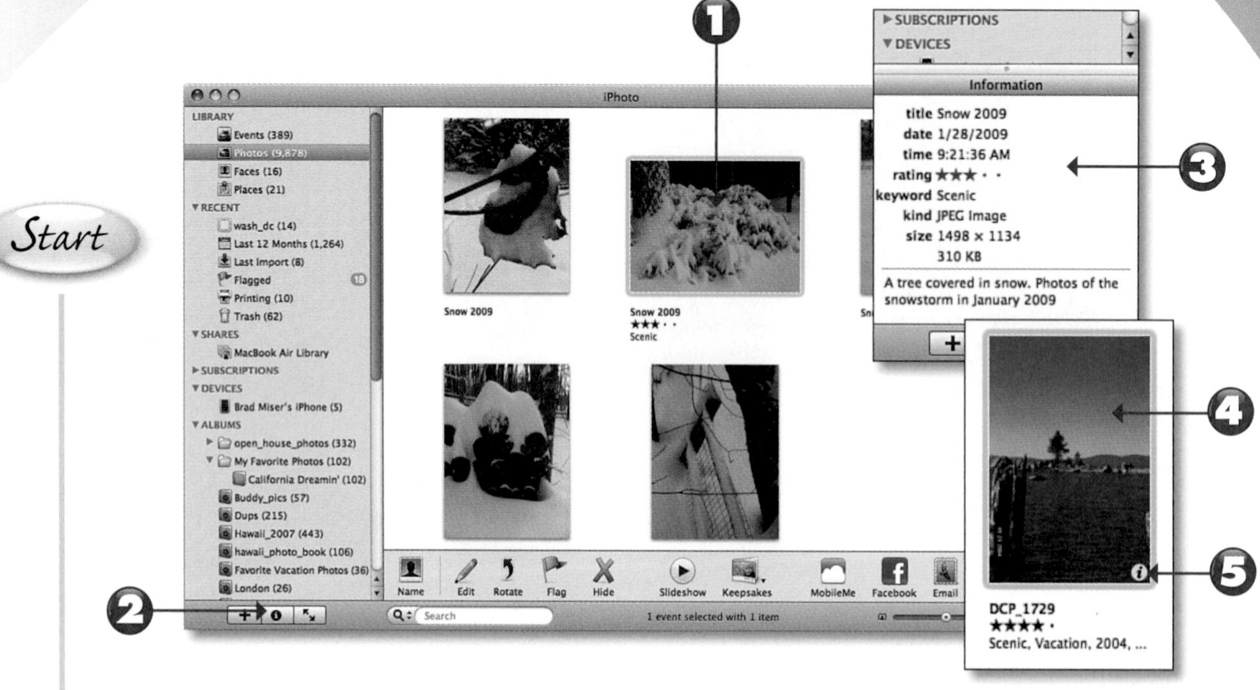

1. Select a photo about which you want to get information.
2. Click the **Info** button in the lower-left corner of the iPhoto window. The Info pane appears.
3. View information about the photo, such as date, time, rating, and so on.
4. Select another photo.
5. Click the **Info** button located on the photo. The Info dialog box appears.

NOTE

Tagging Photos In Chapter 3, you learn how to tag your photos with different kinds of information. ■

TIP

Lots of Info The Info pane displays information about any object you select in the iPhoto window. ■

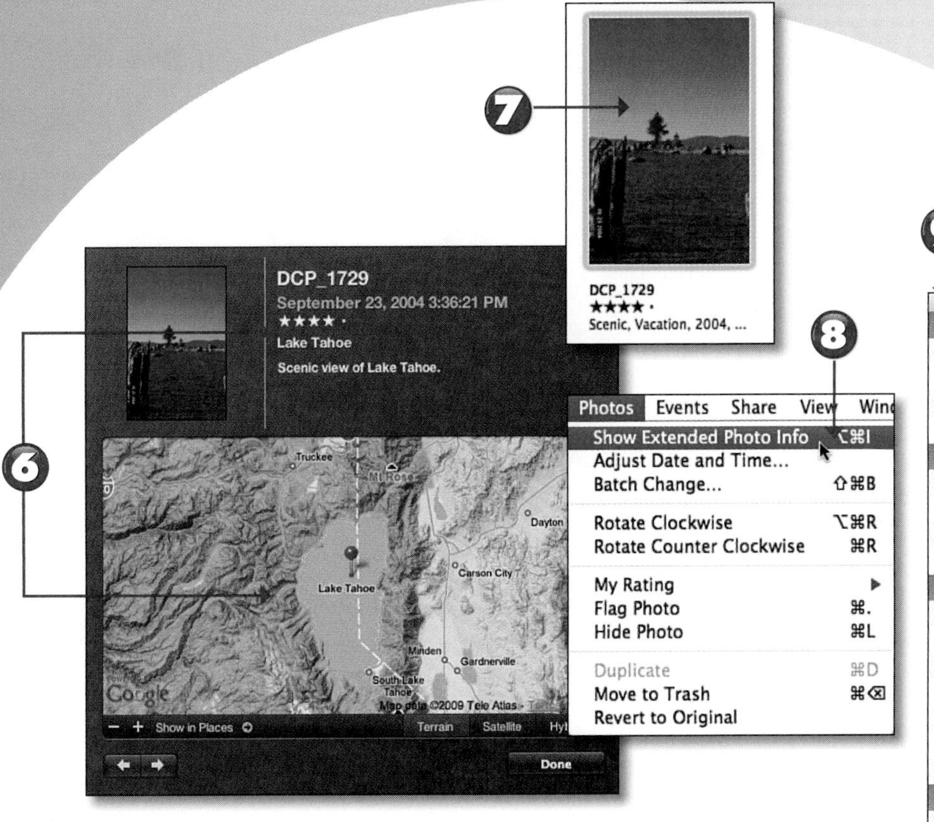

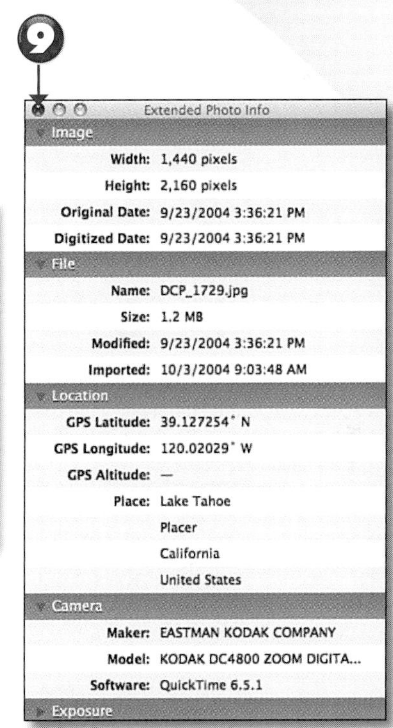

6. View information about the photo and Click **Done**.

7. Select a photo.

8. Choose **Photos**, **Show Extended Photo Info** to see very detailed information about the selected photo.

9. View the detailed information about the photo and click the **Close** button.

End

TIP

Expanding Sections You can expand or collapse the sections of the Extended Photo Info window by clicking the triangle next to the section titles, such as Image or Location. ■

TIP

All Info, All the Time You can leave the Info pane open all the time. As you select different objects, the information it contains changes to reflect the current object. ■

ORGANIZING AND SEARCHING AN iPHOTO PHOTO LIBRARY

Over time, you're going to build up a large iPhoto library containing thousands of photos. It's important that you are able to organize your photos so that you can find specific photos you want to use in projects or just to view in a temporary slideshow.

In Chapter 2, "Getting Started with iPhoto," you learned about a couple of ways, Faces and Places, you can tag photos with information that you can use to find photos using those tags. In this chapter, you're going to take your organization and searching skills to the max by learning about the other tags you can configure. Once your photos are properly tagged, you can search for them in many ways.

You'll also learn how to keep your photos organized with events and a couple of kinds of photo albums. Being able to create albums effectively is useful for both general organization and for creating projects (where your first step is usually gathering the photos you want to use in an album).

Tags you apply to photos include a title, rating, keywords, location, and description

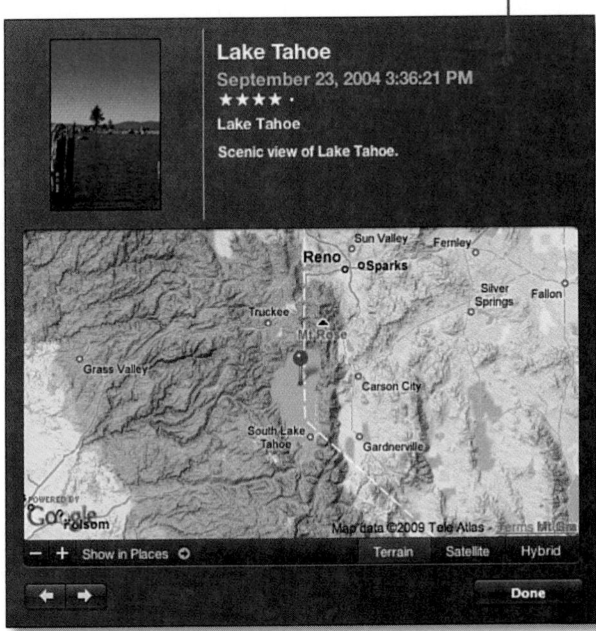

Information

title Lake Tahoe
date 9/23/2004
time 3:36:21 PM
rating ★★★★ ·
keyword Scenic, Vacation, 2004, CA/...
kind JPEG Image
size 1440 × 2160
1.2 MB

Scenic view of Lake Tahoe.

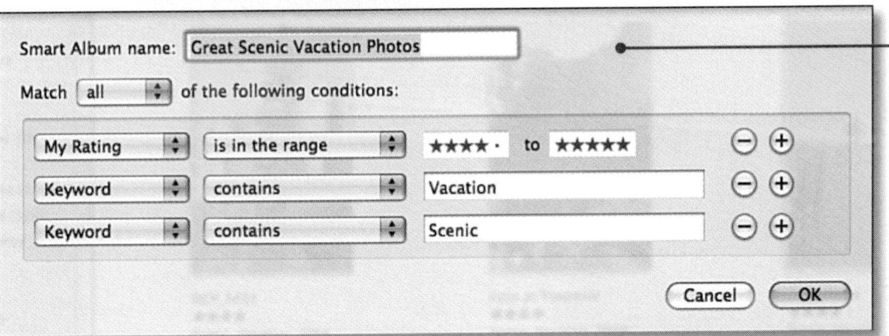

Smart photo albums automatically collect photos based on their tags

By default, events organize photos by date, but you can create events to organize photos any way you want

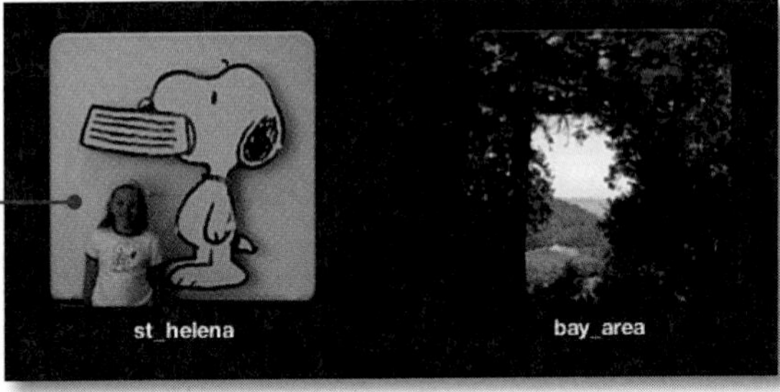

CHANGING A PHOTO'S TAGS USING THE INFO DIALOG BOX

In Chapter 2, you learned how to use the Info dialog box to view a photo's tags and to associate a location with your photos. You can configure a number of other tags with this dialog box, too. These include a title, which is the photo's name; rating, which is how "good" the photo is; and description, which is just what it sounds like it is.

Start

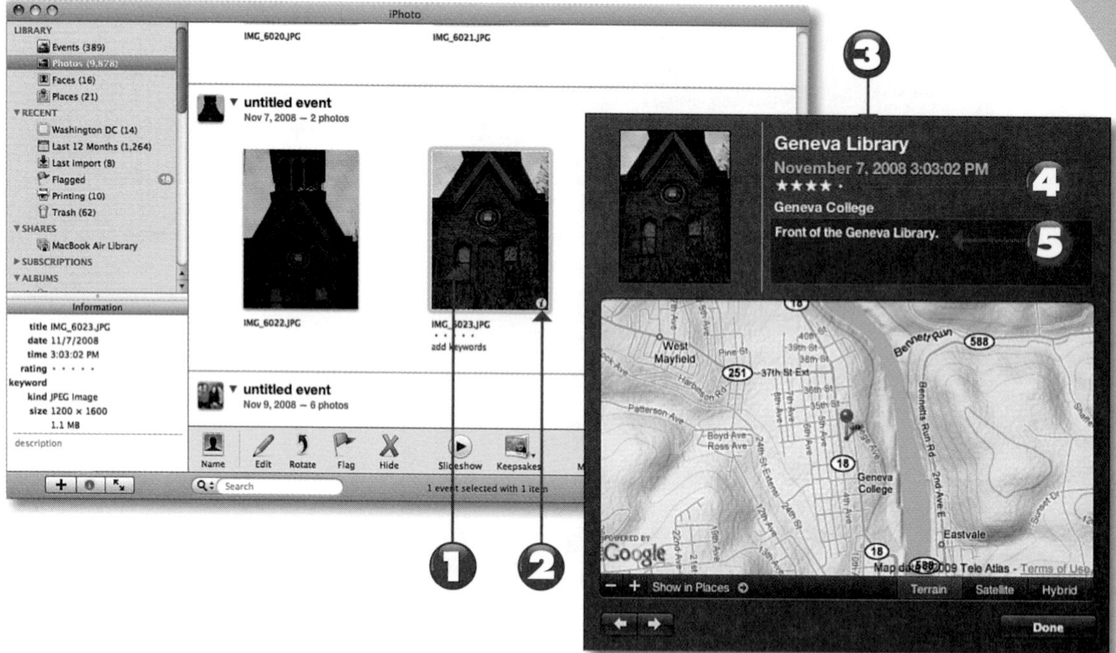

1. Select the photo whose tags you want to configure.
2. Click the **i** button.
3. Enter a title for the photo in the top field.
4. Rate the photo by clicking the number of dots, which become stars, that you want to assign to the photo.
5. Enter a description of the photo.

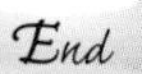

NOTE

Location, Location You can also assign a location to the photo (see Chapter 2). ■

TIP

Finished? When you're done, click **Done**, or to tag the previous or next photo in the same group, click the left- or right-facing arrow at the bottom of the dialog box, respectively. ■

CHANGING A PHOTO'S TAGS USING THE INFO PANE

You can also change a photo's tags in the Info pane. Here, you can change a photo's title, rating, keyword, and description.

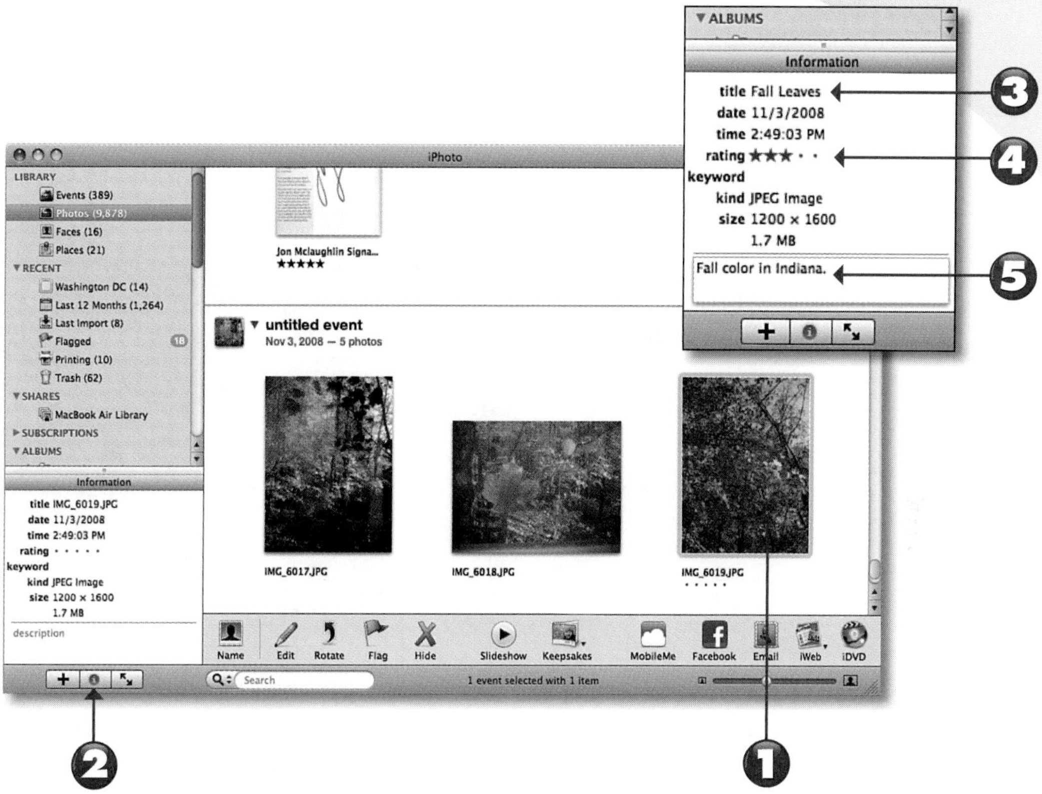

Start

1. Select the photo whose tags you want to change.

2. Click the **i** button.

3. Type a title for the photo in the Title field.

4. Rate the photo by clicking the number of dots, which become stars, to indicate how "good" the photo is.

5. Enter a description of the photo.

End

NOTE

Changing Time and Date You can change the date and time associated with a photo in the Info pane, too. However, you should only need to do this when an error is associated with the photo's current date and time. ■

CHANGING TAGS FOR MULTIPLE PHOTOS SIMULTANEOUSLY

Some tags, such as the location or description of photos associated with a trip, apply to multiple photos. You can select several photos and update their tags at the same time to make the process of tagging photos more efficient.

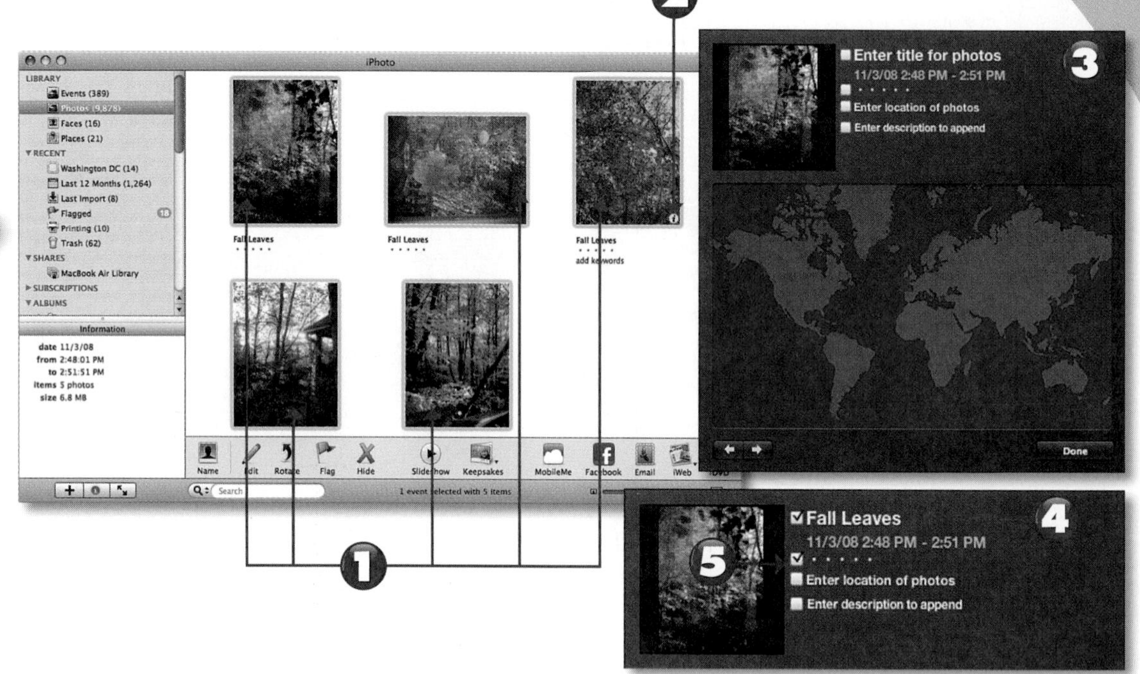

1. Select the photos whose tags you want to change.
2. Click the **i** button for one of the photos.
3. Check the **Enter Title for Photos** check box.
4. Enter a title for all the photos in the top field.
5. To rate all the photos, check the **Rating** check box.

Continued

TIP

Tags To configure the tags you see, open the View menu and enable **Titles**, **Rating**, or **Keywords**. When an option on that menu is checked, such as Titles, you see that tag in the Viewing pane. When an option is not checked, the tags still exist, but you don't see them. ■

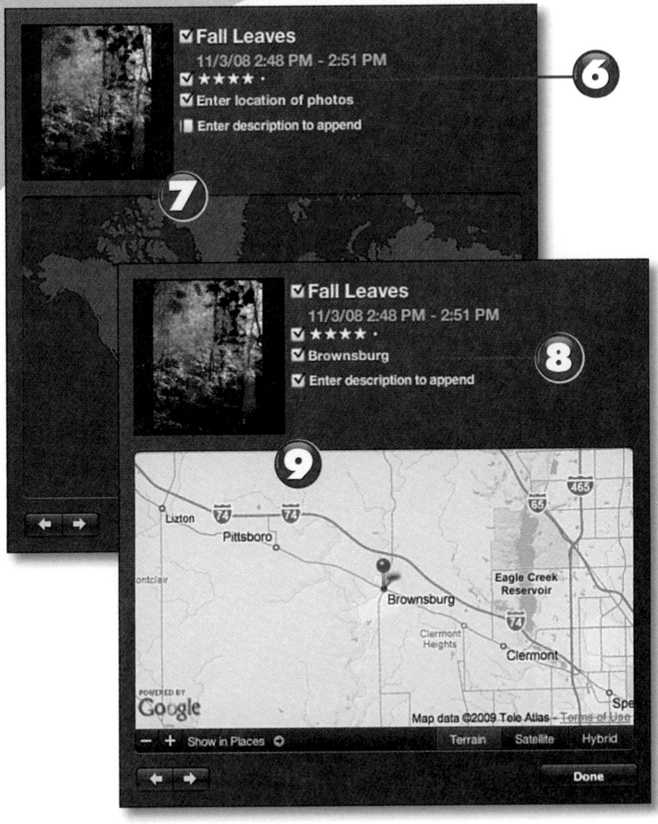

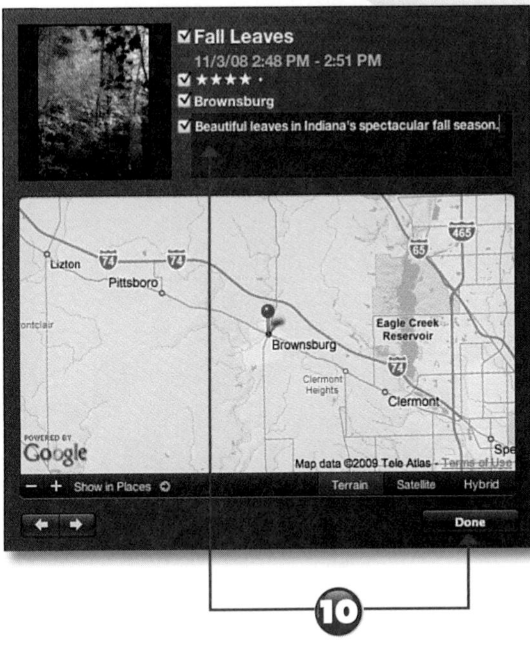

6. Click the dots to represent the number of stars you want to assign to the photos.

7. Check the **Enter Location of Photos** check box.

8. Configure the location of the photos.

9. Check the **Enter Description to Append** check box.

10. Enter the text that you want to be added to each photo's description and click **Done**.

End

NOTE

Appending Text If a selected photo has text in its Description field, any text you enter is added to the end of the existing text. If a selected photo doesn't have any text in the Description field, what you enter becomes the entire entry in that field. ■

CONFIGURING KEYWORDS FOR PHOTOS

Keywords are words or numbers that you can apply to photos as a means to tag them so that you can later find photos by the keywords associated with them. You can apply multiple keywords to the same photo to tag it in several categories at the same time. iPhoto includes a number of default keywords, but in this section you learn how to add your own keywords.

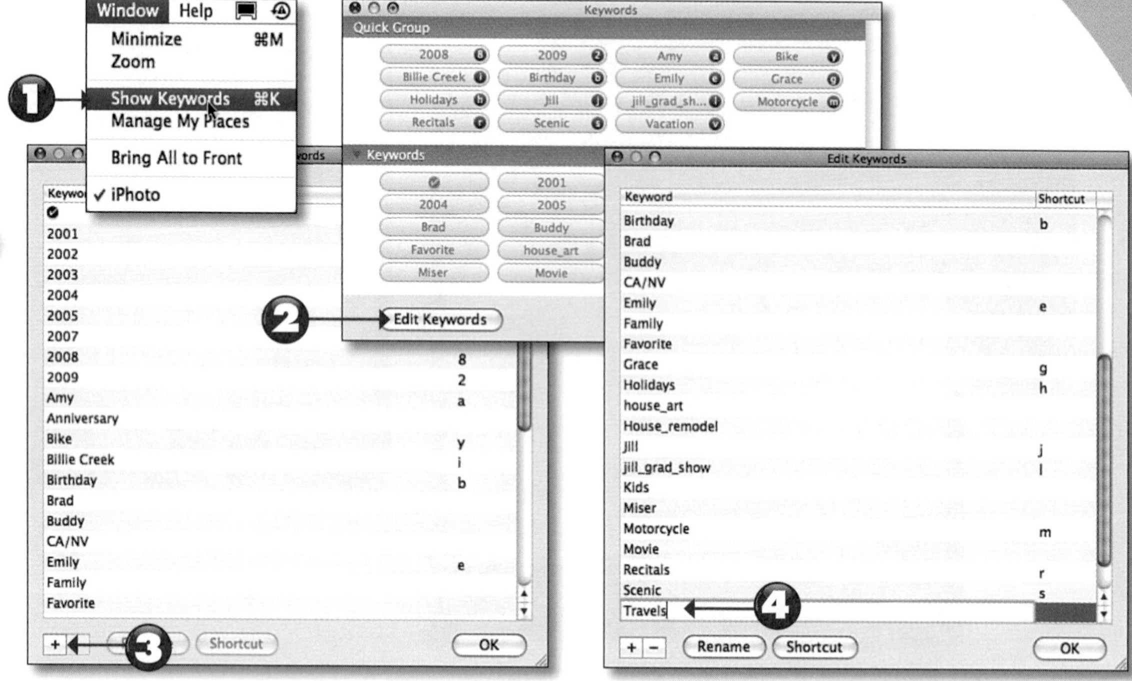

Start

1. Choose **Window**, **Show Keywords**.
2. Click **Edit Keywords**.
3. To add a keyword, click the **Add** button.
4. Type the keyword and press **Return**.

Continued

NOTE

Keyword Panes The Keywords window contains the keywords available to you. It has two panes. In the upper pane, called Quick Group, are the keywords that have shortcuts assigned to them. In the lower pane, labeled Keywords, are the rest of your keywords. ■

TIP

Opening Keywords Quickly You can open the Keywords window by pressing **⌘-K**. ■

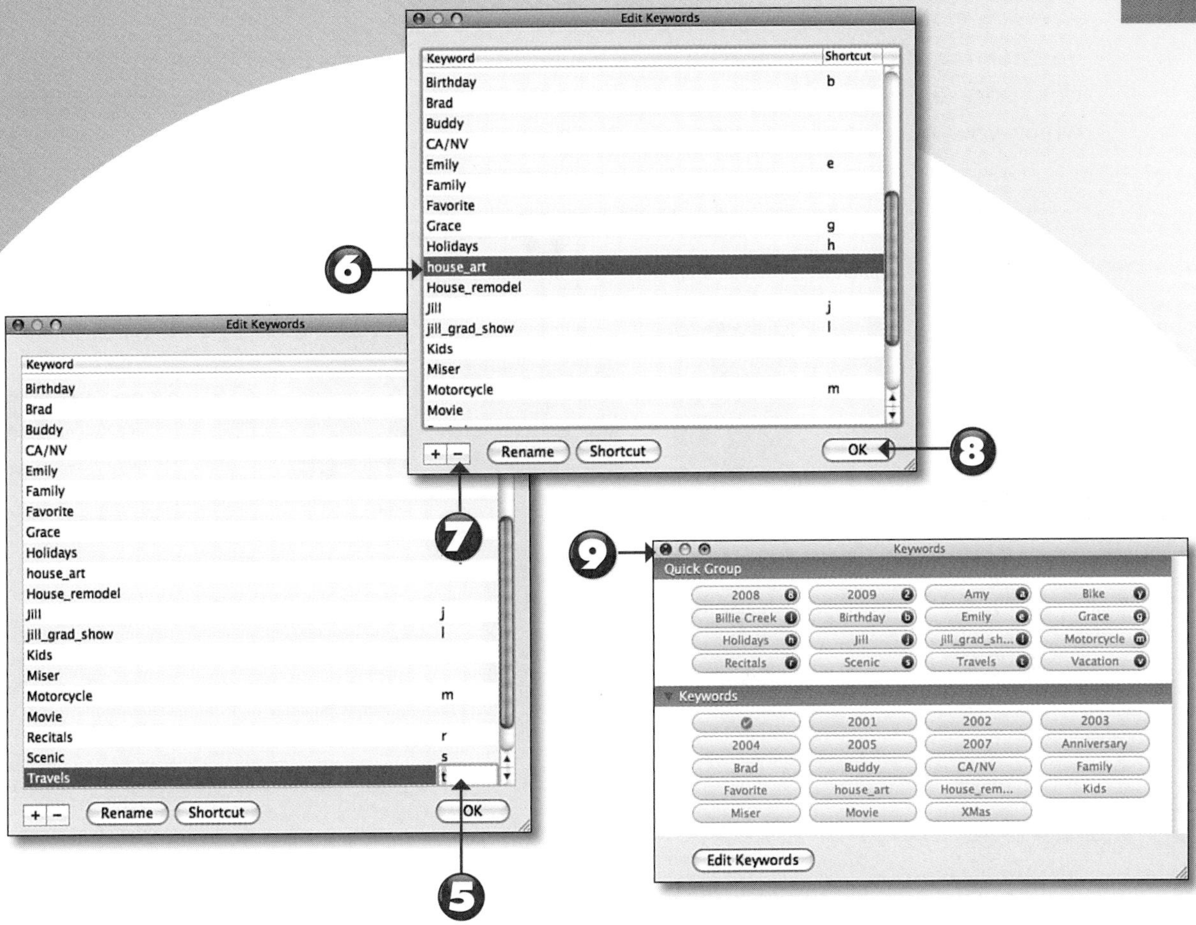

5 To enter a shortcut for the keyword, press **Tab** so that the Shortcut field is highlighted, and then press the key you want to associate with the keyword.

6 To remove a keyword you no longer use, select it.

7 Click the **Remove** button.

8 Click **OK** to close the Edit Keywords window.

9 Click the **Close** button to close the Keywords window.

End

TIP

Automatic Shortcuts You can have shortcuts automatically assigned to keywords by dragging them from the Keywords pane onto the Quick Group pane. ■

NOTE

Alphabetical Keywords Keywords are organized alphabetically in the Keywords window. You can only change the order of keywords by changing their text. ■

APPLYING KEYWORDS TO PHOTOS

You can tag photos with one or more keywords to associate those photos with the categories represented by your keywords. Then, you can find your photos using the keywords with which you've associated them.

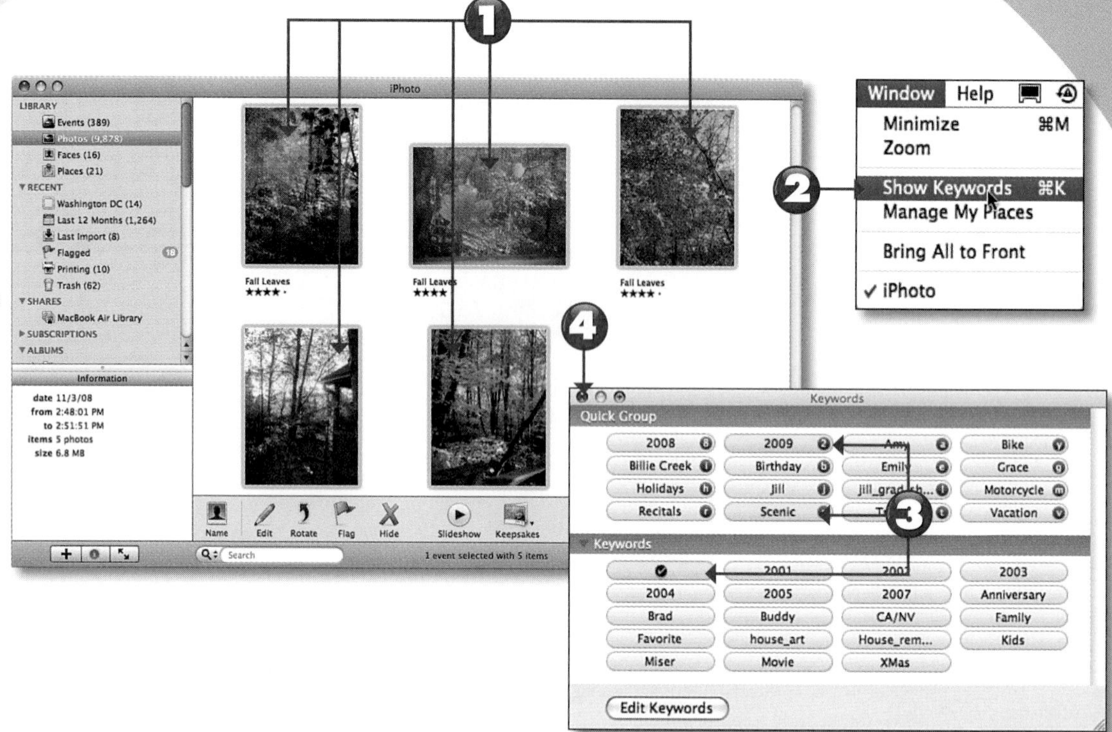

Start

1. Select the photos to which you want to apply one or more keywords.

2. Choose **Window**, **Show Keywords**.

3. Click the keywords you want to apply to the photos.

4. Close the Keywords window when you are done.

End

NOTE

Blue Keywords Keywords that are currently assigned to the selected photos are highlighted in blue in the Keywords window. ■

TIP

Applying Keywords If a keyword has a shortcut, you can apply it by pressing its shortcut key when the Keywords window is open. You can remove a keyword that is applied to the selected photos by clicking it. ■

SEARCHING FOR PHOTOS BY BASIC INFORMATION

Finding photos you want to view or use in a project is always the first step in any iPhoto task. The application includes a number of ways in which you can search for photos. One of these is to search by the "basic" information such as titles and descriptions.

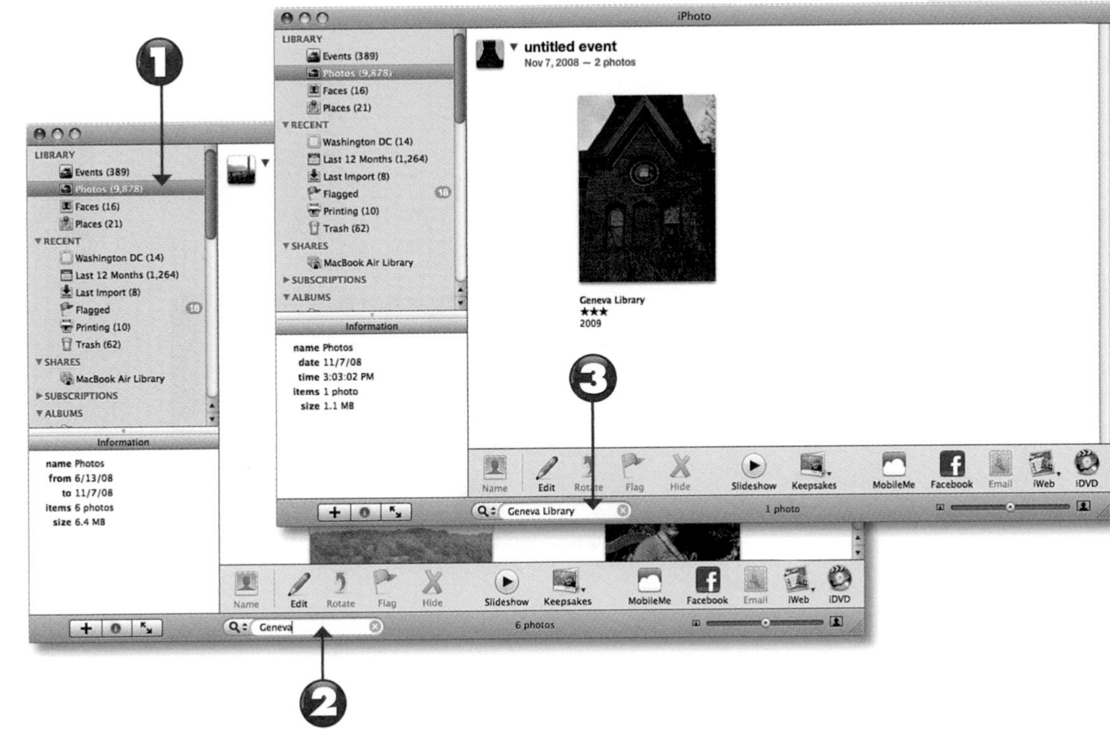

Start

1. Select the source in which you want to search, such as the Photos source to search your entire library.
2. Type the text or numbers for which you want to search in the Search field. As you type, only photos that are tagged with your search term are shown in the Viewing pane.
3. Continue typing until you see the photos you are looking for.

End

NOTE

Searching with Text When you search for basic information, you search both photo and event information. So, if you search for "Colts Football," you'll find photos that are tagged with that information along with any that are included in an event tagged with that information. ■

TIP

Searching by Location You can search for photos by location by typing place names in the Search tool or by people by typing names in the tool. ■

SEARCHING FOR PHOTOS BY KEYWORDS

Keyword searches are easy to perform and are powerful because you can combine several of them during a search, such as a person's name and a holiday.

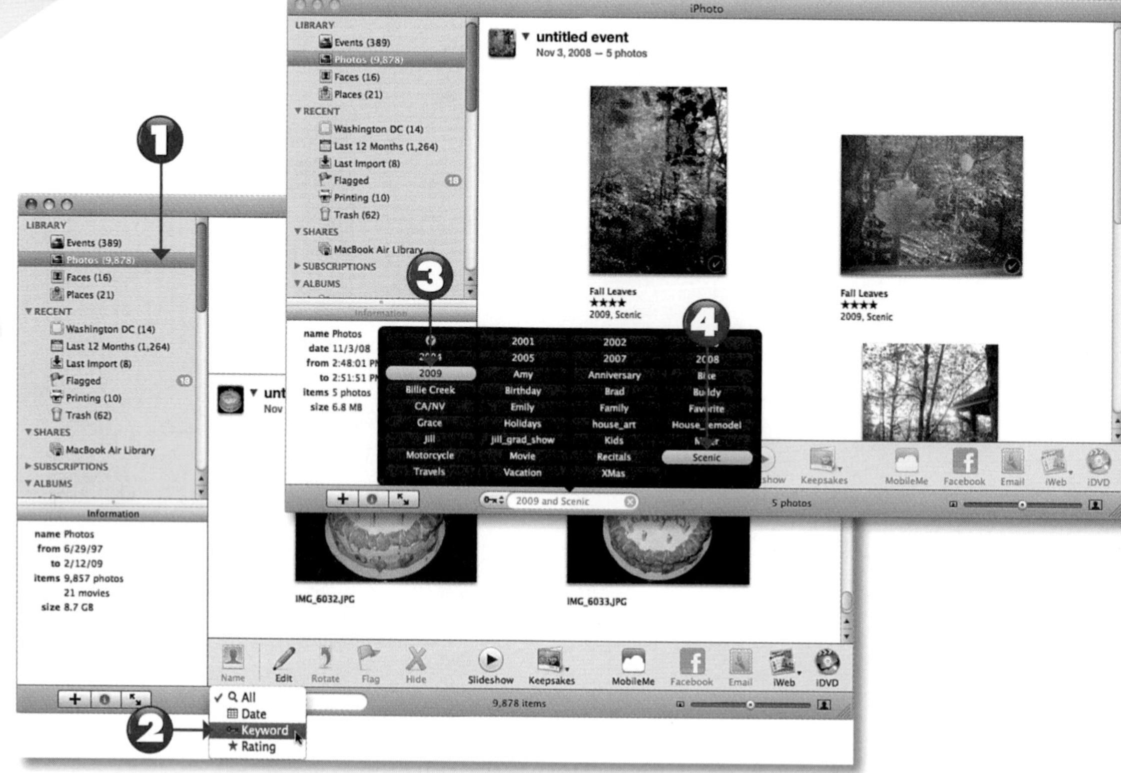

Start

1. Select the source in which you want to search, such as the Photos source to search your entire library.
2. Click the **Search Tool** menu and select **Keyword**.
3. On the Keywords window, click the first keyword for which you want to search.
4. Continue clicking keywords to add them to the search. Photos with which those keywords are associated appear in the Viewing pane.

End

NOTE

Boolean Fun A keyword search is an "and" search, meaning that all the keywords you select must be associated with a photo for it to be included in the results. ■

TIP

How Many? When you point to a keyword on the Keywords window, a pop-up tip indicates how many photos are associated with that keyword. ■

SEARCHING FOR PHOTOS BY DATE

The great thing about date information is that your photos are automatically tagged with a date and time when you take pictures with a digital camera. That means that all the photos in your library have date information by which you can search for photos.

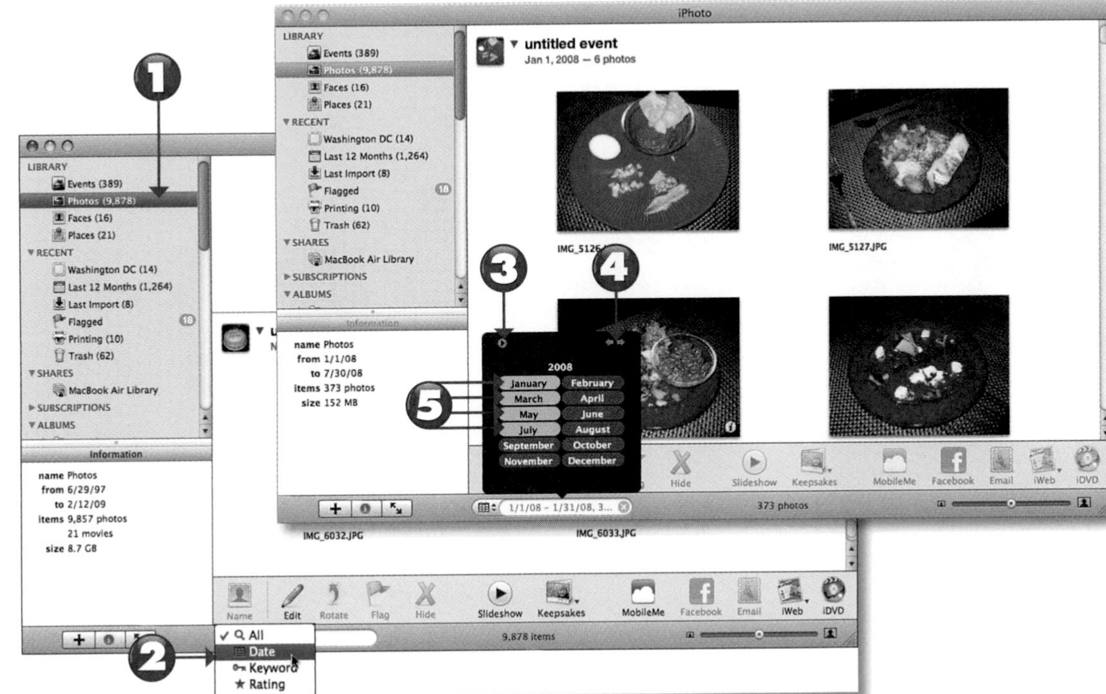

Start

1. Select the source in which you want to search, such as the Photos source.
2. Click the **Search Tool** menu and select **Date**.
3. Click the **Mode** button until the tool shows the 12 months of the year.
4. Click the previous or next arrows to move to the previous or next year, respectively.
5. Click the months in which you want to search for photos; hold the ⌘ key down to select multiple months. Photos in the selected timeframe appear on the Viewing pane.

End

NOTE

How Many Photos? Dates that have photos associated with them are highlighted on the Date tool. Point to a date to see how many photos are associated with it. ■

TIP

Find by Date You can search by specific dates by clicking the **Mode** button until you see the Date view; then select the dates. ■

SEARCHING FOR PHOTOS BY RATING

When you rate photos, you tag them with a rating between one and five stars. Presumably a five-star rating is the "best" kind of photo, while a one-star rated photo isn't as good. But, rating is purely qualitative, so you can make the scale mean anything you'd like. You can search for photos with specific ratings.

Start

1. Select the source in which you want to search, such as the Photos source to search your entire library.

2. Click the **Search Tool** menu and select **Rating**.

3. Click the number of stars for which you want to search. Photos that have that rating or higher appear in the Viewing pane.

End

NOTE

Or More Search When you search by rating, you set the minimum number of stars for a photo to be included in the results. If you click the fourth star in the Search tool, you find photos that are rated with four or five stars. ■

TIP

Clear a Search To clear any search, click the **Clear** button (**x**) in the Search tool. ■

VIEWING AN EVENT'S INFORMATION

Similar to photos, events can also be tagged with information. You can browse and search for events by their tags. And any photos contained within those events are found when you find the events. You can view an event's information using the Info dialog box or the Info pane.

Start

1. Select **Events**.
2. Browse the Viewing pane to find and select an event in which you are interested.
3. Click the event's **i** button.
4. View the event's information.
5. Click **Done**.

End

TIP

Previewing Photos You can preview the photos in an event by dragging across the photo thumbnail in the upper-left corner of the Info dialog box. ■

TIP

Event Info To see an event's information in the Info pane, open the Info pane and select the event. In the pane, you see the event's name, date range, number of photos, file size, and description. ■

TAGGING AN EVENT

Like photos, you can tag events with information so that you can use that information to find and organize your photos. Also like photos, you can use the Info dialog box to configure an event's tags.

Start

1. Select the event you want to tag and click its **i** button.

2. Type a title for the event.

3. Set a location for the event.

4. Enter a description for the event.

End

NOTE

Default Event Names By default, events are named with the date of the photos they contain, but you can name an event anything you'd like. ■

TIP

Set Key Photo To set an event's key photo, which is the photo shown in the event's thumbnail, drag over the thumbnail on the Info dialog box until the photo you want to use is shown. Click the mouse button to set that as the key photo. ■

MERGING EVENTS

The events iPhoto creates might not always organize your photos the way you want them to be organized. For example, you might want all the photos you took on a vacation to be in the same event. However, when you import those photos, iPhoto creates an event for each day of the trip. You can merge events to combine all of their photos into a single event.

1. Select the events you want to merge; hold the ⌘ key down as you click each event you want to include in the merged event.
2. Click the **Merge** button.
3. Click **Merge** at the prompt. The selected events are merged into one event.
4. Click the merged event's **i** button.
5. Enter the event's information and click **Done**.

End

TIP

Don't Bother Me Again Many of iPhoto's warning prompts enable you to skip them in the future by checking the **Don't Ask Again** check box. ■

SPLITTING EVENTS

Events can have too many photos, or may contain photos that you want to separate into two or more events. In those situations, you can split an event into two events. You can repeat this process as many times as needed to create as many events from a single event as you want.

Start

1. View the event that you want to split by double-clicking its frame.
2. Select the photo at which you want the event to be split into two events.
3. Click **Split**. The event is split into two events, and you see both events in the Viewing pane.
4. To split the event again, select the photo where you want the split event and click **Split**.
5. Configure the tags for each event you created.

End

NOTE

First Photo When you split an event, the photo you select becomes the first photo in the new event. ■

CREATING EVENTS

You can create your own events and then add photos to them. (See the next section for the details about adding photos to an event.) For example, you might want to create an event for all of your scenic photos for a given year.

1. Click **Events** on the Source list and choose **Events**, **Create Event**. A new, empty event is created.
2. Click the event's **i** button.
3. Configure the new event's information.

End

NOTE

Can't Create? If you have any events or photos selected, the Create Event command is disabled. If this happens, click outside of any event or photo and then try again. ■

NOTE

No Location If you plan to include photos from different locations in the new event, leave its Location field empty. Each photo within the event can have a location associated with it, and you can use that information to find photos by location regardless of the event they are stored in. ■

MOVING PHOTOS BETWEEN EVENTS

You can organize photos by moving them between events. These can be events that iPhoto created when you imported photos or events you created. When you move a photo from one event to another, that photo becomes associated with the event in which you place it. The event's information also gets updated, such as the date range of the photos it contains.

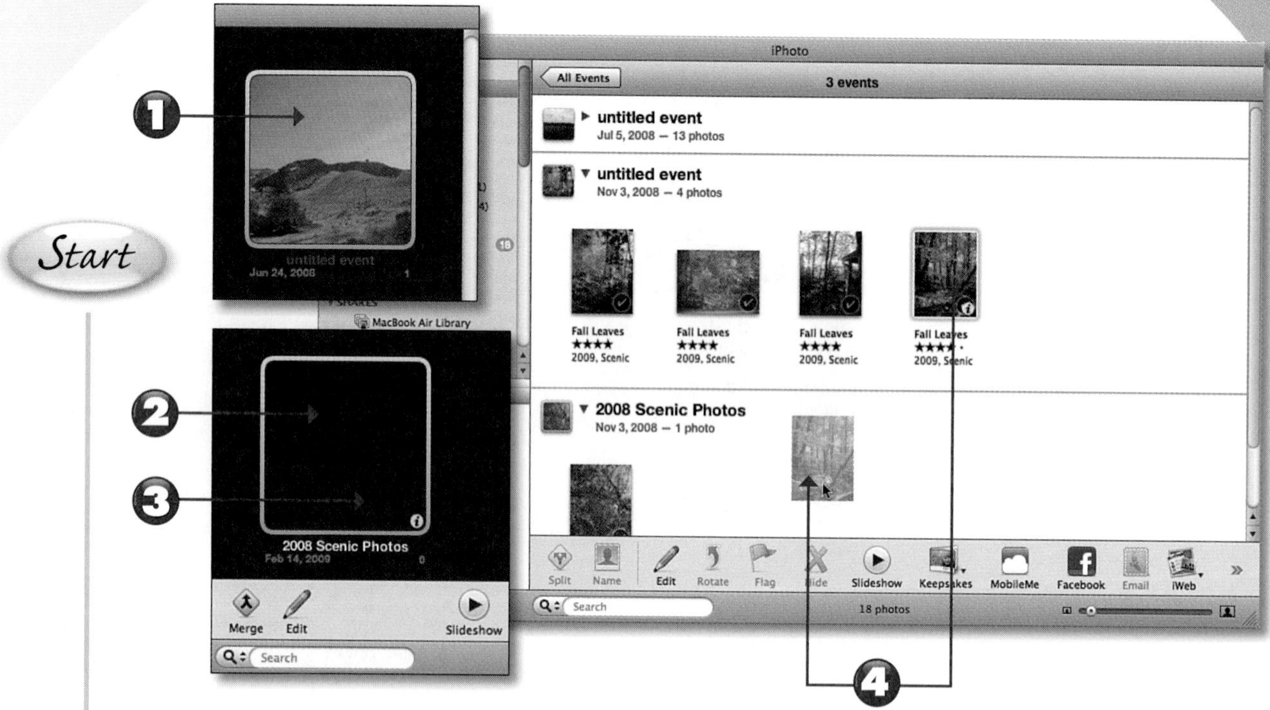

1. Select the event (call this event 1) containing photos you want to move to another event.
2. Hold the ⌘ key down and select the event into which you want to move photos (call this event 2).
3. Double-click **event 2** to view both events.
4. Drag the photos you want to move from event 1 into event 2.

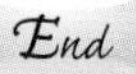

NOTE

Empty Events If you move all the photos out of an event, it is removed from your library. ■

TIP

An Easier Way to Move Photos? You can also move photos between events by selecting the photos you want to move, choosing **Edit**, **Cut**, moving into the event in which you want to place them, and choosing **Edit**, **Paste**. ■

ORGANIZING ALBUMS AND PROJECTS IN FOLDERS

When you start creating photo albums and projects, you'll probably end up with a lot of them, which can clutter up the Source list so that it becomes hard to work with. You can organize your Source list by creating folders and then placing other objects into those folders. You can store photo albums, projects, and even other folders within folders you create.

Start

1. Choose **File**, **New Folder**.
2. Type the name of the folder and press **Return**. The folder is created with the name you entered.
3. Drag items from the Source list onto the folder's icon; when the folder's icon is highlighted by a blue box, release the mouse button.
4. Continue adding items to the folder until it contains everything you want.

End

NOTE

Folder Contents When you select a folder's icon, in the Viewing pane, you see all the photos the albums within the folder contain.

TIP

Expand or Collapse Folders You can collapse or expand folders on the Source list by clicking the triangles next to their icons.

CREATING AND ADDING PHOTOS TO STANDARD PHOTO ALBUMS

Photo albums are a way to collect and organize photos for various purposes. A standard photo album is one you create and then manually add photos. You can then organize the photos in any way you want.

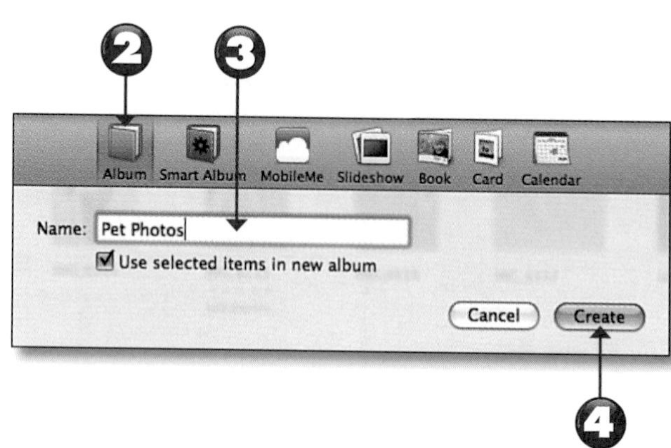

1. Click the **Add** button at the bottom of the iPhoto window.
2. Click the **Album** tab.
3. Enter the name of the album you are creating.
4. Click **Create**. The album is created and appears on the Source list.

Continued

NOTE

One Photo, Many Albums The same photo can be in many photo albums. That's because when you add a photo to a photo album, iPhoto really just places a pointer there. The photo remains in your library. ■

TIP

Start with Photos To include photos in a new album when you create it, select the photos you want to include, and then perform step 1. ■

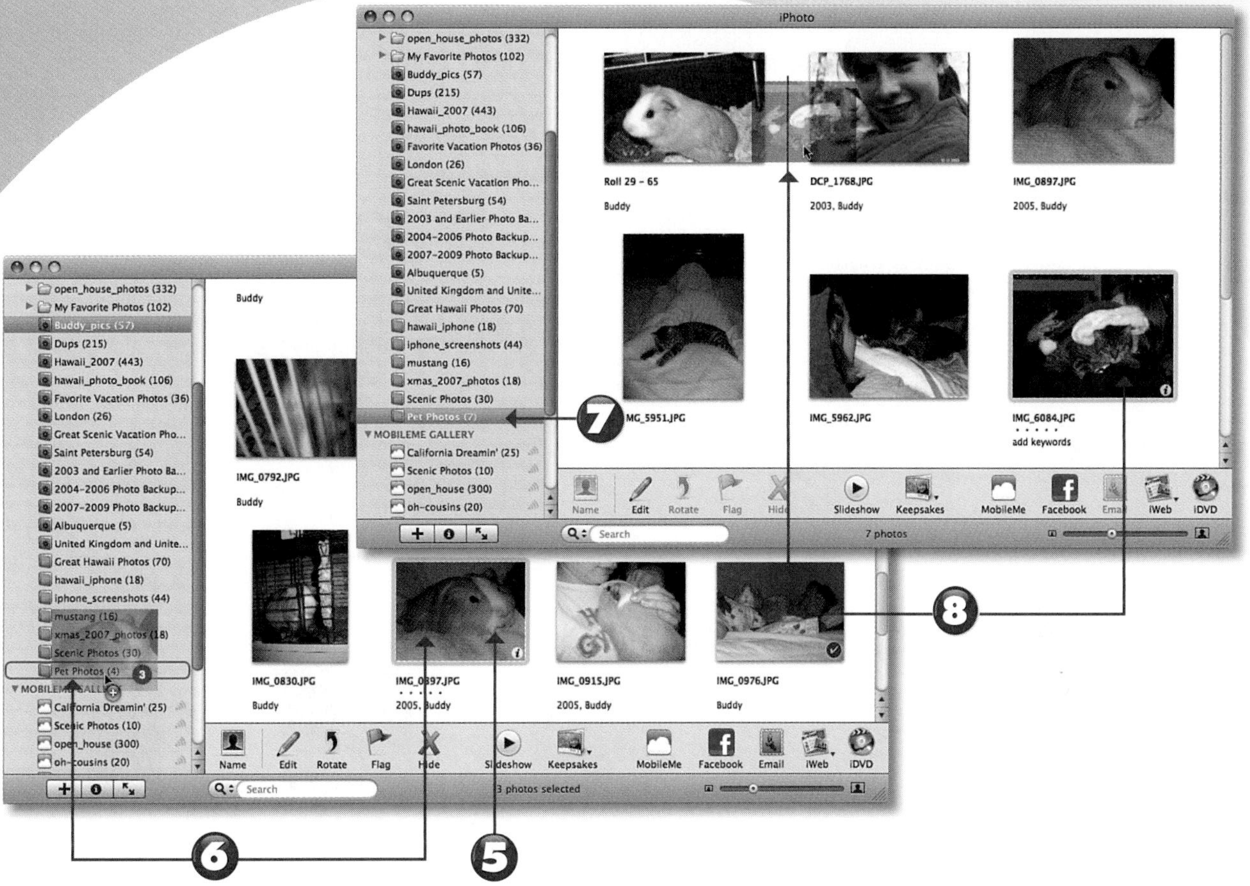

5. Find and select photos you want to add to the new album. You can use any of the techniques you've learned to locate photos you want to place in the new album.

6. Drag the photos from the Viewing pane onto the album's icon; release the mouse button when the green circle containing a + appears and the album is highlighted.

7. Select the album you created.

8. Drag the photos around the Viewing pane to place them in the order you want them to appear. As you move a photo between photos, they slide apart to make room.

End

TIP

Removing Photos To remove a photo from an album, select it and press **Delete**. Because only a pointer is stored in the album, nothing happens to the photo itself. ■

NOTE

Order, Order When viewing the photos an album contains or using their photos in projects, pictures appear in left to right order starting from the upper-left position in the Viewing pane. For example, when you play the photos in a slideshow, the upper-left photo is the first one, and the lower-right photo is the end. ■

CREATING SMART PHOTO ALBUMS

A smart photo album has the same basic purpose as a standard photo album, that being to collect photos for various purposes, including viewing them and using them in projects. However, unlike a standard photo album, you don't place photos into a smart photo album manually. Instead, you define conditions based on tags, and the smart photo album gathers all the photos that meet those conditions automatically.

Start

1. Click the **Add** button at the bottom of the iPhoto window.
2. Click the **Smart Album** tab.
3. Enter the name of the smart album you are creating.
4. Choose the first condition attribute on the left pop-up menu.

Continued

NOTE

Why is Smart, Smart? Another difference between a smart photo album and a standard photo album is that you can't arrange the photos in a smart album by dragging them around. Their order is determined by the Sort Photos command on the View menu. ■

NOTE

Changing Options The choices you make on the smart album window's pop-up menus determine which controls and options are available. For example, if you choose a date condition, you see tools relevant to choosing dates. ■

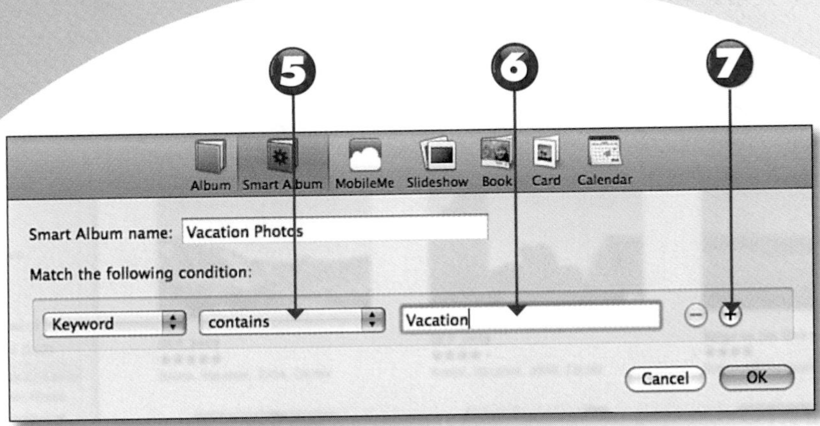

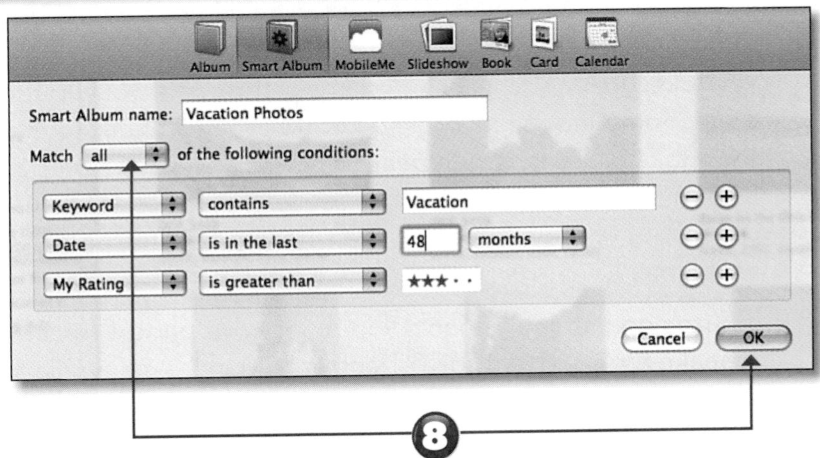

5. Select the comparison you want to use in the condition on the center pop-up menus.

6. Enter the criterion in the fields that appear or make choices on pop-up menus.

7. Click the **Add Condition** button. Repeat steps 4 through 6 to add all the conditions you want to use for photos to be included in the smart album.

8. If you want all the conditions to be met for a photo to be included, choose **All** on the Match pop-up menu. If you want only one condition to have to be met for a photo to be included, select **Any** instead. Click **OK**.

End

NOTE

Gathering Photos After you click **OK** to create a smart photo album, the photos that meet its conditions are collected within it, the album is selected on the Source list, and you see the photos it contains. ■

TIP

Changing Smart Albums To change the contents of a smart photo album, select it on the Source list and choose **File**, **Edit Smart Album**. On the resulting window, you can make changes to the album's conditions, and thus change the contents of the album. ■

IMPROVING PHOTOS IN iPHOTO

One of the best things about using iPhoto is that you can improve the photos you take. Is something included in a picture that you'd rather not see? Just crop it out. Something seem off-kilter? Straighten a photo to make it look right. Do the subjects of a photo appear to have become demon-possessed? You don't need an exorcist; a few clicks of the Red-eye tool will get them back to the light side. Want to apply your artistic creativity to some photos? With iPhoto, it's no problemo.

iPhoto's editing tools enable you to improve photos to correct problems or to make them better, more effective, and more enjoyable to look at. To edit a photo, you select it, and then put iPhoto into Edit mode. You can do this within the iPhoto window, or you can use full-screen editing.

When you edit within the iPhoto window, you see the Source list on the left as you normally do. At the top of the right part of the window, you see the photo browser, where thumbnails of photos you are editing appear. When you select a thumbnail, the photo appears in the largest part of the window, which is where you edit it. At the bottom of the right part of the window, you see iPhoto's editing tools.

Photo being edited
Photos in selected source
Navigation window
iPhoto
Navigation
Rotate
Crop
Straighten
Enhance
Red-Eye
Retouch
Effects
Adjust
Done
Photo 3 of 102
Selected source
Editing tools
Size slider

EDITING PHOTOS

No matter which specific editing tasks you want to do, you follow some common steps. These include selecting the photo you want to edit, moving into the Edit mode, zooming and navigating in the photo, editing it, and saving your changes. You need to perform these general steps when you perform the remainder of the tasks in this chapter.

Start

1. Select Events, Photos, or an album containing the photos you want to edit.
2. Click the **Edit** button.
3. Browse the photos and select the one you want to edit.
4. If you are doing detailed editing (such as retouching), use the size slider to zoom in or out.
5. Drag the box in the Navigation window to focus on the area you want to edit.

Continued

TIP

Editing in Full Screen If you want to try editing in full screen, click the **Full Screen** button (it has two diagonal arrows pointing away from each other). The photo fills the screen. Point to the top of the screen to see the browser and to the bottom to see the editing tools. Press **Escape** to exit. ■

6 Use the editing tools to edit the photo.

7 Click the **Previous** or **Next** button to move to the previous or next photo in the selected source to edit it.

8 Edit the next photo. Repeat until you've edited the photos in the selected source.

9 Click **Done**.

End

TIP

Editing in Full Screen All the Time You can set your default Edit mode (full screen or in the main window) using the Edit Photo pop-up menu on the General tab of the iPhoto Preferences dialog box.

NOTE

Save? Edits to your photos are saved when you select another photo by clicking its thumbnail, the **Previous** or **Next** buttons, and when you click the **Done** button.

ROTATING PHOTOS

This is a simple but extremely useful edit. When you take or import photos in the portrait orientation, they come into iPhoto "on their sides" so that up and down are actually left and right. With the Rotate tool, you can put photos in their proper orientation.

Start

1. In Edit mode, select a photo that needs to be rotated.

2. Click the **Rotate** button until the photo is oriented properly.

End

TIP

Default Direction You can set the default direction of the Rotate button on the General pane of the iPhoto Preferences dialog box. Choose the orientation that is needed most commonly for photos you take by rotating your camera. ■

TIP

Changing Directions When you hold the **Option** key down, the Rotate button switches to the opposite direction. You can also rotate an image by pressing **⌘-R** or **Option-⌘-R** to rotate the photo in the opposite direction. ■

APPLYING EFFECTS TO PHOTOS

iPhoto includes a number of effects you can apply to photos to enhance their appearance for artistic or other purposes. For many of these effects, you can also choose "how much" of the effect you apply.

1. Click the **Effects** button.
2. Click the first effect you want to apply.
3. If applicable, increase or decrease the amount of the effect by clicking the arrows at the bottom of the effect's box.
4. Apply and adjust more effects.

End

CAUTION

Change Once Everywhere Be aware that when you edit a photo, the changes you make apply to *every* use of that photo. If you crop a photo that you use in a photo book and a slideshow, the cropped version will be used in both projects.

TIP

You Can Go Back Again To remove all the effects from a photo, apply the Original effect.

CROPPING PHOTOS

Cropping means to cut out parts of a photo you don't want or to refocus the image more on the part that is of the most interest to you. For example, if you want those who look at a photo to focus mostly on the people in the photo, you should crop it down so that the people fill most of the image. If the background is important, crop out less.

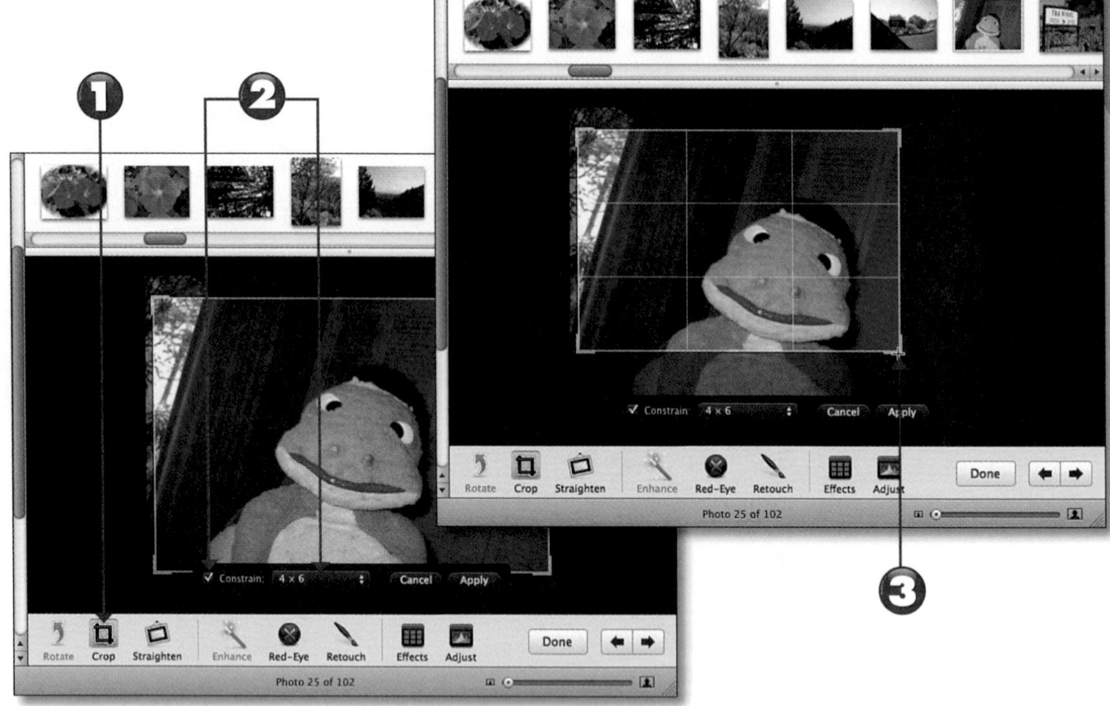

1. Click the **Crop** button.

2. To constrain the cropped photo to specific dimensions, check the **Constrain** check box and choose the proportion you want to maintain on the pop-up menu.

3. Drag the crop box by its Resize handle until it is about the size (and shape if you didn't constrain it) you want the cropped photo to be.

Continued

TIP

Making Copies Earlier, you learned that edits you make on an image, such as a crop, apply to the image everywhere it is used. If you don't want this, make a copy of a photo by selecting it and pressing **⌘-D**. You can edit and use the copy in a project without impacting the versions you've used elsewhere. ■

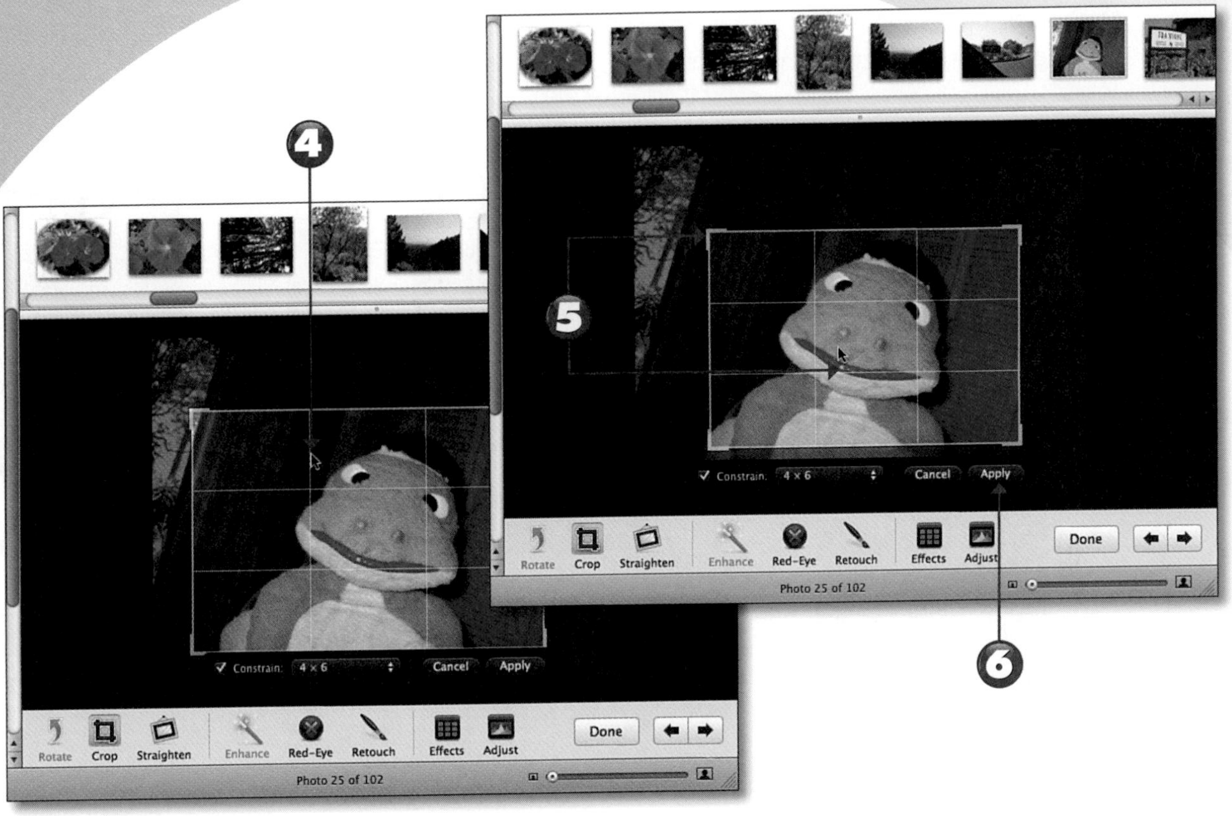

4 Drag the crop box around until the part of the photo you want to keep is within the box. (Everything outside of the box is cropped out.)

5 Continue adjusting the crop box's size and location until the image is just right.

6 Click **Apply**. The image is cropped.

End

TIP

Seeing Changes To see the impact of a crop, or any other edit for that matter, press and hold the **Shift** key down. The most recent edit you made is "undone." Release the key to see the edit again. Press and hold **Shift** to see the image without the edit again. This is a good way to see whether you are making improvements (or not). ■

STRAIGHTENING PHOTOS

Sometimes, photos aren't lined up "square" with the frame of reference and so they look twisted. You might want this for aesthetic reasons, but in some cases, you want to straighten the image up so that it better aligns with the invisible horizontal and vertical grid we all use to judge whether something is "straight."

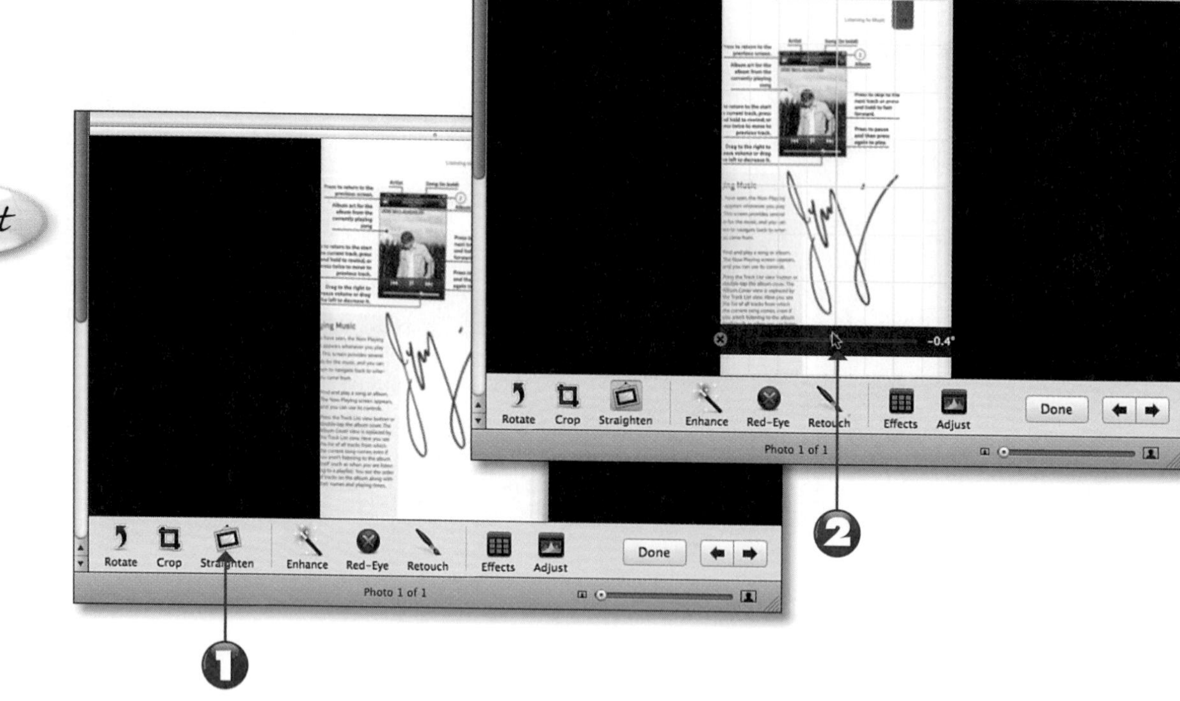

1. Click the **Straighten** tool.
2. Drag the slider to the left to rotate the image to the left or to the right to rotate it to the right. As you move the slider, the image rotates in its frame; the amount of rotation is shown at the end of the slider bar.
3. When the image looks straight, release the mouse button.

End

NOTE

Straighten Scans You can import scanned images into iPhoto. When you scan an image or document, it's not uncommon for the item you scanned to not be quite lined up correctly in the scanner. The Straighten tool is a great way to fix that in iPhoto. ■

TIP

Go Back, Way Back iPhoto always keeps the original version of each photo you import into your iPhoto library, so you can go back to it again; this undoes all the edits you've ever made to a photo. To restore a photo to its as-imported version, select the photo and choose **Photos**, **Revert to Original**. ■

ENHANCING PHOTOS

Sometimes photos are too light or too dark. You can use the Enhance tool to have iPhoto automatically adjust an image's exposure and contrast to improve its appearance. Using the tool is extremely easy.

Start

1. Click the **Enhance** button. The photo's contrast and exposure are adjusted.
2. Continue clicking the **Enhance** button until the photo begins to look worse.
3. Press ⌘-**Z**. The most recent enhancement is undone. The photo should look as good as the tool can make it look.

End

TIP

Going Back to the Previous Version Sometimes as you edit an image with various tools, save it, and then come back to edit it again, you actually make the image worse. You can restore an image to its most recently saved version (the one prior to the current editing session) by choosing **Photos**, **Restore to Previous**. ■

REMOVING RED-EYE

Red-eye is probably the most common problem with photos taken with a digital camera using flash. Nothing spoils a good photo like the evil-looking appearance of eyes when their centers are glowing red. Fortunately, iPhoto includes a Red-eye tool that can help decrease the impact of red eyes. The tool has two modes: Automatic and Manual. Try the Automatic mode first. If that doesn't work, use the Manual mode.

Start

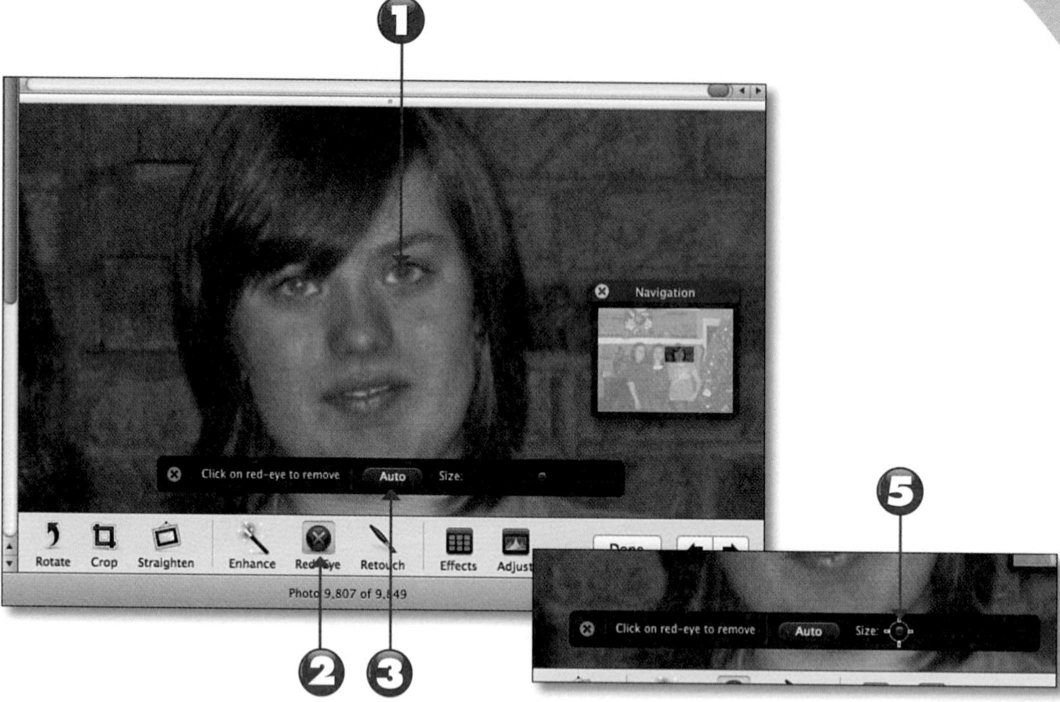

1. Zoom and navigate to focus on some glowing eyes.
2. Click the **Red-eye** button. The Red-eye tool appears.
3. Click the **Auto** button. iPhoto attempts to remove the red-eye. If the problem is corrected sufficiently, you're done. If not, continue.
4. Press ⌘-**Z** to undo the automatic red-eye correction.
5. Drag the slider until the size of the circle (which is the pointer on the screen) is about the size of the red circles in the first eye you want to correct.

Continued

TIP

Zoom on Red As you evaluate red-eye correction, make sure you zoom out to see the photo at the size you'll typically view it. Red-eye correction doesn't look its best when you are zoomed in. ■

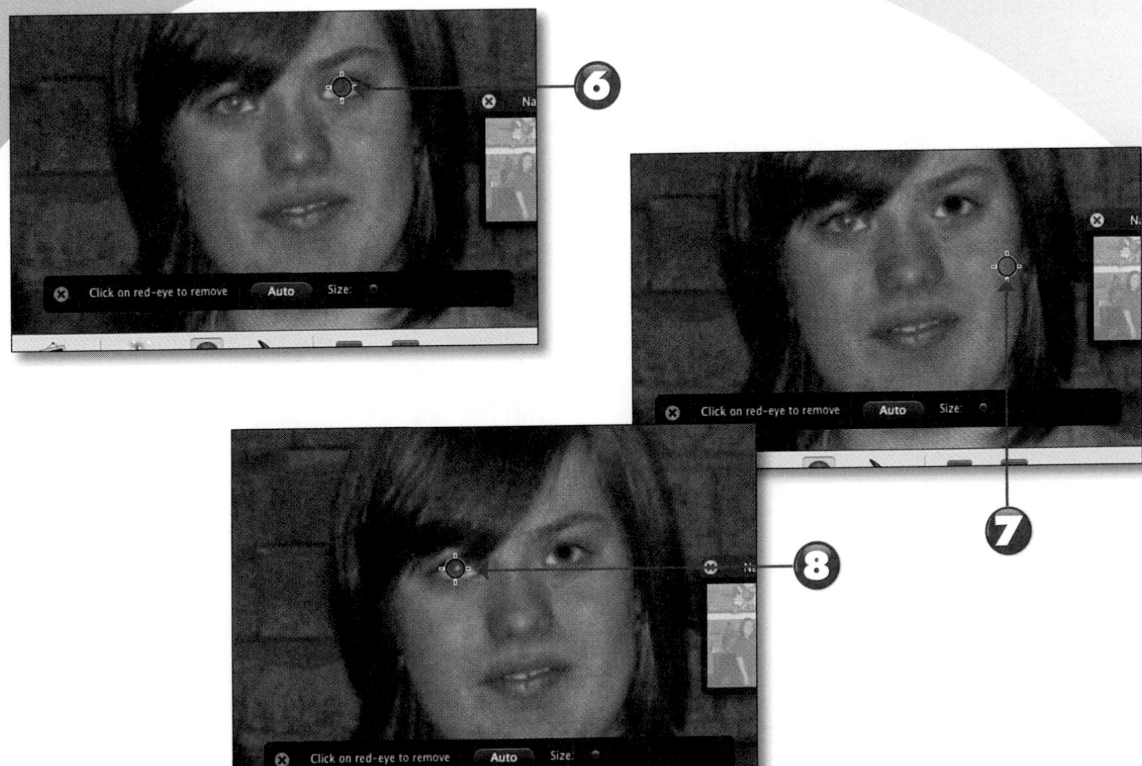

6 Move the pointer over the red part of the eye. Click the mouse button. The red in the circle is replaced with black.

7 Move the pointer out of the way and look at the result.

8 If you're happy with the eye, move to the other eyes in the photo and repeat the process. If not, press ⌘-**Z** to undo the change, make the pointer circle smaller or larger, and try again.

End

NOTE

Seeing Red The red-eye effect occurs because pupils can't close fast enough when a flash occurs. The light from the flash passes though the pupil and hits the fundus at the back of the eye, which reflects red. The red-eye effect is more pronounced in light-colored eyes. ■

TIP

Prevention The best cure for red-eye is to avoid it. Because flash is the cause of red-eye, avoid needing to use flash by using direct or indirect lighting instead. If you have to use flash, don't point the flash in a straight line with the eyes. ■

RETOUCHING PHOTOS

Photos sometimes end up with blemishes, often from a problem with the camera's lens, such as it being dirty or scratched. You can use the Retouching tool to hide the resulting blemishes in a photo.

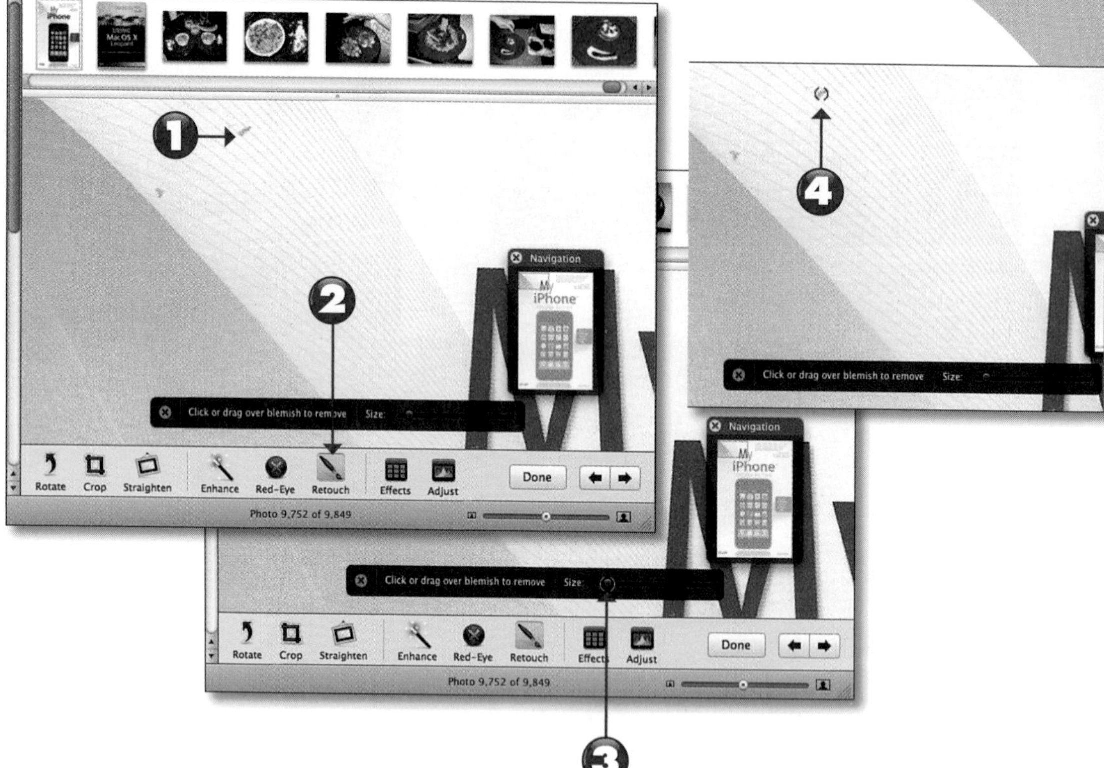

Start

1. Zoom and navigate to focus on the blemish.
2. Click the **Retouch** button. The Retouch tool appears.
3. Drag the size slider until the pointer, which is now a partial circle, is about the size of the blemish.
4. Move the pointer over the blemish.

Continued

NOTE

Smudge It The Retouch tool works by smudging or smearing the blemish so that it blends in with the surrounding part of the image. ■

TIP

Less is More For best results, you want to use as little of the Retouch tool as possible. The more retouching you do, the larger area you "smudge" or "smear," and the retouched area can be worse than the blemish was. ■

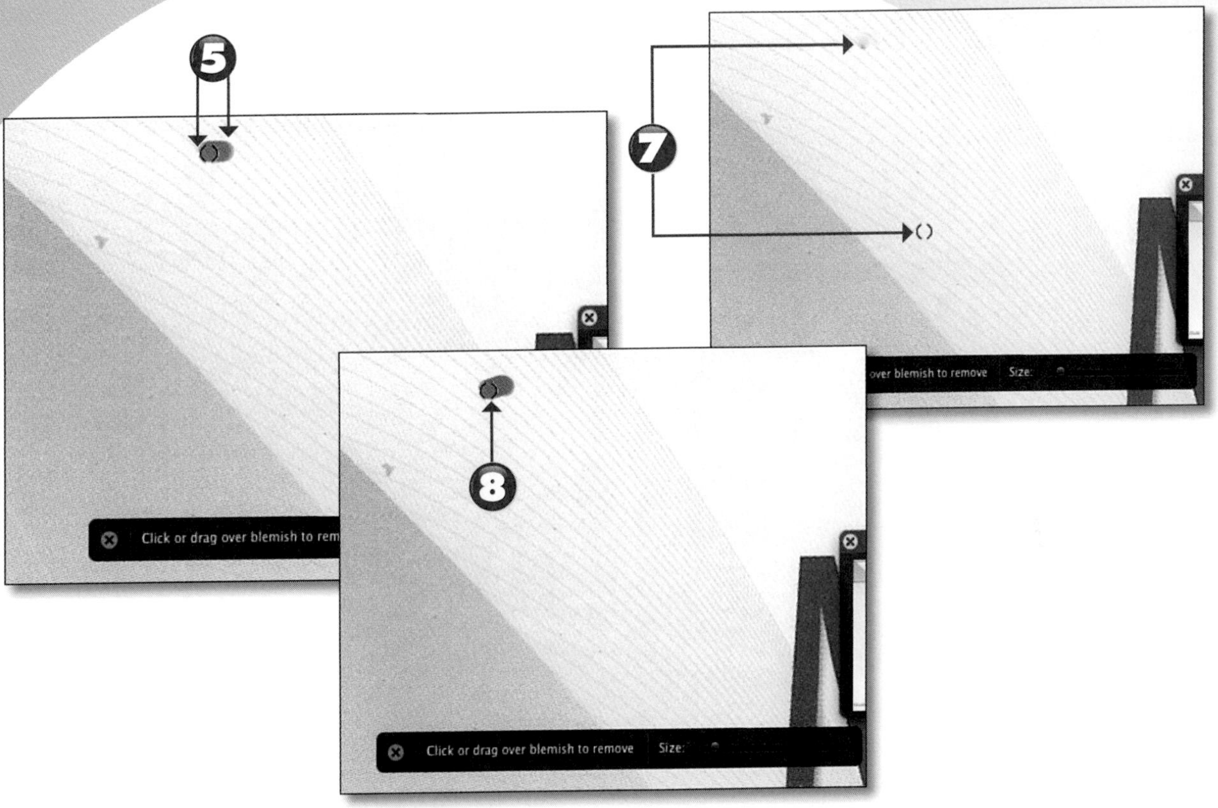

5 Drag the pointer over the blemish. As you drag, a brown swath shows you the part of the image that you are dragging over.

6 When you've covered the blemish, release the mouse button.

7 Move the pointer out of the way and evaluate the results.

8 If the blemish is gone, you're done; if not, repeat the process until it is.

End

TIP

Click instead of Drag Instead of dragging over a blemish, you can just click on it repeatedly. Try both methods to see which has the best result. ■

NOTE

Improving Scans Scanned images are more likely to have blemishes than images you capture with a digital camera. Using the Retouch tool is a great way to clean up these images. ■

ADJUSTING PHOTOS

The Adjust tool is the most complicated because it has many controls that are somewhat technical, such as Contrast, Saturation, and Temperature. Plus, each time you adjust one control, it can impact the appropriate setting of the other controls. Using the Adjust tool is a balancing act of sorts.

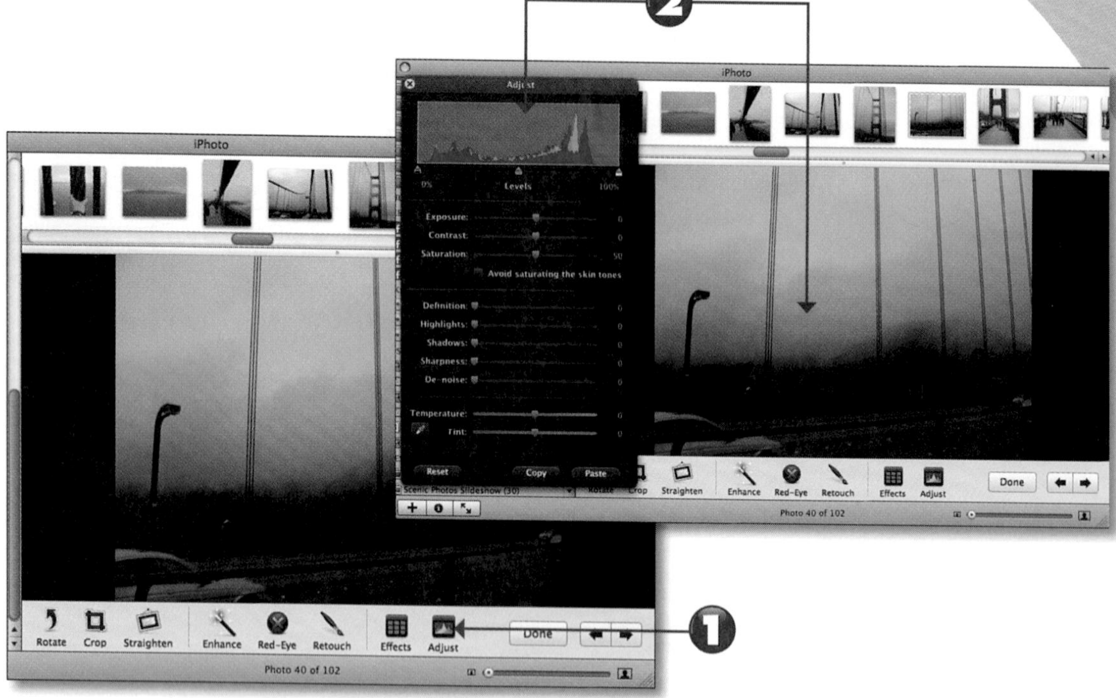

1. Click the **Adjust** button. The Adjust tool appears.
2. Drag the tool on the screen so that you can see it and the photo you are editing.

Continued

NOTE

Technicalities The properties that you can adjust are fairly technical and can be difficult to understand. Some, such as Contrast (which is the amount of distinction between dark and light areas), aren't too difficult to grasp, but others, such as Definition, are harder to define (pun intended). ■

TIP

Experiment The best way to see what impact changing a property has is to drag its slider all the way to the left and then slowly drag it all the way to the right, while looking at the photo. ■

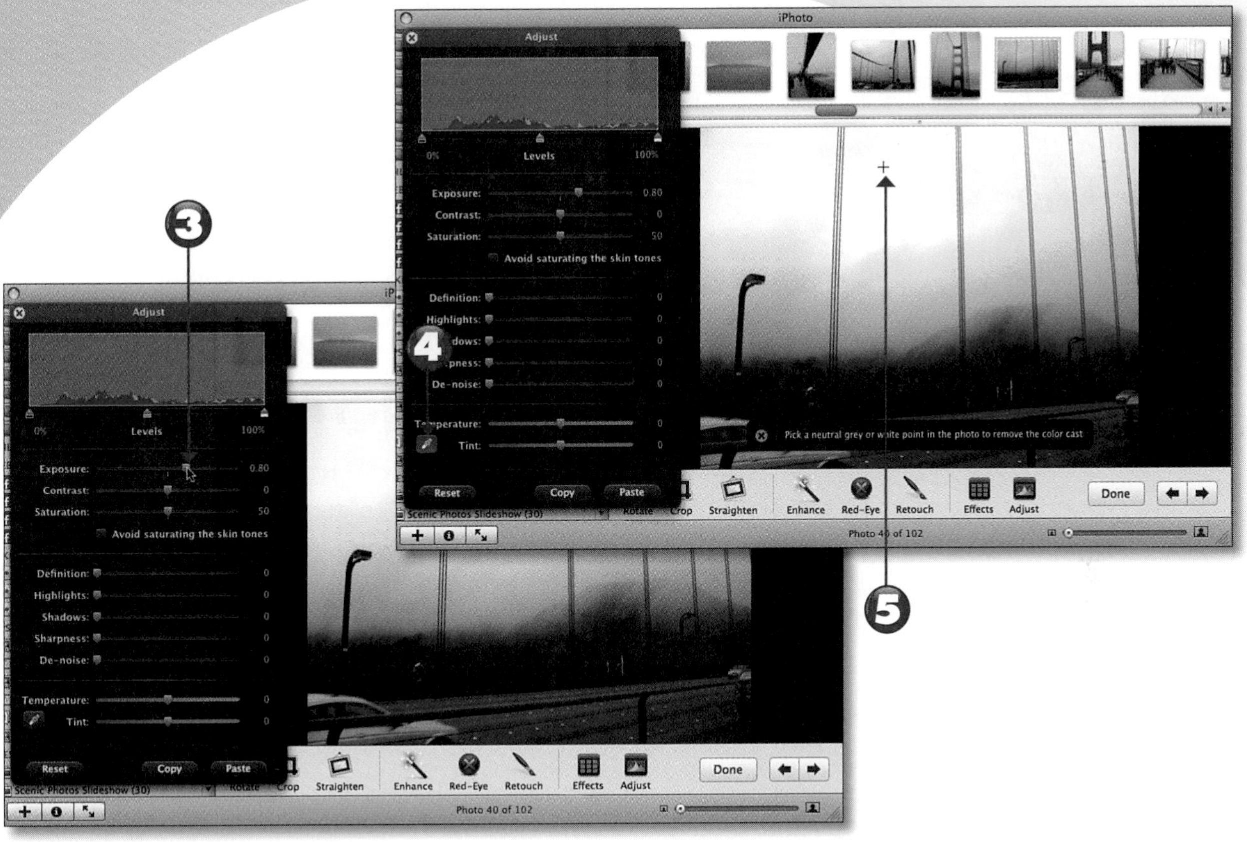

3. Use the sliders to change various properties of the image by moving them from the left to the right. As you move a slider, you see its impact on the image. The relative amount of change is indicated by the position of the slider and the numeric value at the right end of its bar.

4. To try to remove color cast (poor whites) from an image, click the **Eyedropper** button.

5. Point to the neutral gray or white and click the mouse button. iPhoto attempts to reset the colors accordingly.

End

TIP

Copying is Good If you find a set of adjustments that work well, click **Copy**. Move to a similar image and click **Paste** to apply those same adjustments. ■

NOTE

Try, Try, and Try Again The impact of adjusting the same property on different images can be unpredictable because the property's significance can be lesser or greater on different images. Using the Adjust tool well requires a lot of experimentation. ■

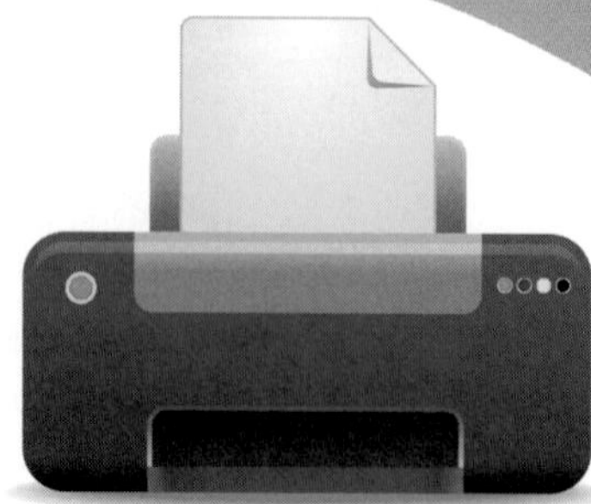

SHARING PHOTOS WITH iPHOTO

You shouldn't keep all your great pictures to yourself; iPhoto provides many ways to share your photos with other people. If you want to go old-school analog, you can print your photos using your own printer, or you can order professionally printed photos through Apple. While being the lowest-tech method, hard copies of photos are still a good way to share them.

There are also many ways to share photos digitally. You can email photos to other people. Or, to enable lots of people to view your photos online, you can publish your photos to the Web using MobileMe, iWeb, and Facebook.

If your Mac is on a local network, you can share your iPhoto library with other people on the network, and you can access photos they share with you. If you put your photos on DVD, other people can use the photos on that DVD within iPhoto on their computers.

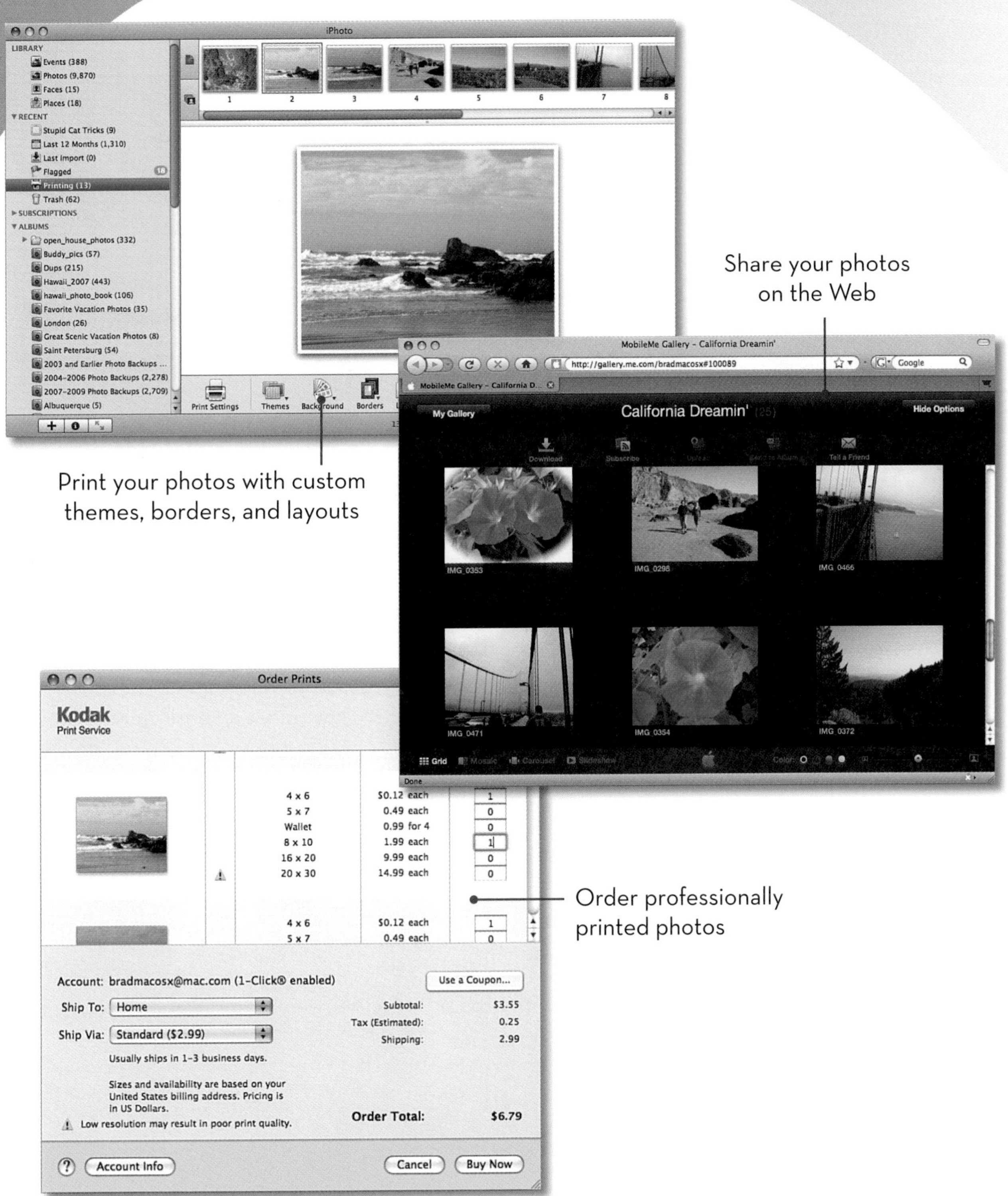
iPhoto
Print your photos with custom themes, borders, and layouts
Share your photos on the Web
MobileMe Gallery - California Dreamin'
California Dreamin'
Order Prints
Kodak
Print Service
4 x 6 $0.12 each
5 x 7 0.49 each
Wallet 0.99 for 4
8 x 10 1.99 each
16 x 20 9.99 each
20 x 30 14.99 each
Order professionally printed photos
Account: bradmacosx@mac.com (1-Click® enabled)
Use a Coupon...
Ship To: Home
Ship Via: Standard ($2.99)
Usually ships in 1-3 business days.
Sizes and availability are based on your United States billing address. Pricing is in US Dollars.
Low resolution may result in poor print quality.
Subtotal: $3.55
Tax (Estimated): 0.25
Shipping: 2.99
Order Total: $6.79
Account Info
Cancel
Buy Now

PRINTING PHOTOS

With all due respect to the higher-tech ways of sharing photos, printing your photos is a great way to share the fruits of your photographic labors with others. And you might want to have a few prints around for yourself.

Start

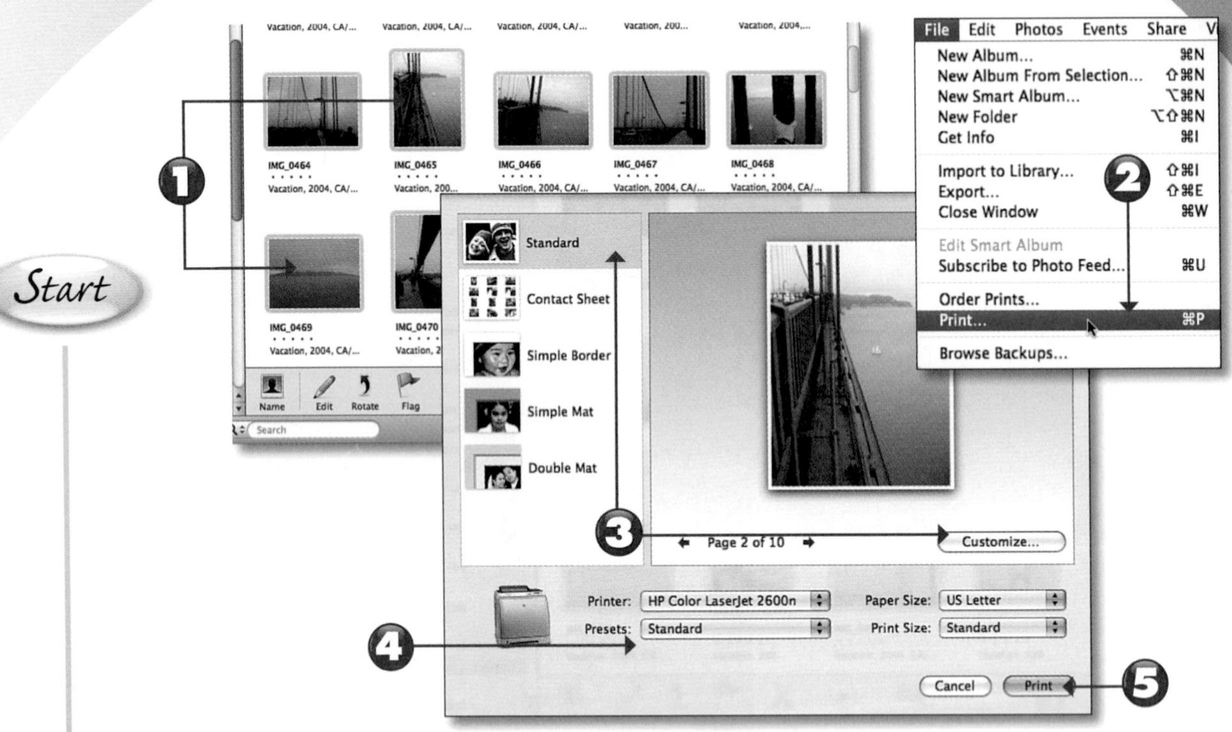

1. Select the photos you want to print. You can select them individually (hold the ⌘ key down while you click photos to select multiple photos at once) or select an entire photo album.

2. Choose **File**, **Print**. The Print sheet appears.

3. Select the theme of the photos you want to print, such as Standard or Contact Sheet, or click **Customize** for more advanced control over the printing and skip to step 6.

4. Configure your printer settings.

5. Click **Print** to print your photos. Your photos print to the selected printer and you're done.

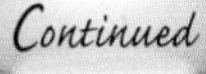

TIP

Print with a Shortcut You can also print by pressing **⌘-P**. ■

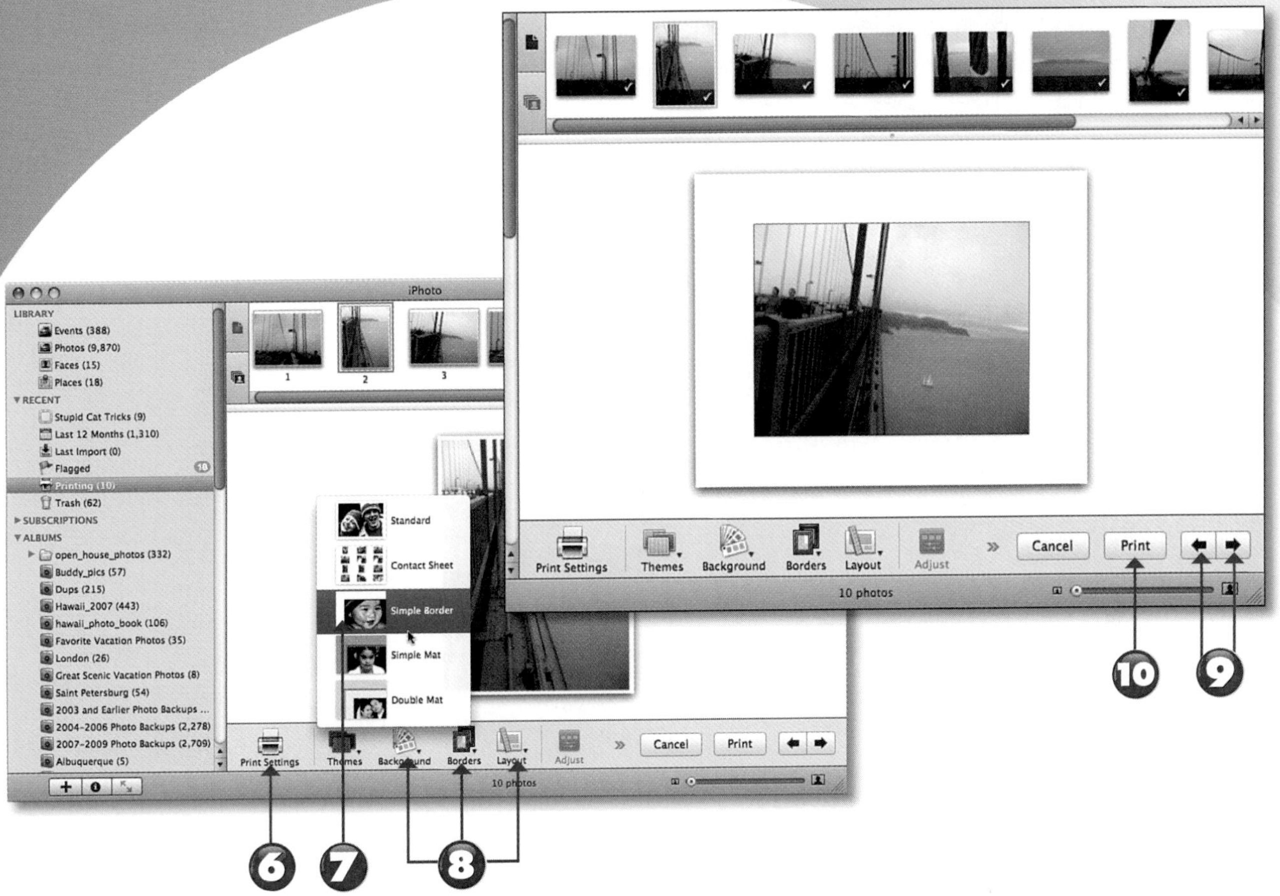

6 Click **Print Settings** to configure your printer.

7 Select the theme you want to use to print the photos.

8 Choose background, borders, and layout options.

9 Click the **Previous** and **Next** arrows to preview each of the photos with the selected options.

10 Click **Print**.

End

NOTE

Printing on the Source List When you use the Customize option, an object called Printing appears in the Recent section of the Source list. This remains until you select and print more photos or delete it. You can print the photos by selecting this object. ■

ORDERING PRINTS OF PHOTOS

Printing your own photos can be expensive and time-consuming. Plus, if you don't have the right mix of paper and toner, the results might be a bit disappointing. Instead of printing photos yourself, you can use iPhoto to send photos to Kodak to be printed. Once printed, the photos are shipped anywhere you'd like. The results you get with this technique are high quality, convenient, and inexpensive. To do this, you have to have an Apple ID, which you can get via the Apple Store, iTunes Store, or from within iPhoto.

Start

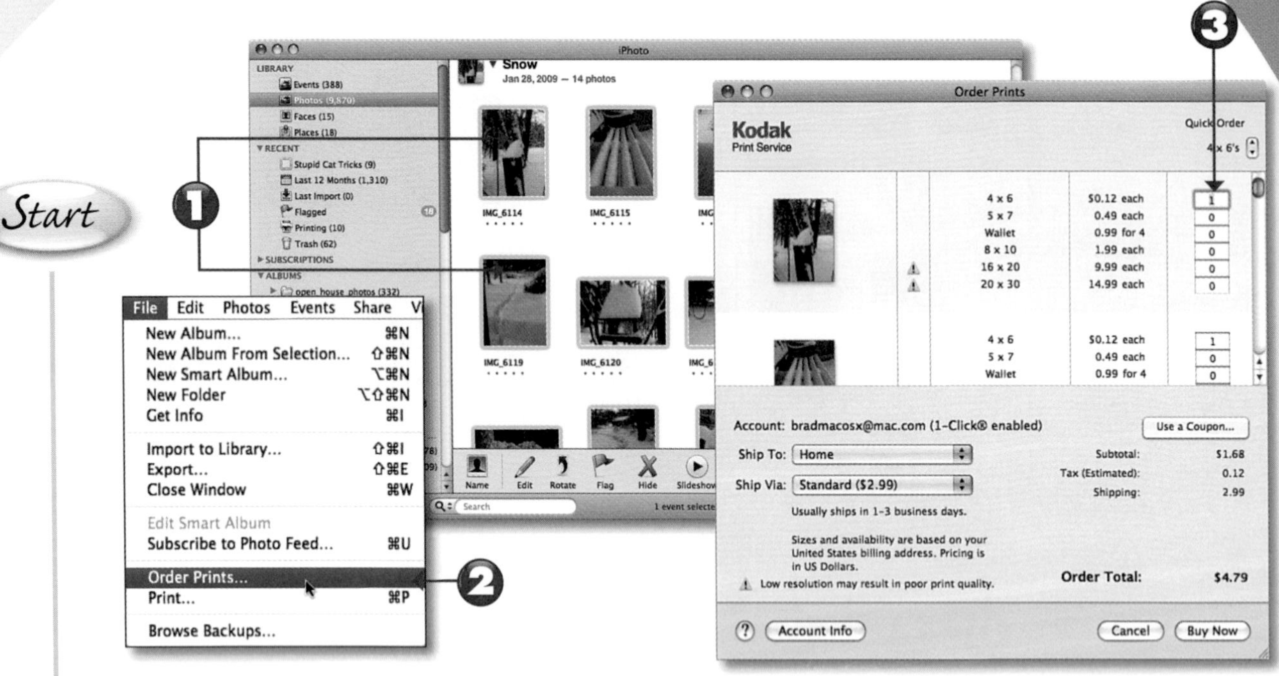

1. Select the photos you want to order. You can select them individually (hold the ⌘ key down while you click photos to select multiple photos at once) or select an entire photo album.

2. Choose **File**, **Order Prints**. The Order Prints dialog box appears.

3. Enter the quantity of each size of the first photo that you want to order.

Continued

NOTE

Danger, Danger! If you see the Caution icon (exclamation point in a yellow triangle) next to a size, the photo is not high enough resolution to be certain that it will print at good quality at that size. ■

TIP

Standard Prints To order 4x6 prints of all the photos, use the up and down arrows in the upper-right corner of the Order Prints dialog box. Each time you click the arrow, the quantity of the 4x6 prints you are ordering increases or decreases. ■

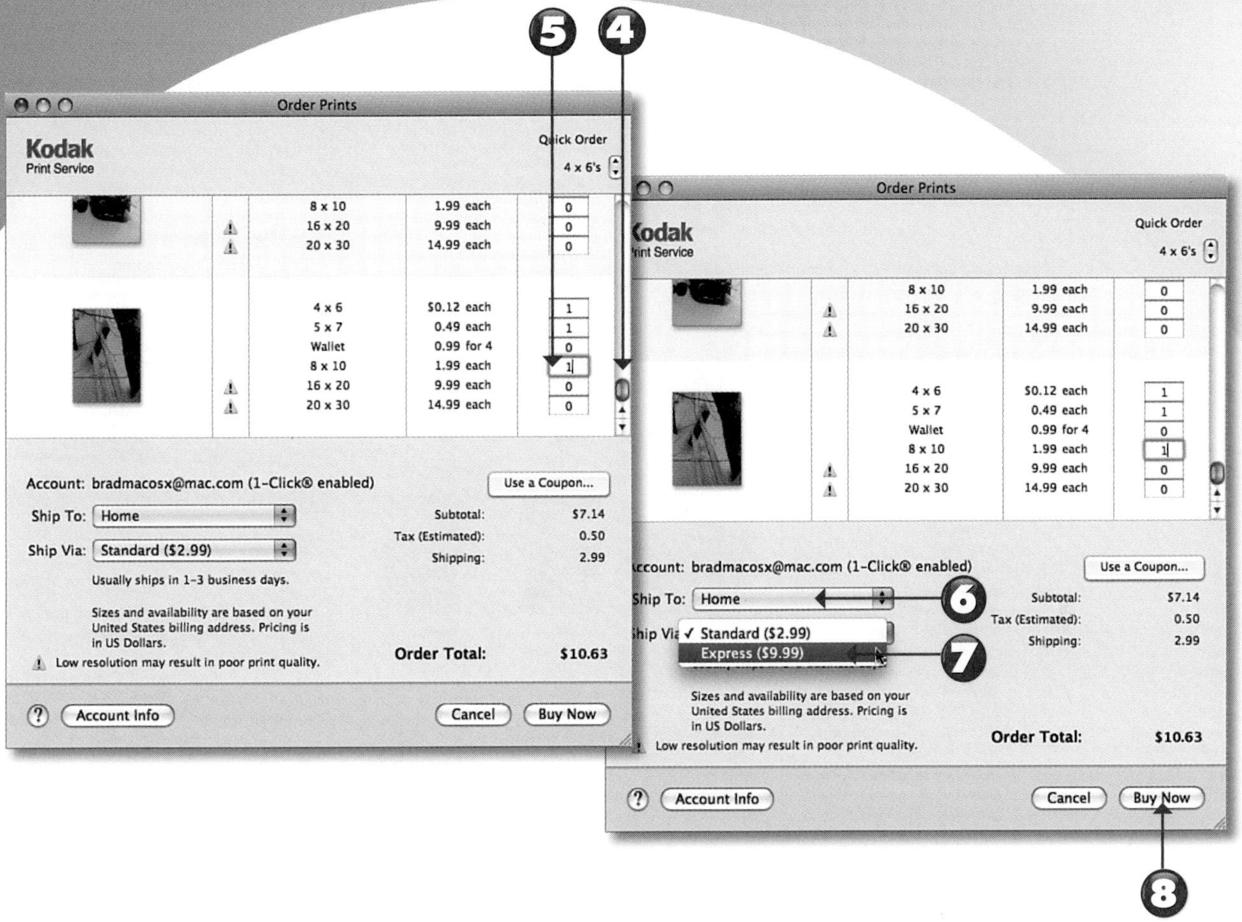

4 Use the scrollbar to browse down to see the rest of the photos you've selected.

5 Continue entering quantities of the sizes of each photo you want to order.

6 On the Ship To pop-up menu, choose the location where you want the prints to be shipped.

7 On the Ship Via pop-up menu, choose how you want the photos shipped.

8 Click **Buy Now**. The photos are printed and delivered to the address you specified.

End

NOTE

Apple ID Required You have to have an Apple ID to be able to order photos. This is the same account information that you use in the iTunes Store or to order from the Apple Web site. ■

TIP

Shipping When you choose the **Add New Address** option on the Ship To pop-up menu, you can configure additional addresses to ship your prints to. ■

EMAILING PHOTOS

Emailing your photos is great way to share them with other people. When you email photos from within iPhoto, the photos you select are attached to a new email message created in your default email application. You then complete and send the message. The recipient gets the message with your photos attached.

Start

1. Select the photos you want to send. You can select them individually or select an entire photo album.
2. Click **Email**.
3. Choose the size of the photos you send on the Size pop-up menu.
4. Check the check boxes for the photo information you want to include in the files you send.
5. Click **Compose Message**. A new message is created with the selected photos attached.

Continued

NOTE

Better is Bigger Making the photos you attach larger makes them higher quality, but also increases their file size. ■

NOTE

Consider Size When you select a size for your photos, the total size of the photos is shown under the Size pop-up menu. You should keep this to 5MB or less to ensure your photos can be received. ■

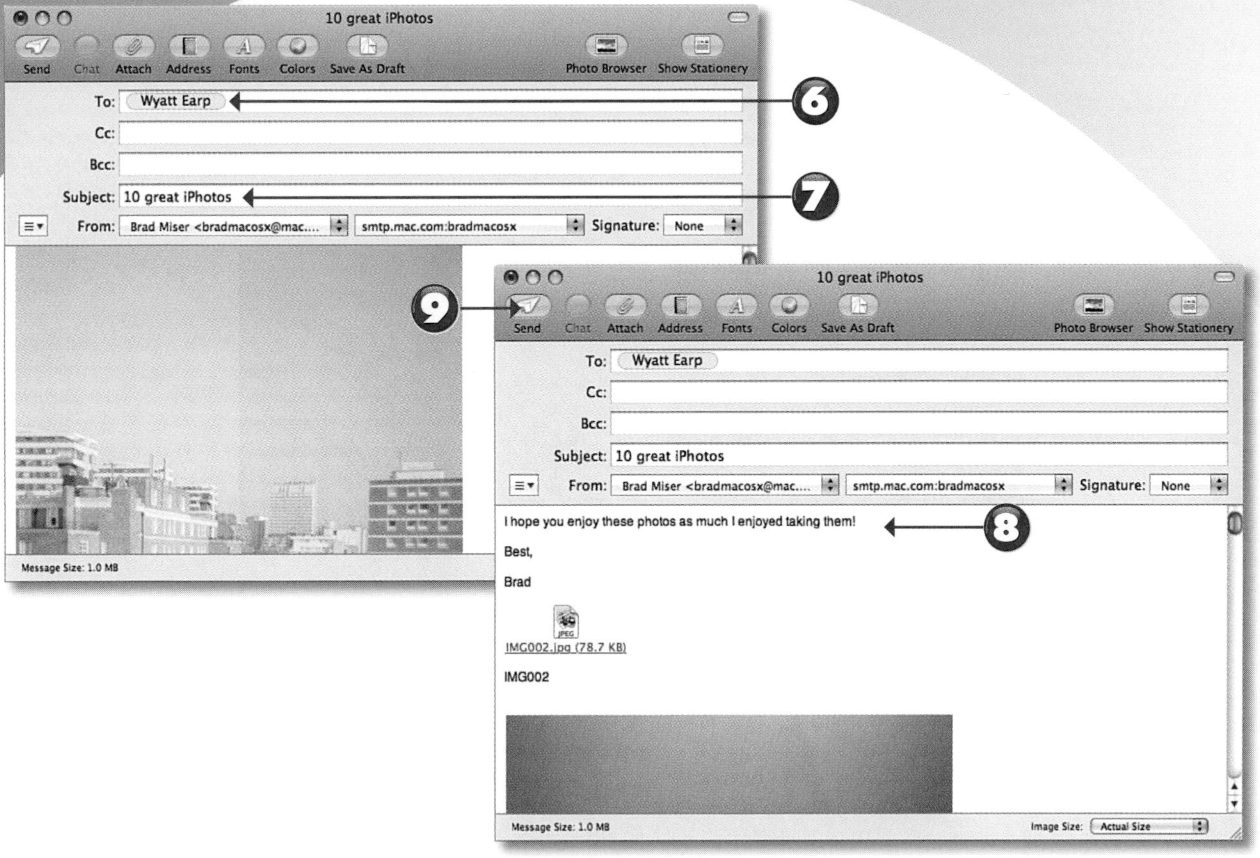

6. Address the message.

7. Replace the subject if you want to. The default subject is "*X* great iPhotos," where *X* is the number of photos you are sending.

8. Type a message in the body.

9. Click **Send**. The message is sent. The recipient can view the photos you send, print them, and so on.

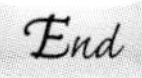

TIP

Viewing Icons In Mail, if you want to see a photo as an icon in the message body instead of seeing the photo, **Ctrl-click** it and choose **View as Icon**. ■

NOTE

Windows Friendly If you use the Mail application, you can send photos to people who use Mac or Windows computers. By default, Mail configures attachments so that either kind of computer can use them. ■

PUBLISHING PHOTOS TO A MOBILEME GALLERY

If you have a MobileMe account (to learn more about getting one, see Chapter 1, "Preparing iLife 09") you can easily post photos to your MobileMe gallery, where they can be viewed by anyone with a Web browser and an Internet connection.

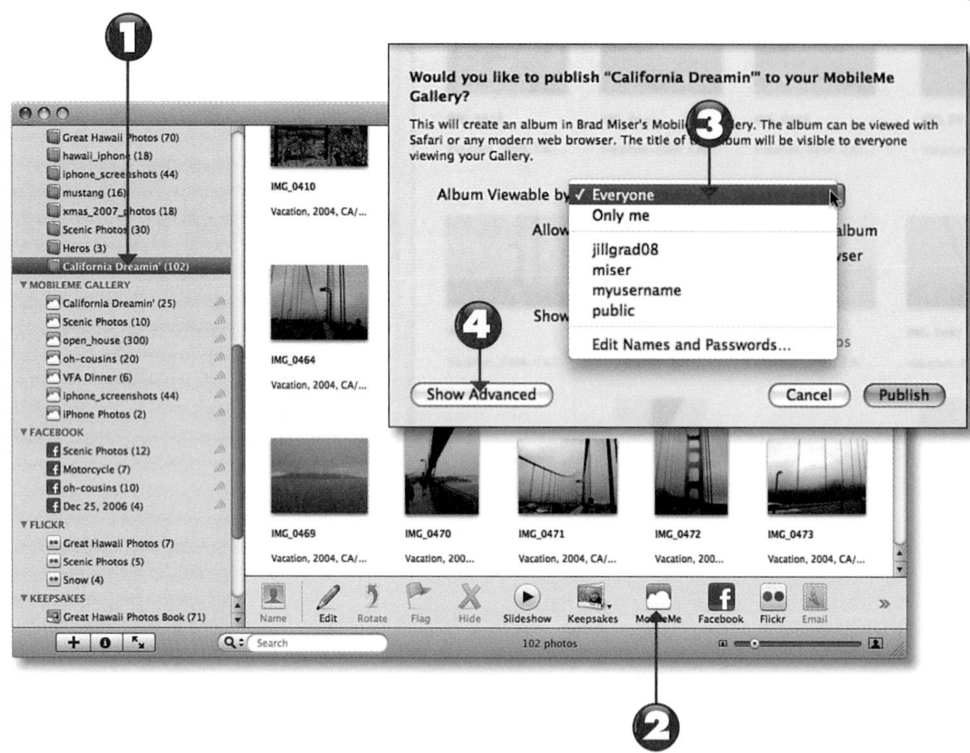

Start

1. Select the photos you want to share online via MobileMe. You can select them individually or select an entire photo album.

2. Click **MobileMe**.

3. On the Album Viewable By pop-up menu, choose **Everyone** if everyone who visits your site should be able to see the photos, **Only Me** to limit them to only you, or a username to require a username and password to view them.

4. Click **Show Advanced**.

Continued

NOTE

MobileMe Login For these steps to work, you must be logged in to your MobileMe account on the MobileMe pane of the System Preferences application. See Chapter 1 for help with this task. ■

TIP

Make it Secure Choose **Edit Names and Passwords** on the Album Viewable By pop-up menu to password-protect your photos. ■

5 Check the check boxes for the actions you want to allow people to do.

6 Check the check boxes for the information you want to show.

7 Click **Publish**. The photos are published to a page on your MobileMe gallery Web site. When the process is complete, you see the URL to your published photos.

8 Click the **URL** to visit your photos on the Web.

9 View your photos.

TIP

Share it Click the **Tell a Friend** button to send an email with your site's URL.

NOTE

Allow to Download You can allow people to download photos from your site to their computers so that they can add them to their iPhoto library.

PUBLISHING PHOTOS TO AN iWEB WEB SITE

With iWeb and a MobileMe account, you can easily create and publish a Web site. You can include iPhoto photos on pages on your site by publishing them from iPhoto to iWeb.

Start

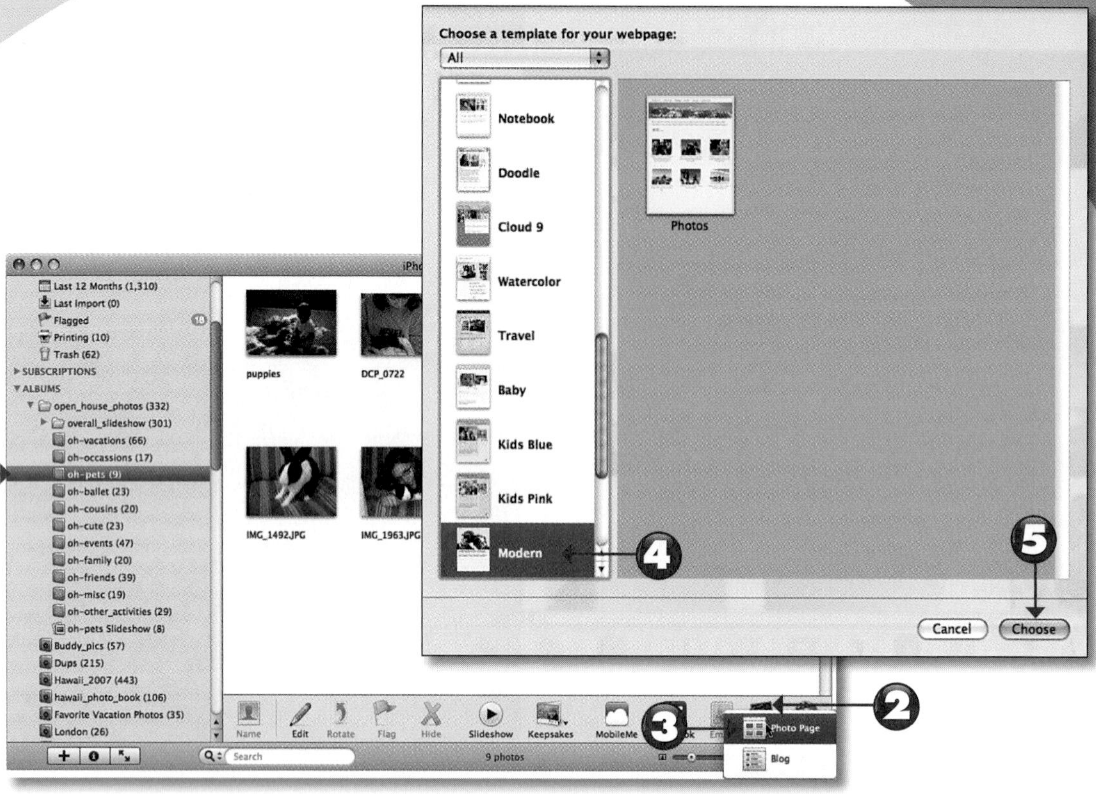

1. Select the photos you want to put on an iWeb Web page. You can select them individually (hold the ⌘ key down while you click photos to select multiple photos at once) or select an entire photo album.
2. Click the **iWeb** button.
3. Select **Photo Page**. The selected photos are sent to iWeb.
4. Select a theme for the photo page.
5. Click **Choose**.

Continued

NOTE

Lots of Buttons If you have a lot of buttons on your iPhoto toolbar, the iWeb button appears under the Keepsakes menu. ■

6. Edit the text on the page.

7. Click a photo to select it.

8. Use the Album style, Columns, Spacing, Photos per page, and Caption lines controls on the Photo Grid tool to design the layout of the page.

9. Click the **Inspector** button.

10. Use the Photos sub-tab of the Photos Inspector to configure download and other options.

End

NOTE

Publish It After you've configured the photo page, you publish your site to make it available on the Web. See Chapters 11 through 13 for more information about iWeb. ■

SHARING PHOTOS ON FACEBOOK

Facebook has become a social phenomenon. Everybody seems to have a Facebook these days, from people you'd expect, such as teenagers, to people you wouldn't, such as grandmothers. If you have a Facebook account, you can easily publish your photos to your Facebook pages, where people can view them. (If you don't already have an account, iPhoto leads you through setting it up the first time.)

Start

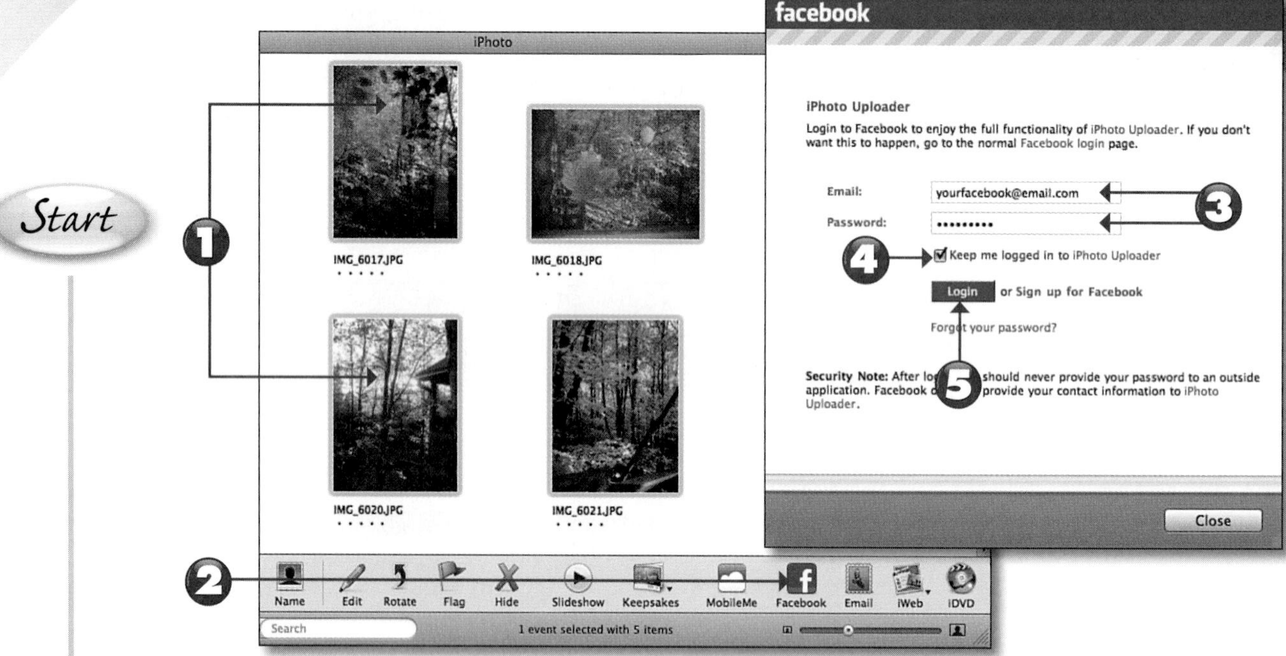

1. Select the photos you want to share on your Facebook site. You can select them individually (hold the ⌘ key down while you click photos to select multiple photos at once) or select an entire photo album.
2. Click **Facebook**.
3. Enter your Facebook email address and password.
4. Check the **Keep Me Logged In To** check box.
5. Click **Login**. After you are logged in, click **Close** to close the Login sheet.

Continued

NOTE

No Log In Required You only have to log in to your Facebook account the first time you share photos there. After that, you skip steps 3 through 5. ■

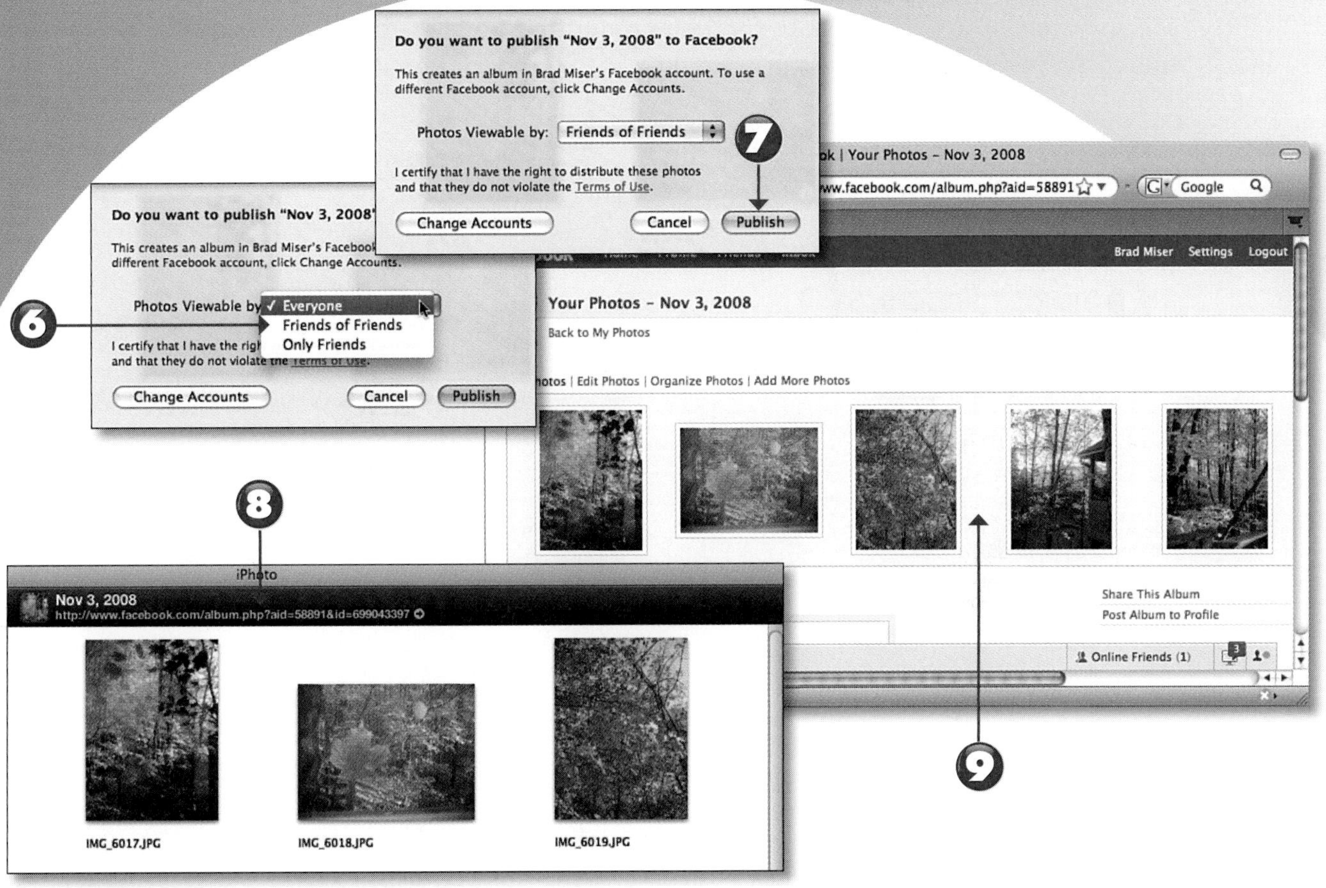

6 On the Photos Viewable By pop-up menu, choose who should be able to see your photos.

7 Click **Publish**. The selected photos are sent to Facebook. You see the Facebook album with the URL you visit to see the photos.

8 Click the **URL**.

9 View your photos on your Facebook page.

End

TIP

Flickr You can also publish photos to a Flickr account. This process is quite similar to publishing photos using Facebook. To get started, select the photos you want to publish and click the **Flickr** button. You can create or log in to your Flickr account and then publish your photos online. ■

NOTE

Letting Your Friends Know When you share photos on Facebook, your friends get notified. They can leave comments about your photos. If they tag your photos, those tags move back into iPhoto so that people in your photos are identified with names. ■

SHARING YOUR PHOTOS ON A LOCAL NETWORK

If your Mac is on a local network with other Macs, you can allow people on your network to access your photos using iPhoto on their computers. To allow this, turn **Photo Sharing** on, select the parts of your library you want to share, and (optionally) configure a password.

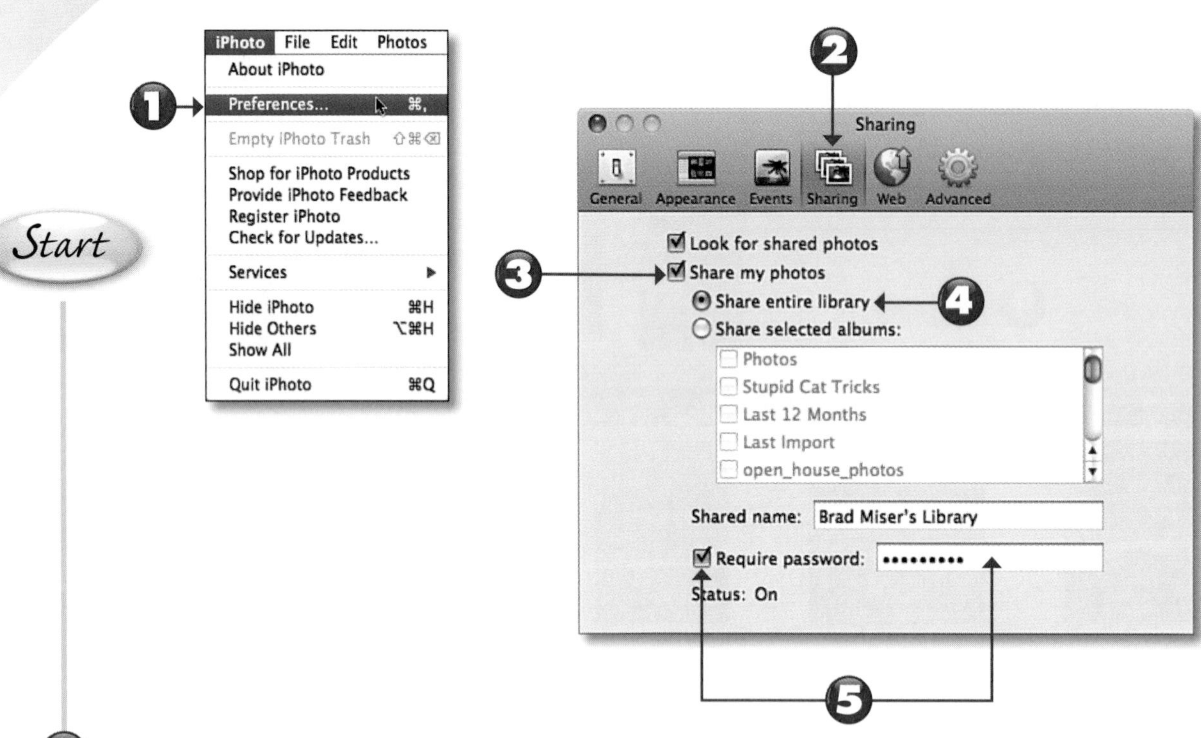

1. Choose **iPhoto**, **Preferences**.
2. Click the **Sharing** tab.
3. Check the **Share My Photos** check box.
4. To share all the photos in your library, select the **Share Entire Library** radio button.
5. To require a password, keep the **Require Password** check box and enter the password.

End

TIP

Be Selective If you want to share only some of your photos, select the **Share Select Albums** radio button and check the check box next to each album you want to share. ■

ACCESSING PHOTOS SHARED WITH YOU ON A LOCAL NETWORK

You can view the contents of iPhoto libraries being shared with you, and you can import photos from those shared libraries into yours. First, configure iPhoto to look for shared photos. Second, select and work with shared sources.

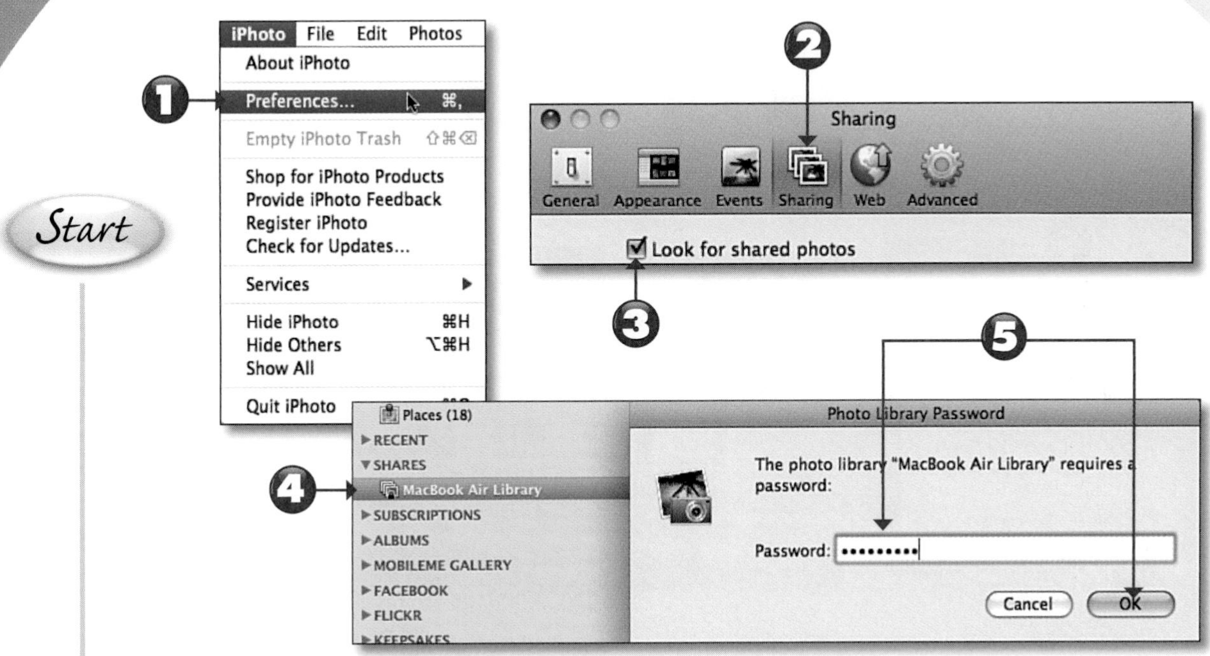

1. Choose **iPhoto**, **Preferences**.
2. Click the **Sharing** tab.
3. Check the **Look for Shared Photos** check box.
4. Select a shared source.
5. If required, enter the password and click **OK**.

End

NOTE

Shared Sources After you select a shared source, its photos appear on your Source list just like photos in your own library. ■

NOTE

Share Five You can have up to five shared sources available at the same time. ■

BURNING PHOTOS TO DISC

It can be useful to burn photos to a DVD to share them with other people. Or, you can burn them to a disc to back them up. (If they are ever lost from your computer, you can import them from the DVDs to restore them.) To burn photos to DVD, they must take up less than or an equal amount to the space available on a blank disc, which is about 4.7GB.

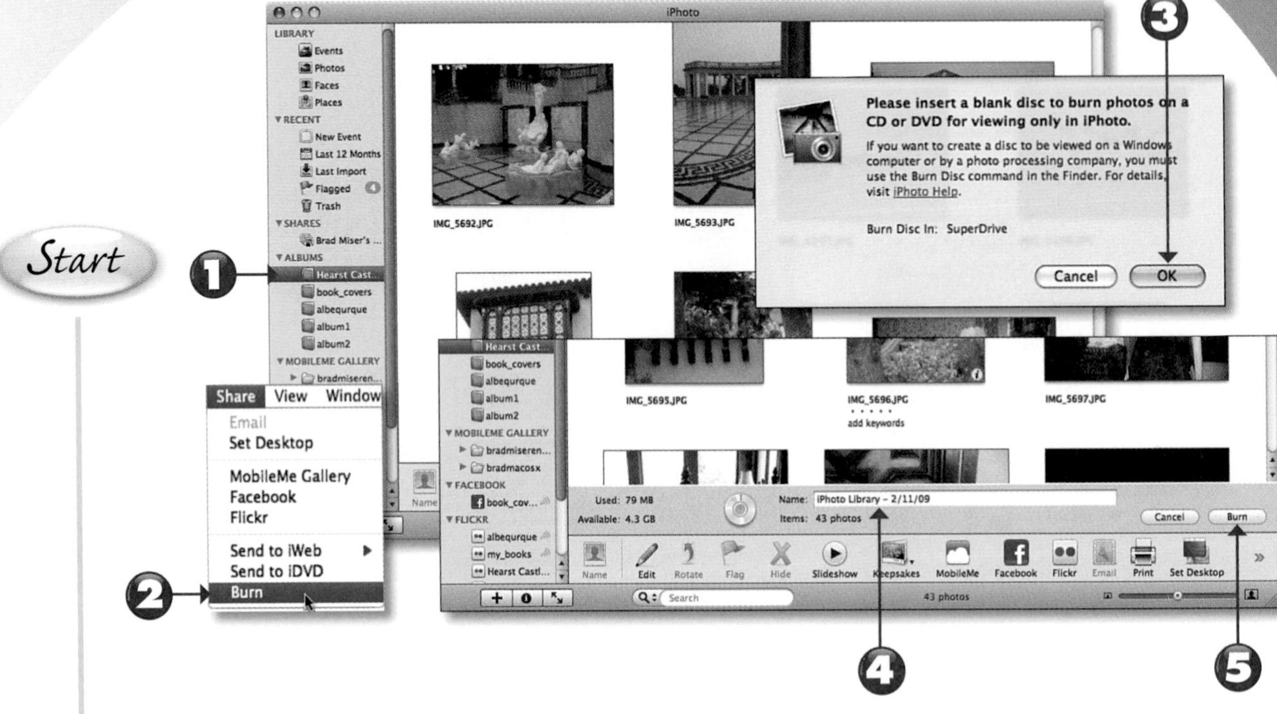

1. Select the source of photos you want to burn to a disc. Burning an album of photos is usually easiest, but you can also select events to burn.
2. Choose **Share**, **Burn**.
3. Insert a blank disc and click **OK**.
4. Enter the name of the disc you want to burn.
5. Click **Burn**.

Continued

NOTE

Check the Space The Disc icon to the left of the Name field indicates how much space on the disc you will use. If the disc is red, there are too many photos selected, and they won't fit on the disc. You have to remove photos from the selection to be able to burn the disc. ■

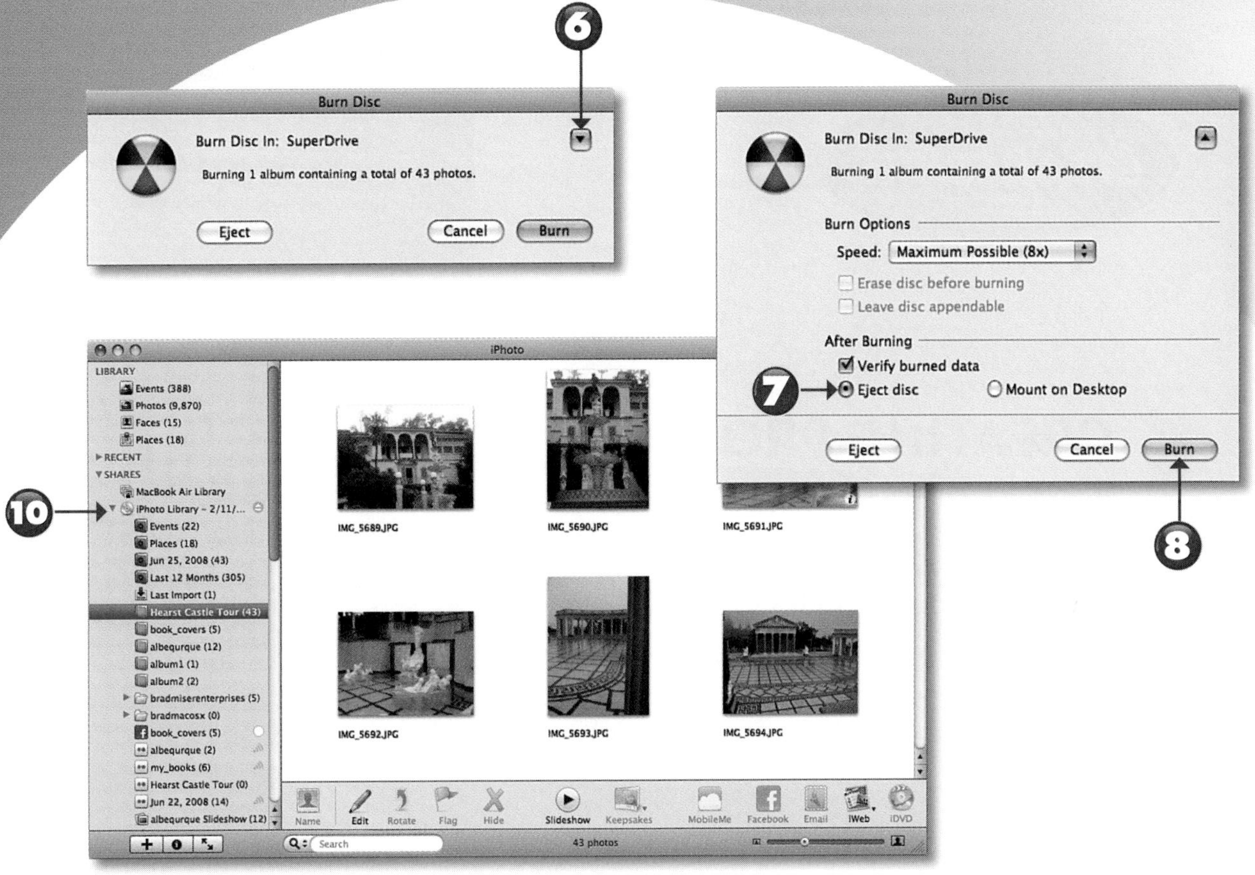

6 Click the **Expand** button.

7 Select **Eject Disc**.

8 Click **Burn**. iPhoto starts the burn process, and you see progress information in the sheet at the top of the window. When the process is complete, the disc is ejected.

9 Insert the disc into your Mac. It mounts on your computer.

10 Select and expand the disc on the iPhoto Source list. The photos it contains appear in the Viewing pane.

End

NOTE

iPhoto Structure The DVD maintains the structure of the library in which you burned it, but only the photos you selected are moved onto the disc. ■

CREATING PROJECTS IN iPHOTO

To this point in the book, you've learned that iPhoto is a great way to store, organize, view, share, and improve your photos. You can also use iPhoto's tools and your own creativity to make amazing projects featuring your photos. These projects include slideshows, calendars, greeting cards, and photo books.

The slideshows you create can include special effects, music, and customized transitions. They can be viewed within iPhoto. You can also export them in various formats so that you can enjoy them in other ways and on other devices, including iPods or an iPhone.

Calendars, cards, and photo books can have a variety of themes and layouts that you customize to create truly unique results. You can then have your work professionally printed (and bound) and shipped anywhere in the world.

iPhoto slideshows show off your photos dynamically on many kinds of devices, including Macs, iPods, and iPhones

Calendars transform your photos into practical and pleasurable gifts that people will love

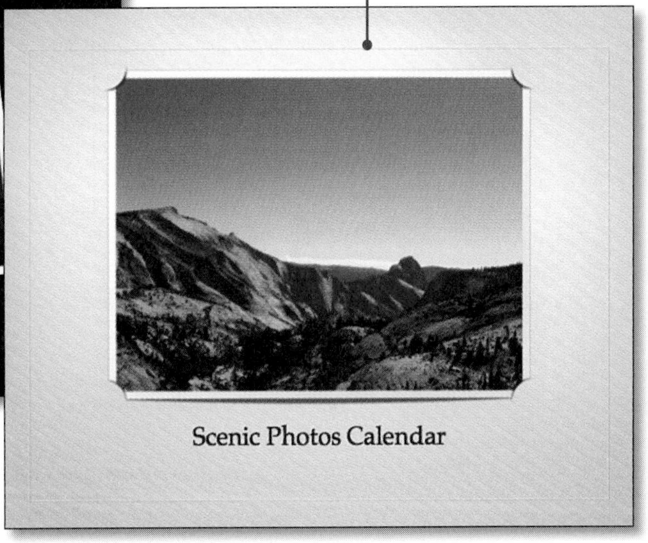

Scenic Photos Calendar

Professionally bound and printed photo books are a great way to view and share your photos

Forget Hallmark, you can use iPhoto to create your own greeting cards

CREATING SLIDESHOWS

A slideshow project presents your photos in a dynamic slideshow that can use a variety of themes and which you can customize by adding music and selecting options, such as the transitions between slides. Once complete, you can watch a slideshow within iPhoto or export it out to other devices.

Start

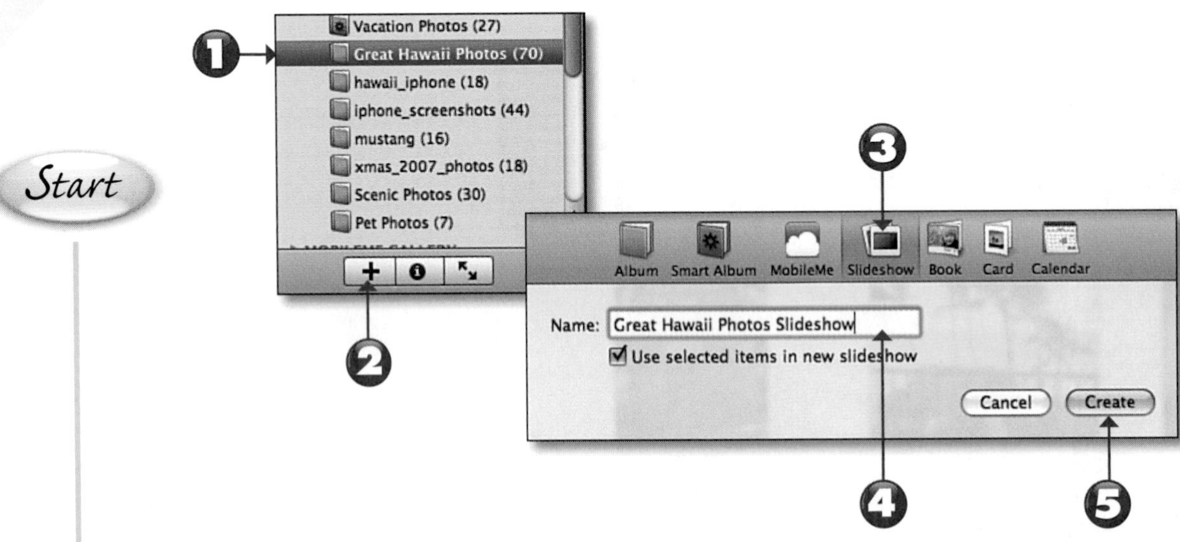

1. Select the photo source containing the photos you want to include in a slideshow.
2. Click the **Add** button.
3. Click the **Slideshow** tab.
4. Enter a name for the slideshow.
5. Click **Create**.

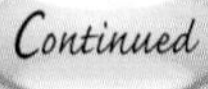

NOTE

Collect and Organize In most cases, you're better off collecting and organizing the photos you want to use in a project within a standard photo album before you start the project. ■

6 Click **Themes**.

7 Select a theme for the slideshow, and click **Choose**.

8 Click **Music**.

9 Select the music you want to hear during the slideshow.

10 Click **Apply**.

Continued

TIP

Music Sources If you open the Source menu on the Music Settings window, you see a number of sources. One of the most useful is iTunes, which enables you to use any of the music in your iTunes library in an iPhoto slideshow. ■

TIP

Quiet Please If you don't want a slideshow to have sound, uncheck the **Play Music During Slideshow** check box. ■

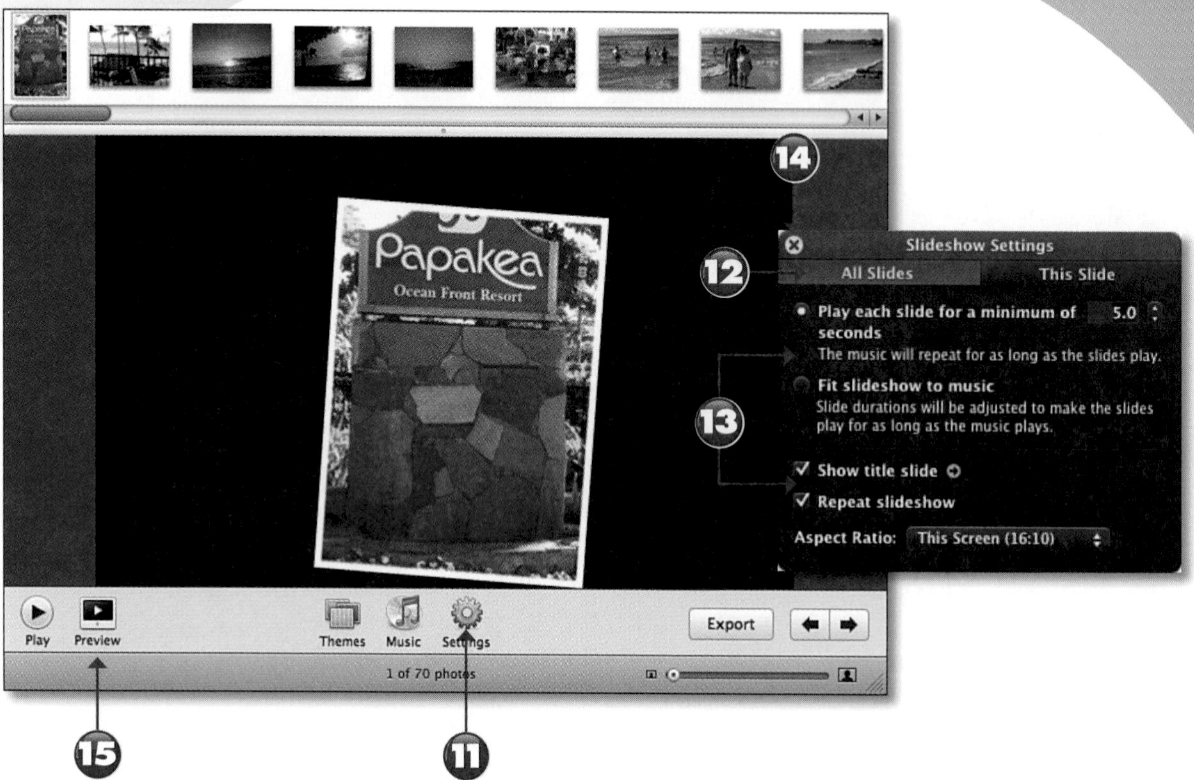

11 Click **Settings**.

12 Click **All Slides**.

13 Configure the settings, such as duration and transition effects.

14 Close the window or move it out of the way.

15 Click **Preview**.

Continued

TIP

Set to Music If you want the slideshow to last exactly the same length as its music, select the **Fit Slideshow to Music** radio button.

TIP

Editing in Full Screen You can override the slideshow's general settings for specific slides by selecting a slide, clicking the **This Slide** tab, and configuring options that apply to the selected slide.

16 Watch the slideshow in the iPhoto window; click **Preview** again to stop it.

17 Use the **Themes**, **Music**, and **Settings** tools to make changes to the slideshow. Repeat steps 14 through 16 until the slideshow is what you want it to be.

18 Click **Play** to watch the slideshow in full screen on your Mac.

19 Click **Export** and use the Export window to save your slideshow in different formats.

End

TIP

Order, Order! To change the order in which slides play, drag them around the browser at the top of the Slideshow tool's window. To add slides to the show, drag them onto the browser. To delete slides from the show, select them on the browser and press **Delete**. ■

CREATING CALENDARS

A calendar is a useful and pleasant way to display photos. You can create custom calendars for yourself or others. When you create a calendar, you choose its layout, the photo it contains, and even how long a time period it covers. You can add text information to each date, such as reminders of important events.

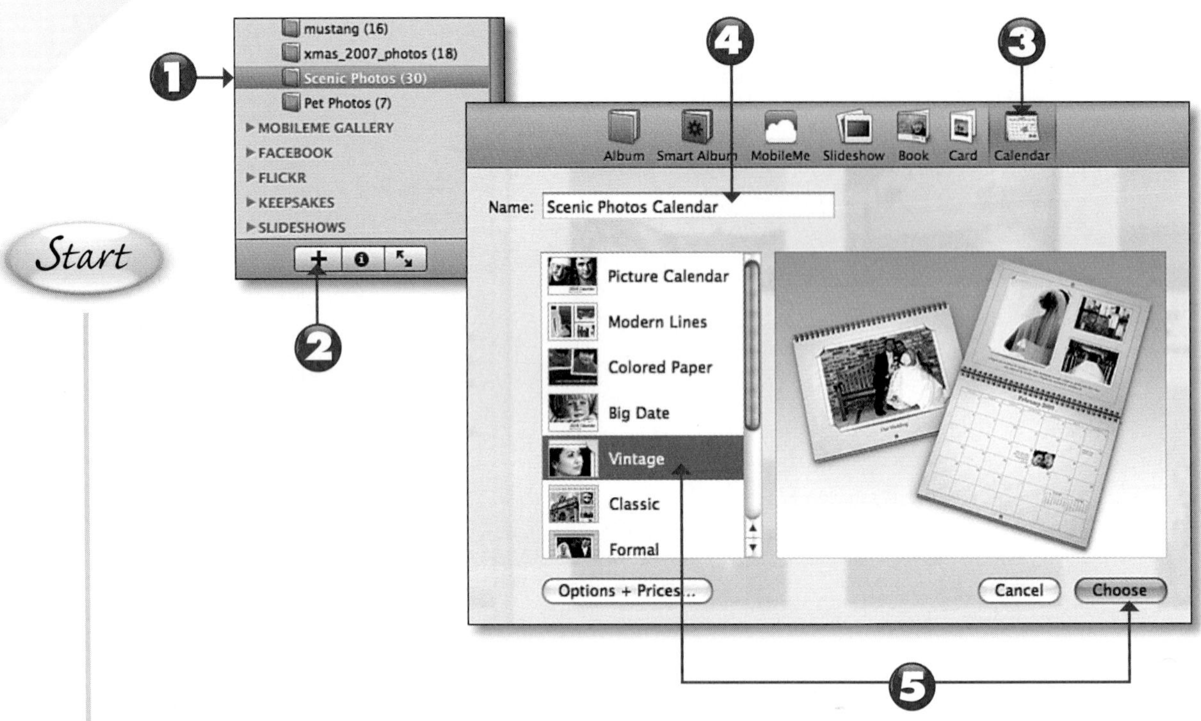

Start

1. Select the source of photos you want to include in the calendar.
2. Click the **Add** button.
3. Click the **Calendar** tab.
4. Enter a name for the calendar.
5. Select a theme for the calendar and click **Choose**.

Continued

NOTE

Adding iCal Info You can include information from your iCal calendars on calendars you create in iPhoto. ■

TIP

How Much Will It Be? To see current prices for calendars and other projects that you print, click the **Options + Prices** button. ■

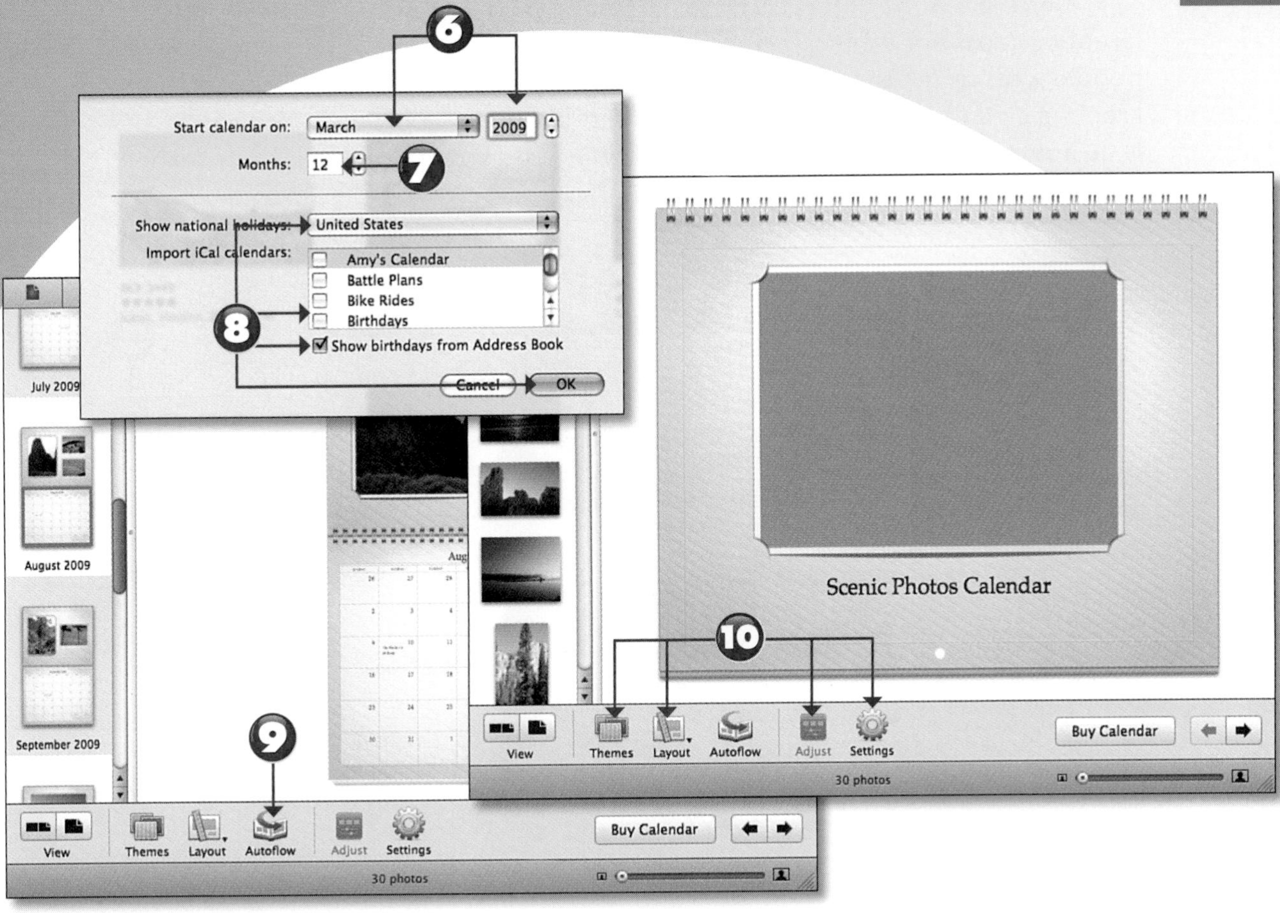

6. Select the month and year on which you want the calendar to start.

7. Select the number of months you want to include.

8. Configure the holidays, iCal information, and birthdays you want to be shown and click **OK**.

9. Click the **Autoflow** button.

10. Use the calendar tools to make changes to the automatic layout.

End

NOTE

Designing a Calendar The Autoflow tool lays out the photos you've included in the calendar according to the theme you selected. You can change the automatic layout, for example, to move photos around, make adjustments to photos, and so on. ■

CREATING GREETING CARDS

Greeting cards are a great way to let other people know about important events, to wish people well, or just to let them know you are thinking about them. The more specific a greeting card is, the more impact it has on the person receiving it. You can create completely customized greeting cards in iPhoto that include your photos and your text.

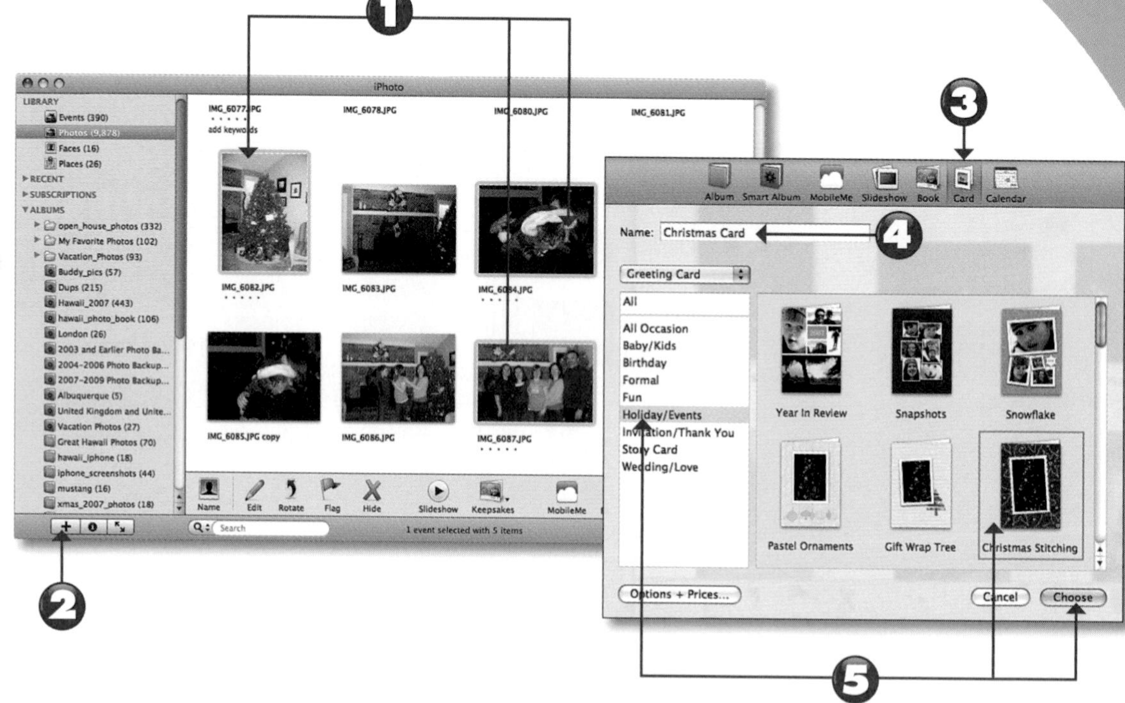

Start

1. Select the photos you want to include in the card (cards include fewer photos than other kinds of projects so you can select them directly instead of working with a source).
2. Click the **Add** button.
3. Click the **Card** tab.
4. Enter a name for the card.
5. Select a theme for the card and click **Choose**.

Continued

NOTE

The Envelope Please When you order a greeting card (see the last task in this chapter), you also get envelopes. ■

TIP

Post Cards You can create a greeting card or a post card by making a selection on the pop-up menu just under the Name field. Greeting cards have four sides with a fold; post cards have only two sides. ■

6 Select and edit the card's text.

7 Select a photo.

8 Use the size slider to set its zoom in its frame.

9 Drag the photo to set the part that is displayed in the frame.

10 Click **Adjust** and use the palette to change the appearance of the photo.

End

TIP

Setting the Order You can change the order of photos on the card, its design, and other aspects using the browser at the top and the toolbar at the bottom of the window. ■

TIP

Copy and Paste You can write the text for a card in another application and copy it. Then you just paste that text into the text placeholders on the card. ■

BUILDING PHOTO BOOKS

A photo book is a great way to enjoy your pictures. You can create many different kinds of books using the many format and layout options that iPhoto offers. Combined with your own photos and creativity, there's no limit on what you can do with your photo books. After you've created a book, you can have it professionally printed and bound. If you've never done this, prepare to be amazed at the results.

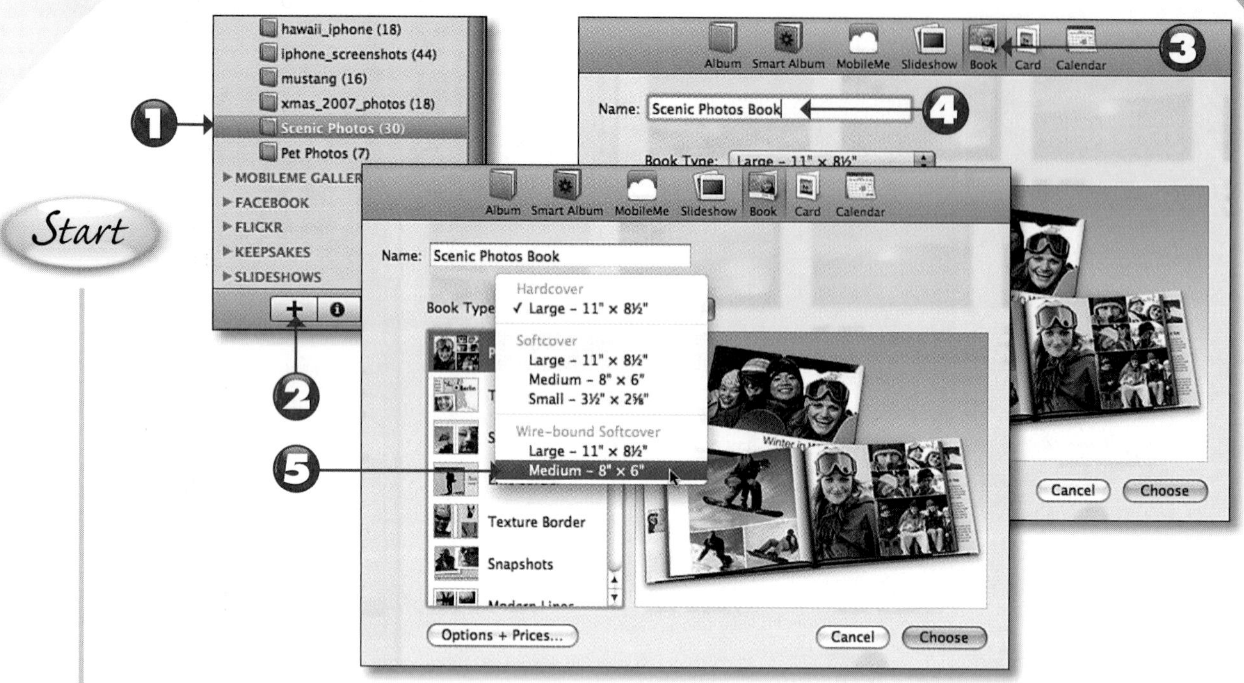

1. Select the photos you want to include in the book.
2. Click the **Add** button.
3. Click the **Book** tab.
4. Enter a name for the book.
5. Select the type of book you want to create on the Book Type pop-up menu.

Continued

NOTE

Projects on the Source List Projects that you create, including calendars and photo books, appear in the Keepsakes section of the iPhoto Source list.

TIP

Options, Options... To see the book options you have and the printing costs of each, click the **Options + Prices** button.

6. Select the theme you want to use for the book.

7. Click **Choose**.

8. Click **Autoflow**. iPhoto automatically lays out the selected photos using the book's design.

9. Select and edit the text in the placeholders on the cover.

10. Click the **Next** button.

Continued

NOTE

Spelling Correctly iPhoto uses the Mac OS X spell checker that is configured by default to check your spelling as you type. ■

NOTE

Manual Works You don't have to use Autoflow to design a book. You can manually lay out each page by dragging photos from the photo browser at the top of the window. ■

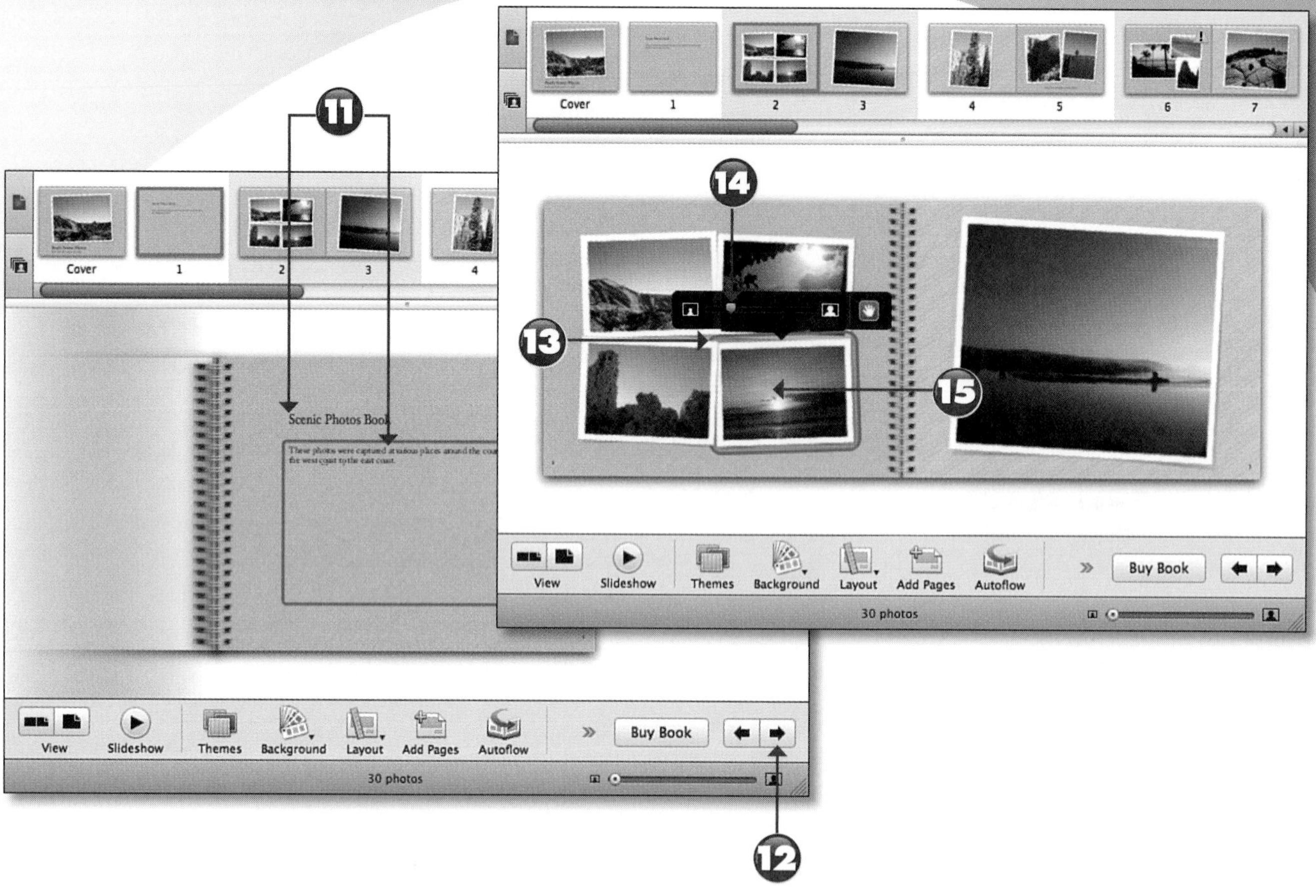

11 Edit the text in placeholders on the page.

12 Click the **Next** button.

13 Select a photo on the page.

14 Drag the size slider to the left to zoom out or to the right to zoom in.

15 Drag the photo within its frame to determine which part of the image is displayed.

Continued

NOTE

Warning! If you see an image marked with the Caution icon, that means the image is not high enough resolution to print at the current size. ■

TIP

Adjust It You can change how an image looks by selecting it and clicking the **Adjust** button. Use the resulting palette to change various properties of the image. ■

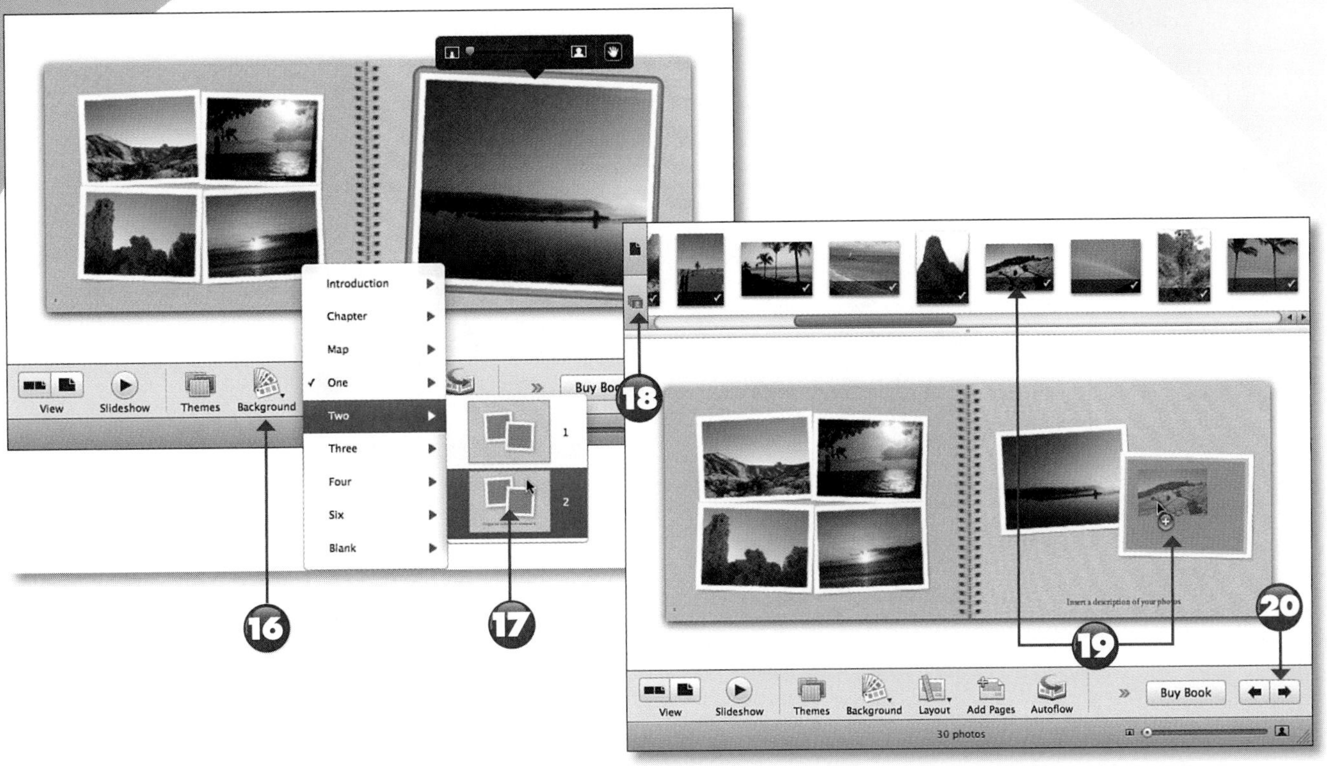

16 Use the Background menu to apply a background to the page.

17 Use the Layout menu to change the number and configuration of the photos on a page.

18 Click the **Photo Browser** tab.

19 Drag a photo into a placeholder to add it to a page.

20 Click the **Next** button to move to and edit each page in the book.

End

TIP

Handling Low Res Images There are number of ways you can deal with an image flagged with the low-resolution warning: replacing it with a different higher-resolution image, using the image at a smaller size, or zooming out on the image.

PREVIEWING, EDITING, AND ORDERING PROJECTS

You can order professionally printed calendars, greeting cards, and photo books directly through iPhoto. Although you can do this relatively inexpensively considering what you get, it's a good idea to proof your projects before you send them for printing. The exact steps you use vary slightly based on the type of project you order, but these are minor differences.

Start

1. Select the project you want to order.
2. Use the **Next** button to move through each page in the project.
3. If you see any problems, fix them using the tools you have available.
4. Choose **File**, **Print**.
5. Open the PDF menu and choose **Save as PDF**.

Continued

NOTE

Review on Paper You can also preview projects by printing them on your own printer. It's a good idea to preview them on PDF first, so you can catch and correct problems before you commit a project to paper. ■

NOTE

Apple ID Required To order a project, you need to use an Apple ID. If you shop in the iTunes Store, you can use the same ID in iPhoto. ■

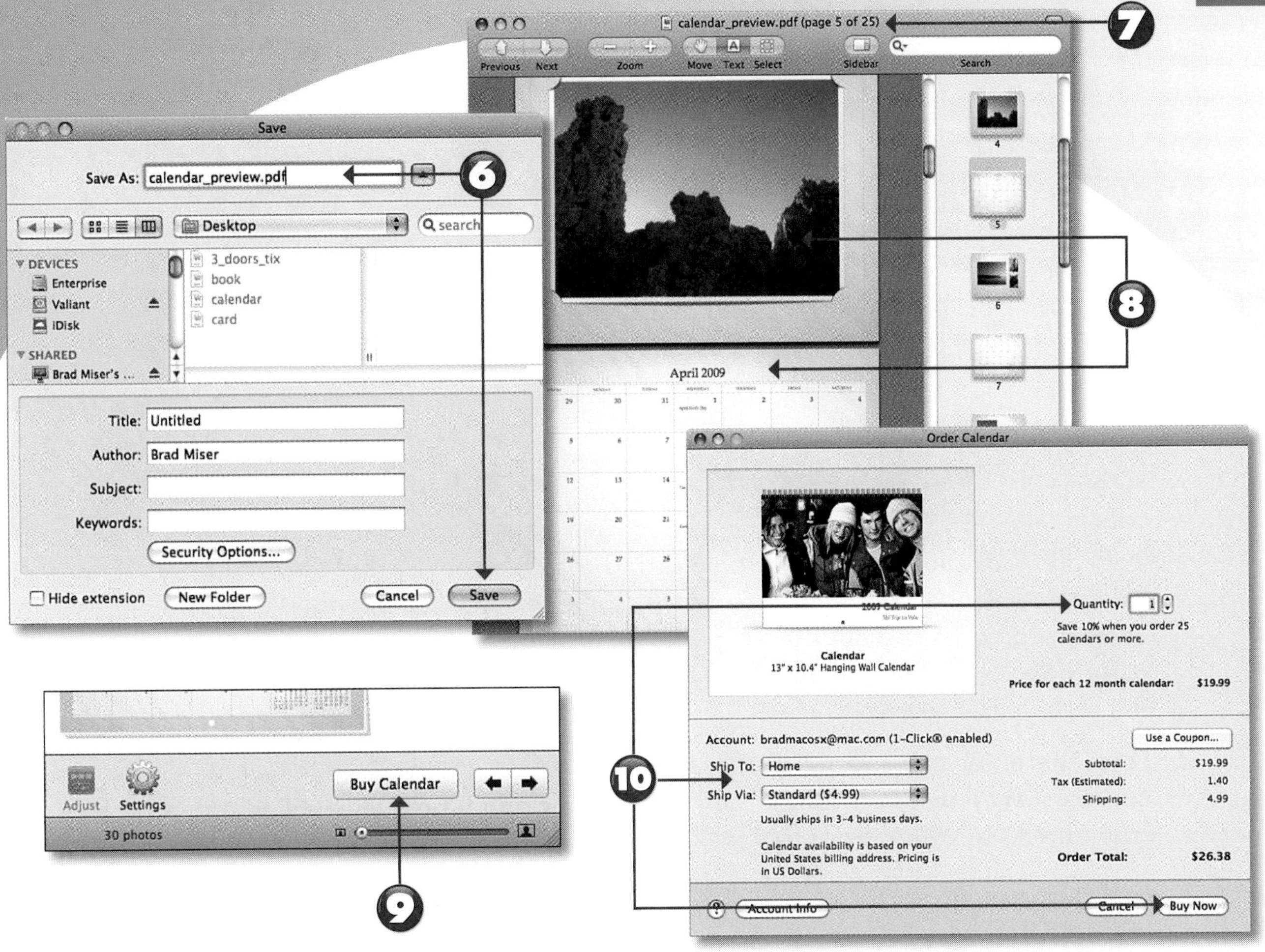

6 Name and save the PDF file.

7 Open the PDF file.

8 Preview the project. If you find problems, move back to iPhoto, fix the problems, and preview the project until you are happy with it.

9 Click the **Buy** button.

10 Use the Order dialog box to configure and place your order.

End

NOTE

Could Be a Problem When iPhoto finds problems with the project that might prevent it from printing with good quality or if there are missing elements, you see notifications and icons marking those problems. If possible, fix the problems before you order the project. You can print the project with the problems if you can't fix them, but the results might not be as good as you hope. ■

GETTING STARTED WITH iMOVIE

iMovie enables you to create your own movies. Your movies can include video from different sources, most notably your own video camera, but also video you've downloaded from the Web or that someone else has provided to you. You can edit clips and put them together in projects. After you've created a basic video track, you can add all sorts of interesting transition effects between the clips in your movies.

From there, you can add still images, titles, and other visual elements. Of course, silent movies are long a thing of the past; with iMovie, you can add soundtracks to your movies that include music, sound effects, and narration.

In this part, you get started with iMovie by adding the content you'll use to build a movie to the Event Library and starting a new project.

In the preview window, you can watch clips or projects

You create movies from projects that contain clips, titles, transitions, effects, and audio

Use the Open Import Window button to import video from a camera

Events contain video clips you've imported into your Event Library

When you select an event, you see the clips it contains

ADDING VIDEO TO THE EVENT LIBRARY

iMovie's Event Library is where you store the video content that you'll use in your movie projects. In many cases, you'll get that content from a video camera that you connect to your Mac; you can import video directly from the camera into the iMovie Event Library. Once that content is in the Event Library, you can use it in your projects.

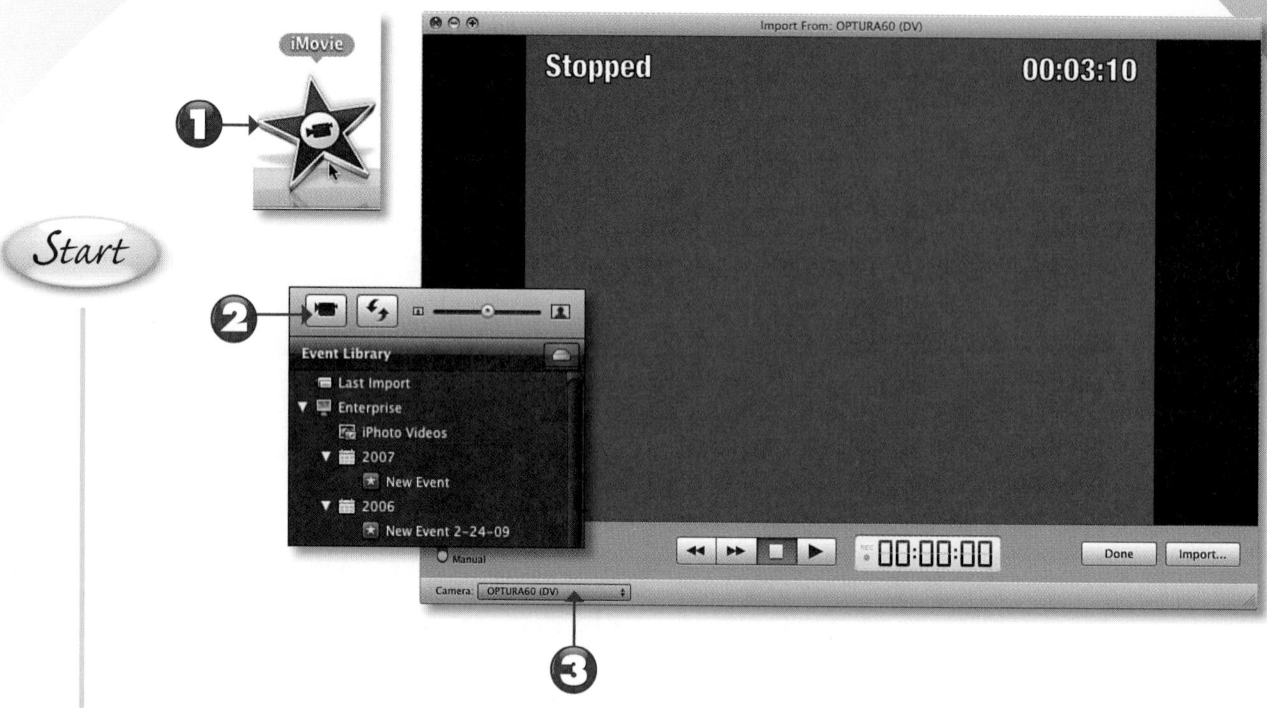

1. With your video camera connected and in **Playback** mode, click the **iMovie** icon on the Dock.
2. Click the **Open Camera Import Window** button.
3. Select the video camera on the Camera pop-up menu.

Continued

NOTE

Tape Media Cameras The steps here describe importing video from a video camera that uses a tape to store video. If you use a camera that uses a different medium, the steps differ slightly, but the general process is the same. ■

TIP

Importing Selected Clips from Tape To import specific clips from a tape, leave the mode switch on Manual and use the **Import** playback controls to position the tape in the camera to where you want to start importing clips. Then click **Import**. ■

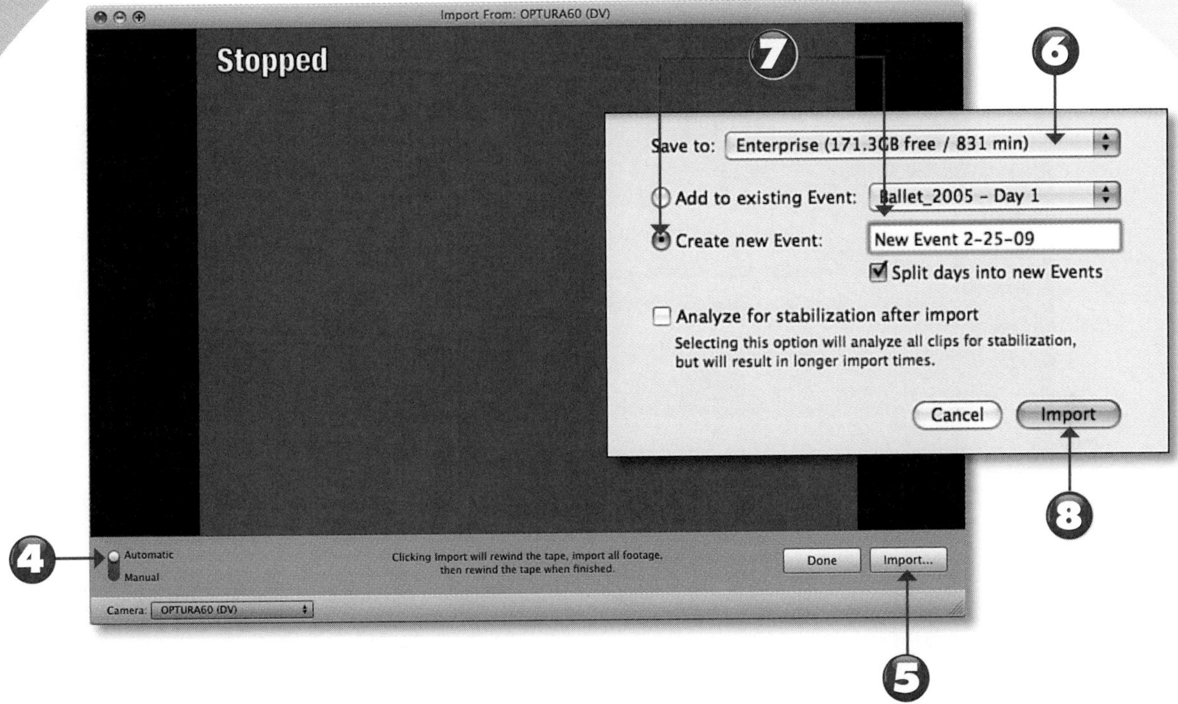

4 Flip the mode switch to **Automatic**.

5 Click **Import**.

6 On the **Save To** pop-up menu, select the disk on which you want to save the imported clips.

7 Click **Create New Event** and name it if you don't want to accept the default name.

8 Click **Import**. The video is imported to iMovie and added to the Event Library.

End

TIP

Importing Clips from Memory On a memory-based camera, leave the mode switch on Manual. Select the clips you want to import and click **Import Selected**. ■

NOTE

Video Clips Are Large Storing video clips requires a lot of disk space. If you are going to create many iMovie projects, consider adding a large external hard drive to your system. ■

PREVIEWING CLIPS IN THE EVENT LIBRARY

The Event Library is where your imported video content is stored and organized. You can use the same content from the Event Library in multiple iMovie projects, and the Event Library is the starting point for all iMovie projects. You can preview your clips in the Event Library to see the content available to you.

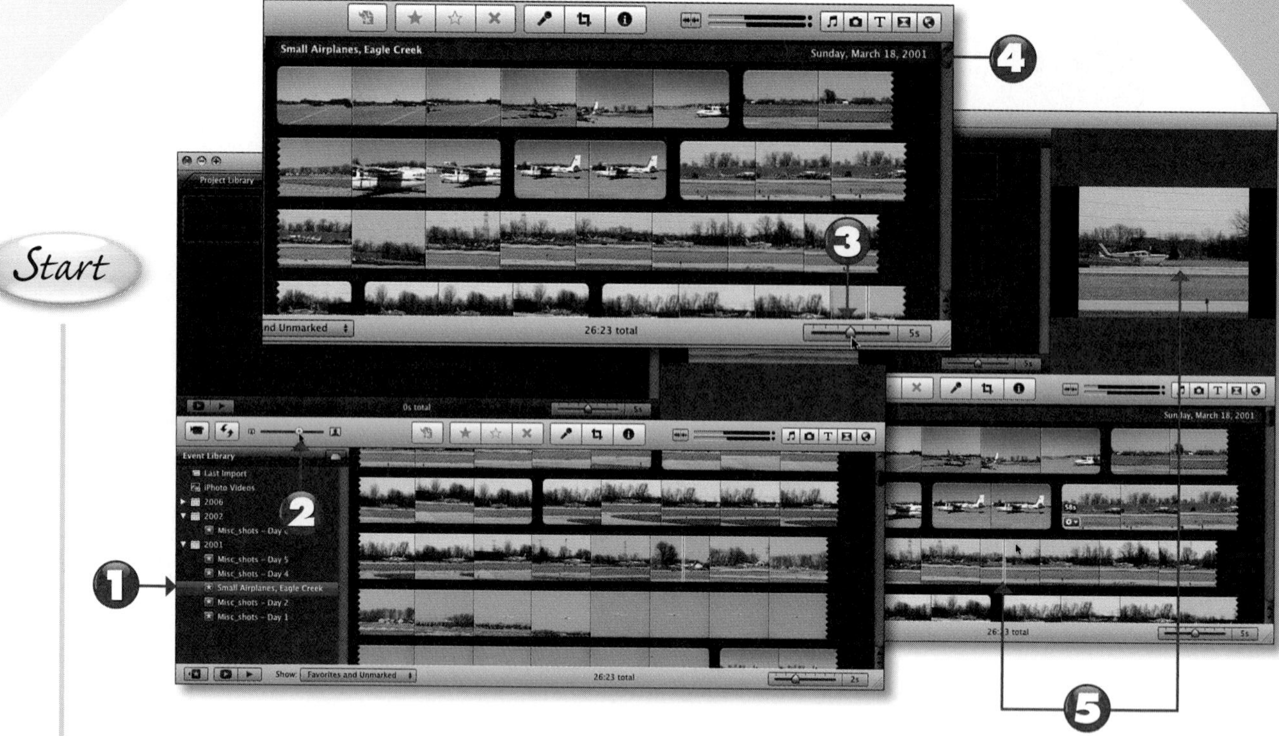

1. Select the event you want to preview.
2. Drag the size slider to the right to make the thumbnails of the clips in the event larger or to the left to make them smaller.
3. Drag the **Clip** size slider to the left to display more frames of the clip in the event's film-strips or to the right to display fewer frames in the event's filmstrips.
4. Drag the scrollbar up or down to browse all the filmstrips in the event.
5. Drag across a filmstrip to see it in the preview window located in the upper-right corner of the iMovie window. The red line represents your current location in a filmstrip.

Continued

TIP

Changing Filmstrip Detail You should become familiar with the Clip size slider. Set toward the right to browse the filmstrips in an event to find specific clips for a project. Move it to the left to make more precise selections. ■

6 When you want to watch the clip in detail at its normal speed, press the **spacebar** and watch the clip in the preview window. Press the **spacebar** again to stop playback.

7 To watch all the clips in the event in order, click the **Play** button.

8 To watch all the clips in full-screen view, click the **Full Screen** button.

9 Use the tools in the full-screen view to select and preview clips (move the mouse or drag on a trackpad to make the controls appear). (Press **Esc** to exit Full-Screen mode.)

End

TIP

Previewing with Speed The faster you drag across a filmstrip, the faster its preview plays.

NOTE

Preview Within a Filmstrip, Too When you drag across a filmstrip, the preview also plays within the filmstrip itself. If you have a large display, you can make the filmstrips large so that you can preview them effectively within the Event Browser.

ORGANIZING THE EVENT LIBRARY

You can change the way events are shown in the Event Library in several ways, including how the clips are organized and whether you see disk information for your clips.

Start

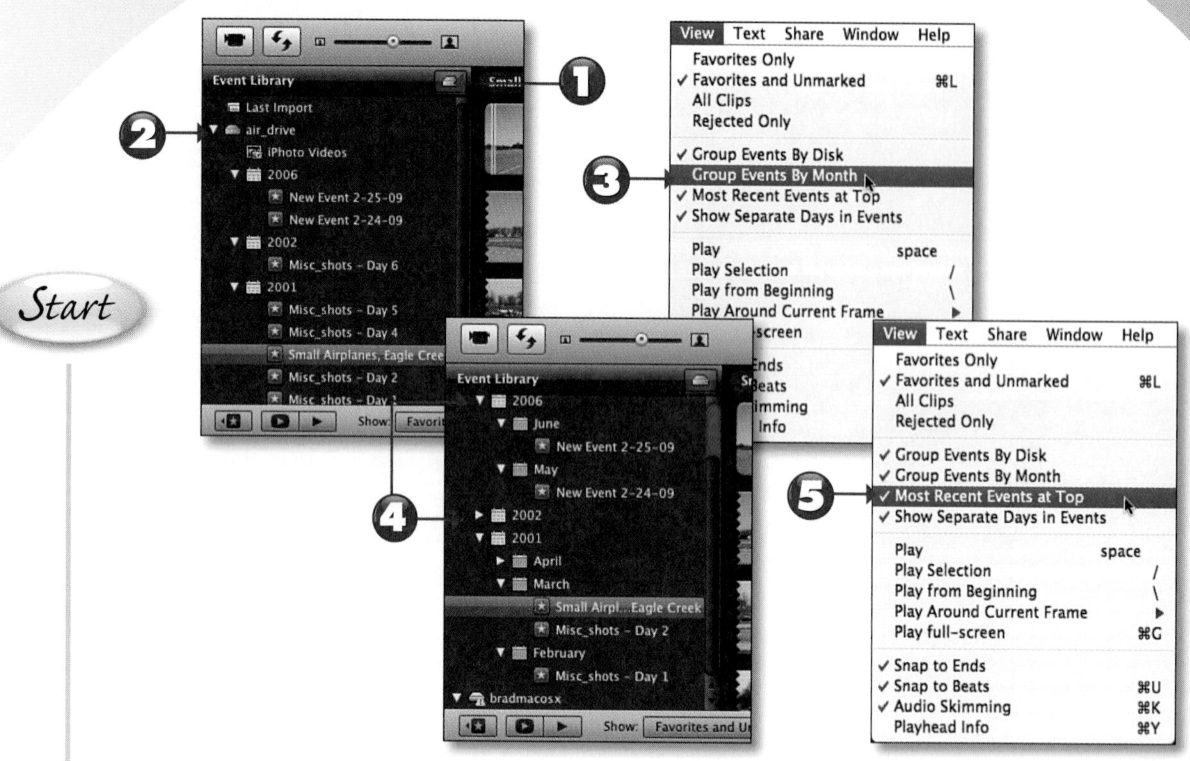

1. To organize clips by the disk on which they are stored, click the **Disk** button.

2. Expand or collapse the contents of a disk by clicking its expansion triangle.

3. To organize clips by month, choose **View**, **Group Events by Month**.

4. To expand or collapse the contents of months or years, click their expansion triangles.

5. To list newer clips at the top of the Event Library, choose **View**, **Most Recent Events at Top**.

End

NOTE

Clip Time Point to a filmstrip in the Event Browser to see the total time of the clip. ■

TIP

Previewing Recent Clips To preview the clips you've recently imported, select Last Import in the Event Library. ■

RENAMING EVENTS

As you start to accumulate clips in the Event Library, the resulting events can be named based on the date associated with the clips you are importing or based on the date you import the clips. You should give your events meaningful names so that you can more easily find clips that you want to use in specific projects. For example, if you have clips from a vacation, name the event with some text that reminds you what those clips are.

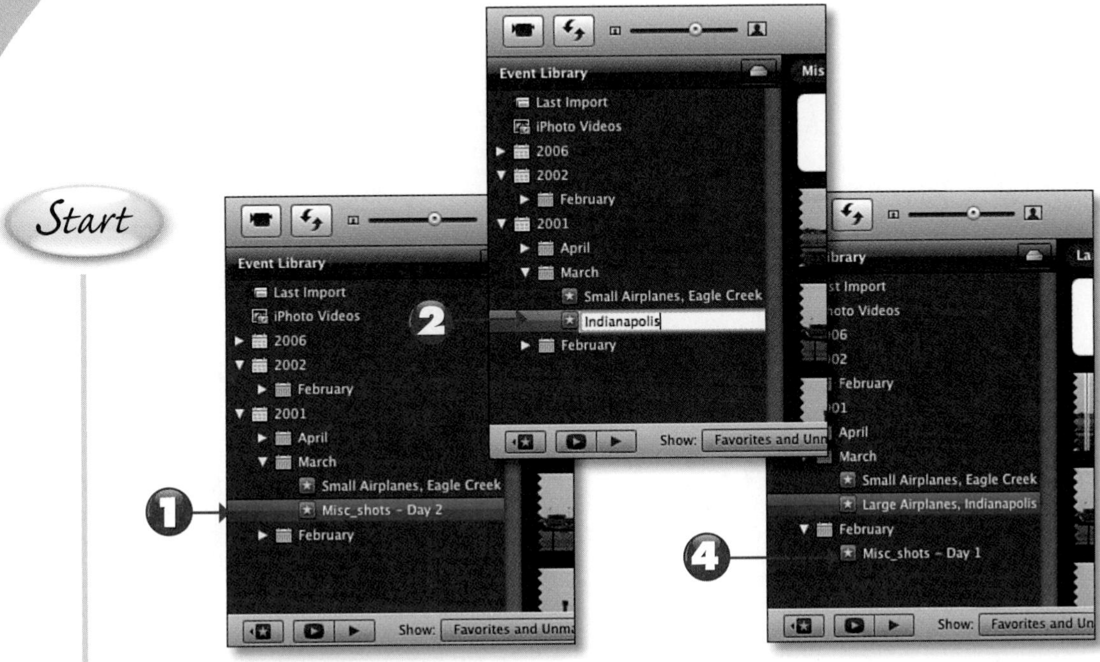

1. Double-click the event you want to rename.
2. Type a new name for the event.
3. Press the **Return** key.
4. Rename other events as needed.

End

NOTE

Event Equals Date (by default) By default, iMovie creates events based on the date associated with clips you import with one event for each date. You learn how to reorganize your events in other ways in this section, to make your clips easier to use in your projects. ■

TIP

See the Full Name If an event's name is too long to see all of it in the Event Library, point to it and the full name appears in a pop-up tooltip. ■

SPLITTING EVENTS

As you read earlier, iMovie collects clips you import into events based on the dates associated with those clips. This might or might not make sense for a group of clips that you happen to capture on the same day. For example, suppose you video a child's first bike ride in the afternoon and a party in the evening. You might not want those clips in the same event, figuring that it is unlikely that you'll use them in the same projects. You can split a single event into two events to help you keep your events organized into logical collections of clips.

Start

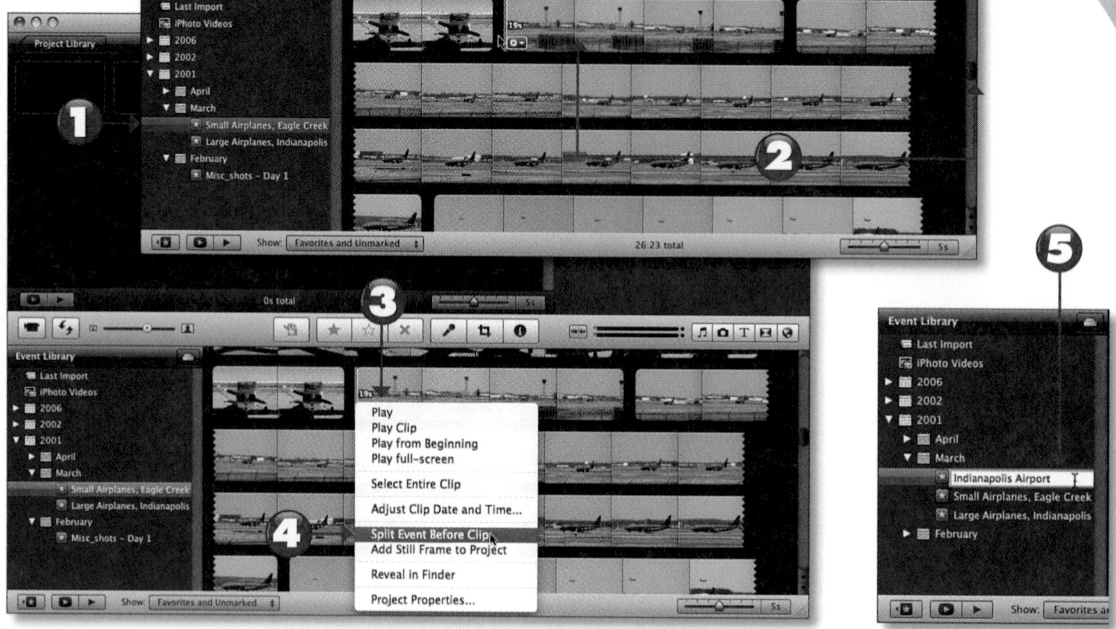

1. Select the event that you want to split.
2. Browse and preview the clips until you find the point at which you want to split the event.
3. **Ctrl-click** or **right-click** before the clip you want to be the first clip in the new event.
4. Choose **Split Event Before Clip**.
5. Rename the split clips.

End

NOTE

Event Name and Date When you select an event and scroll to the top of the Event Browser, you see the event's name and the date associated with the clips it contains. ■

TIP

Multiple Splits You can split an event as many times as you want, even down to putting each clip into its own event. ■

MERGING EVENTS

When you merge events, the clips in the events you merge become part of a single event. This can be a useful way to collect related clips into a single event. Suppose you took a trip over a period of several days. By default, each day's clips will be placed into its own event. You might want to merge all the events containing clips for that trip to make them easier to place into a project.

Start

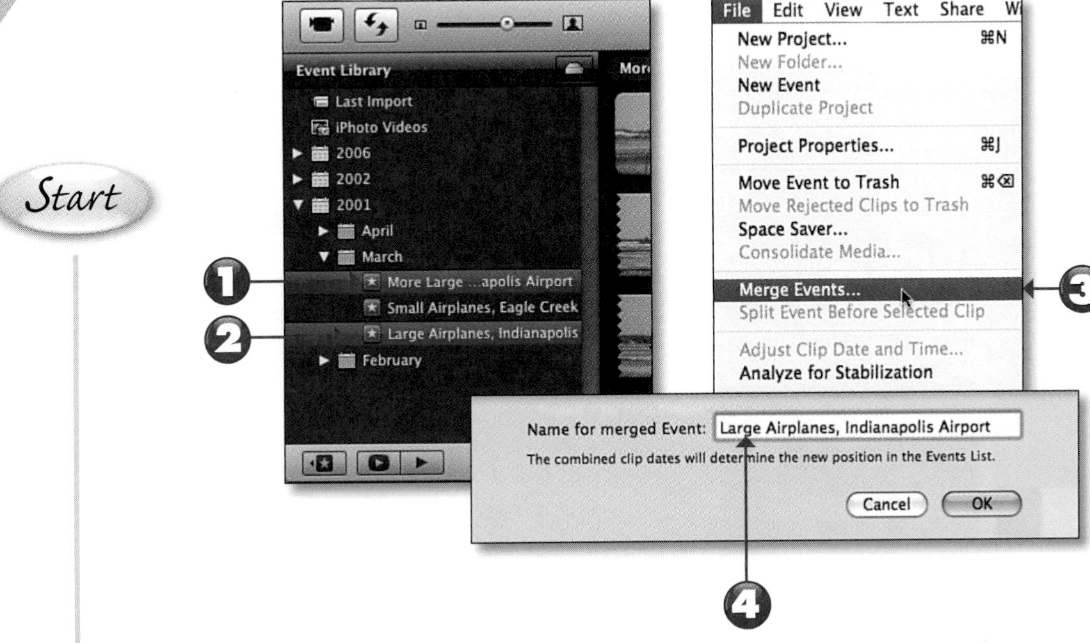

1. Select the first event you want to merge.
2. Hold the ⌘ key down and select the next event you want to merge.
3. Choose **File**, **Merge Events**.
4. Enter a name for the merged event and click **OK**.

End

NOTE

The Dates Remain After you merge events, the resulting event has sections for each of the previous events based on their dates. If you browse the merged events, you see that the previously separate events are divided within the merged event and that each event's clips retain their original dates. ■

TIP

Merging Three Events at a Time You can merge three events at a time by selecting two and dragging them on top of the third. ■

STARTING A NEW iMOVIE PROJECT

In iMovie lingo, a project is a movie that you build by adding video clips from the Event Library and using effects, titles, transitions, audio, and so on to transform those clips into a work of art of your very own. You can create many projects with iMovie, and you can use the same content in the Event Library in more than one project.

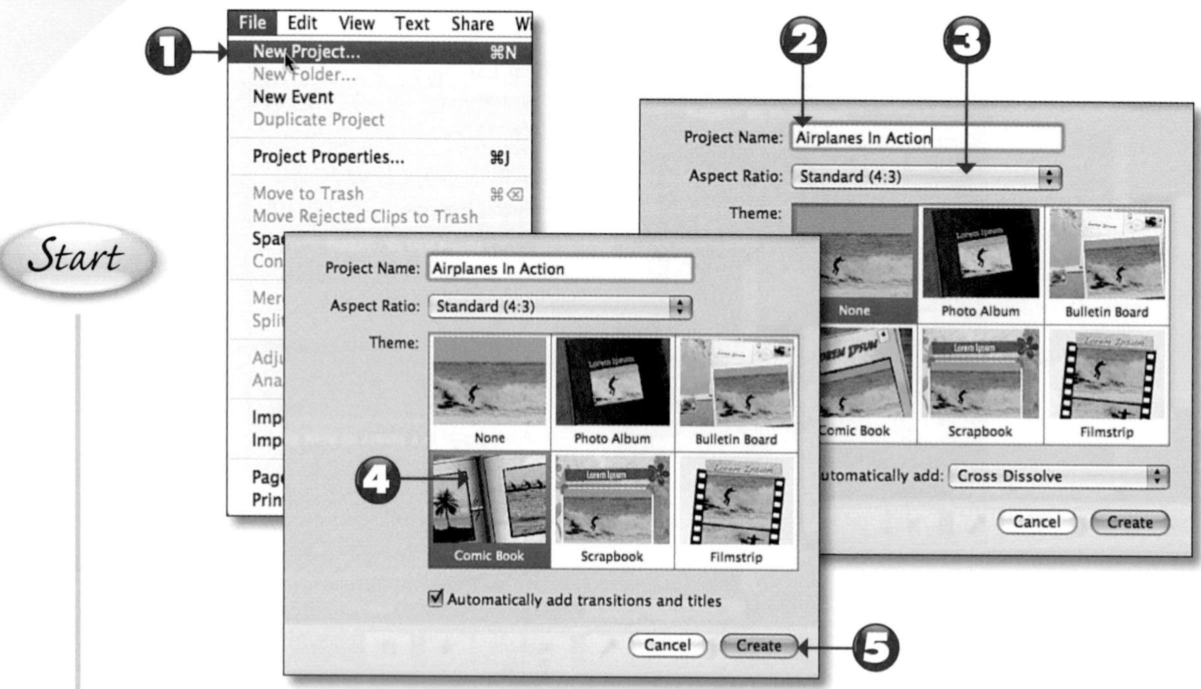

Start

1. Choose **File**, **New Project**.
2. Name the project.
3. Use the **Aspect Ratio** pop-up menu to set the movie's proportions.
4. Select the theme you want to use for the movie.
5. Click **Create**. The new project appears at the top of the Project Library.

End

NOTE

Themes Themes are a style that is applied to a project. Themes include frames in which your content is presented, automatic transitions, and title placeholders. ■

TIP

Preview Themes If you drag across the themes on the New Project window, you see a preview of their look and effects. ■

WORKING IN THE PROJECT LIBRARY

The Project Library is where you store your iMovie projects. When you want to work on a project, you first select it in the library.

Start

1. Click **Project Library**.
2. To preview a project, select it and drag across its filmstrip; you see a preview in the preview window.
3. To watch a project, select it and click **Play**.
4. To work on a project, select it and click **Edit Project**.

End

TIP

Creating Projects When you are viewing the Project Library, you can create a new project by clicking the **New Project** button, which is the + located in the lower-right corner of the Project Library pane. ■

TIP

Useful Project Commands If you select a project and **Ctrl-click** or **right-click** it, you see a menu with very useful commands. For example, choose **New Folder** to create folders to organize your projects. Just drag a project onto a folder's icon to place it within the folder. ■

BUILDING A MOVIE'S VIDEO TRACK

After you've created a project, you can build its video track. Start by adding clips to the project. You edit those clips so that they contain precisely the frames you want to include in your movie. You can also crop or rotate clips, adjust them, and apply effects to determine how the clips appear in your movie.

You can also add photos from your iPhoto library to include static images within your movie for content or visual effect. To smooth the flow of your movie or just to add visual interest to it, you can add and configure transitions between your clips. You can provide information about your movie or as part of your movie by adding and configuring titles.

As you build your movie, use the Precision Editor to make it flow exactly as you want. Along the way, you constantly preview your movie to see how it is coming along.

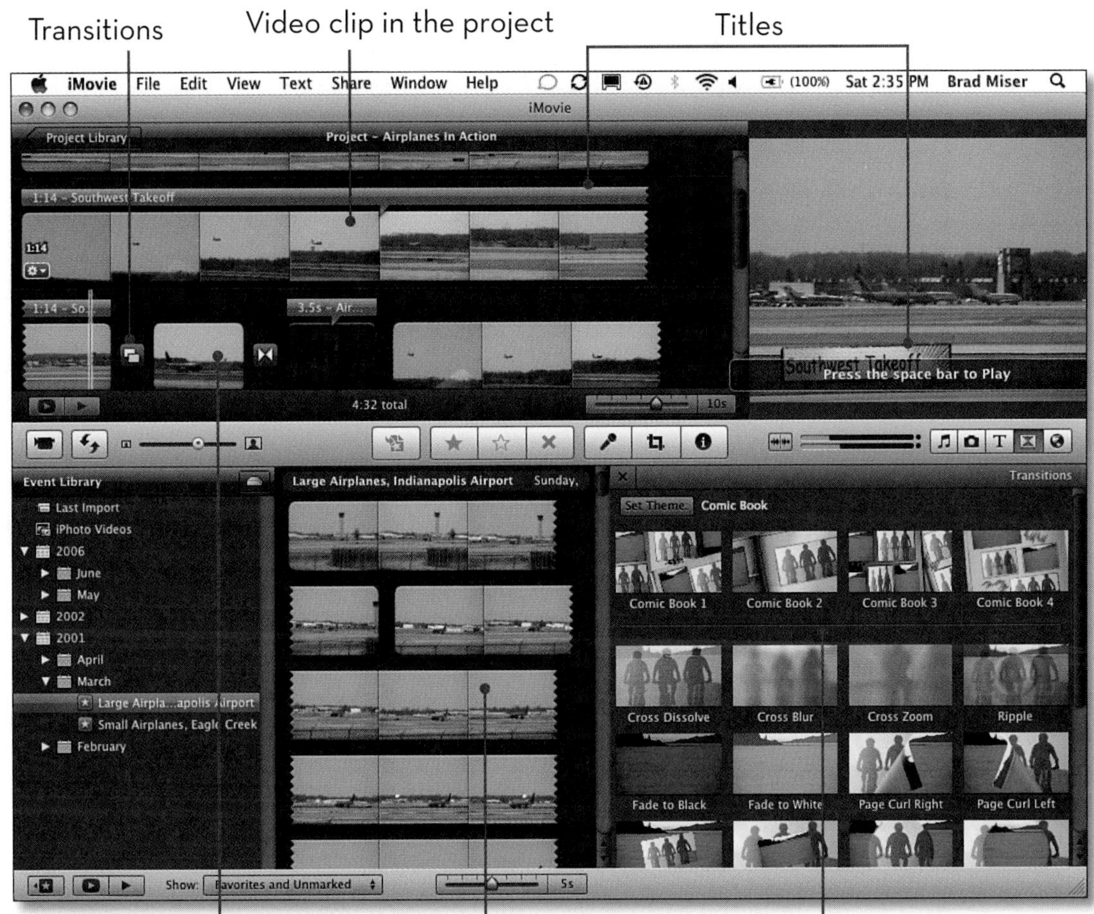
Transitions
Video clip in the project
Titles
iMovie File Edit View Text Share Window Help
Project Library
Project - Airplanes In Action
1:14 - Southwest Takeoff
Southwest Takeoff
Press the space bar to Play
4:32 total
Event Library
Last Import
iPhoto Videos
2006
June
May
2002
2001
April
March
Large Airpla...apolis Airport
Small Airplanes, Eagle Creek
February
Large Airplanes, Indianapolis Airport
Transitions
Set Theme: Comic Book
Comic Book 1
Comic Book 2
Comic Book 3
Comic Book 4
Cross Dissolve
Cross Blur
Cross Zoom
Ripple
Fade to Black
Fade to White
Page Curl Right
Page Curl Left
Show: Favorites and Unmarked
Photo
Video clips that can be added to the project
Transition Browser

ADDING VIDEO CLIPS TO A PROJECT

Most movie projects include video clips that are stored in the Event Library. To add clips to a project, move into the Event Library and find the clip you want to add. Then, select the part of the clip you want to be in the project, and drag it onto the project where you want it to play.

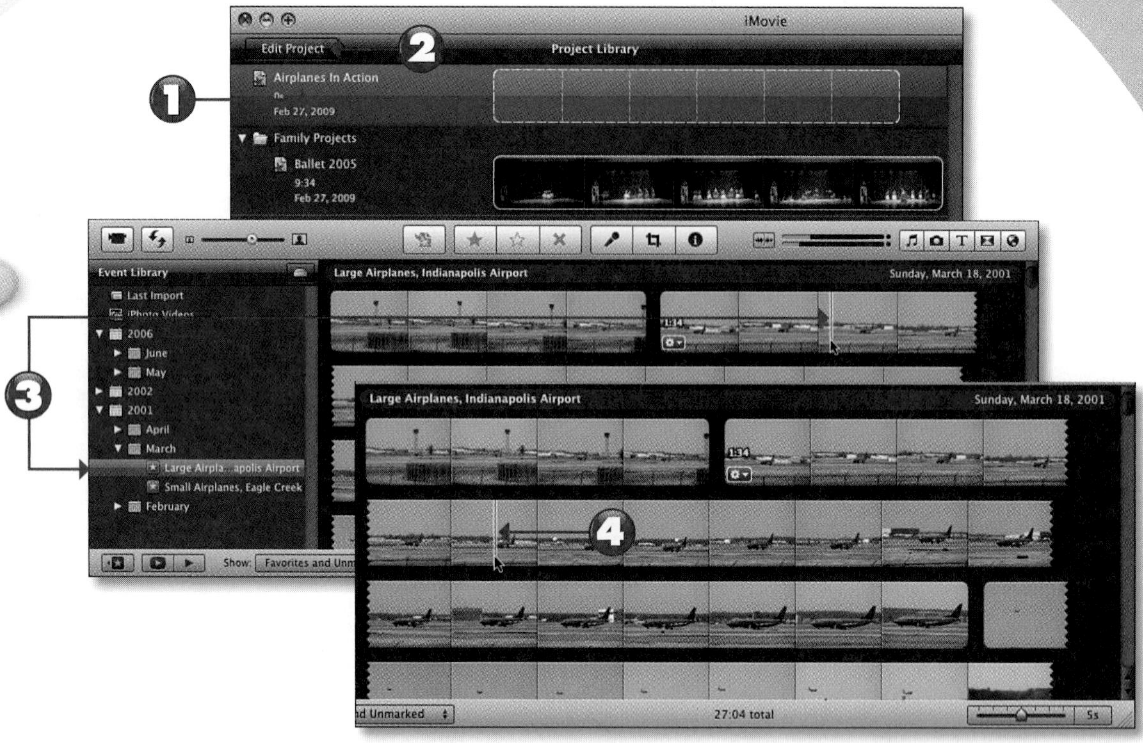

Start

1. Select the project on which you want to work.
2. Click **Edit Project**.
3. Select and browse the event containing the clips you want to add to the movie.
4. Drag across the clip until the red line is at the beginning of the part of the clip you want to use in the movie.

Continued

NOTE

Use the Preview Window Remember that the frame you see in the preview window is where the red line is on a filmstrip. This larger view makes it easier to select a more precise start or end point for a selection. ■

TIP

Time As you select frames within a clip, the amount of time you've selected is shown at the end of the selection box. ■

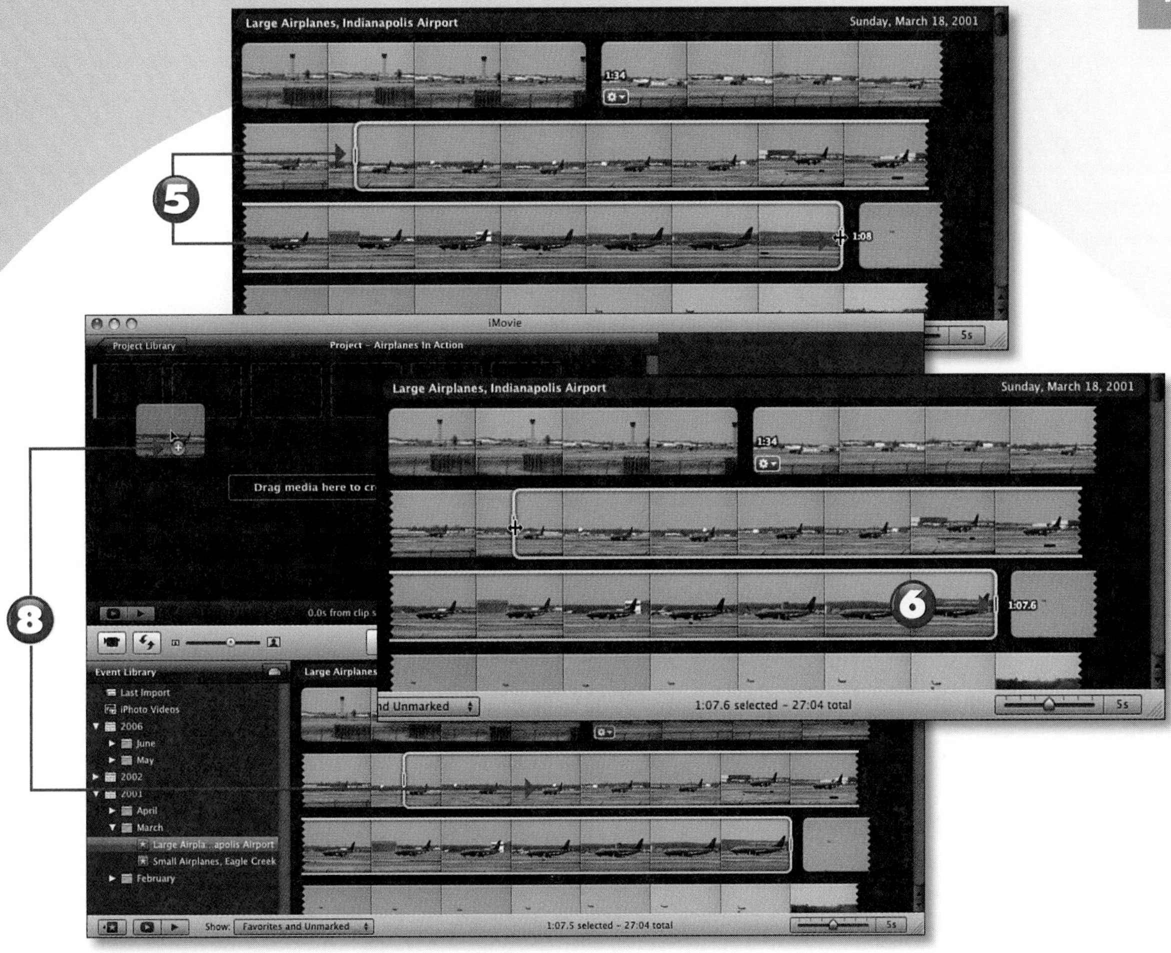

5. Hold the mouse button down and drag in the filmstrip until the part of the clip you want to use in the movie is enclosed in the yellow box.

6. To adjust the selection end point drag the right end of the selection box left or right.

7. To adjust the selection start point drag the left end of the selection box left or right.

8. Drag the selection box from the Event Browser and drop it onto the project at the location where you want it to appear in your movie.

End

TIP

Use the Slider, Luke Remember to use the slider in the lower-right corner of the project window to change the number of frames, and thus the size, of the thumbnails in the filmstrips in the project window. ■

NOTE

Automatic Transitions and Titles If the project has a theme applied and contains automatic transitions, you see a transition box at various points in the movie. If a theme has automatic titles, you see brown title boxes above the clips. ■

TRIMMING VIDEO CLIPS IN A PROJECT

As you edit your movie, you might discover that you want a clip to start later or end sooner than it currently does. In such cases, you can trim the clip to remove frames from either end, and thus from your movie. (Note that trimming a clip in a project doesn't change that clip in the Event Library.)

1. In the project window, select the clip you want to trim.
2. Drag the right end of the selection box to the left until the frames you want to remove from the end of the clip are outside the selection box.
3. Drag the left end of the selection box to the right until the frames you want to remove from the beginning of the clip are outside the selection box.
4. Choose **Edit**, **Trim to Selection**. The frames outside the selection box are removed from the clip and from the movie.

End

TIP

More Precise End Trimming To trim the end of a clip frame by frame, select the clip and press **Option-left arrow** to move the end of the clip to the left or **Option-right arrow** to move the end to the right. ■

NOTE

Preview, Edit, Preview Building a movie is a continuous process of making changes, previewing, making changes, previewing, and so on until you are happy with the project. ■

CROPPING VIDEO CLIPS IN A PROJECT

You can crop a clip so that the image you want to focus on fills the screen. This is useful for removing parts of the image you don't want to include in the movie, or to change the focus of a scene by making the focus point a more prominent part of the clip's images.

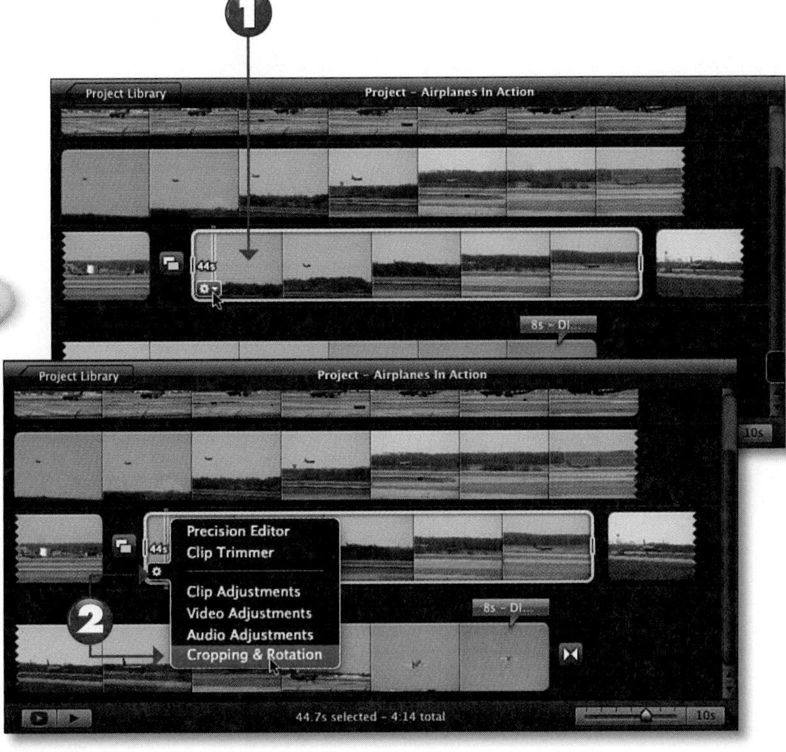

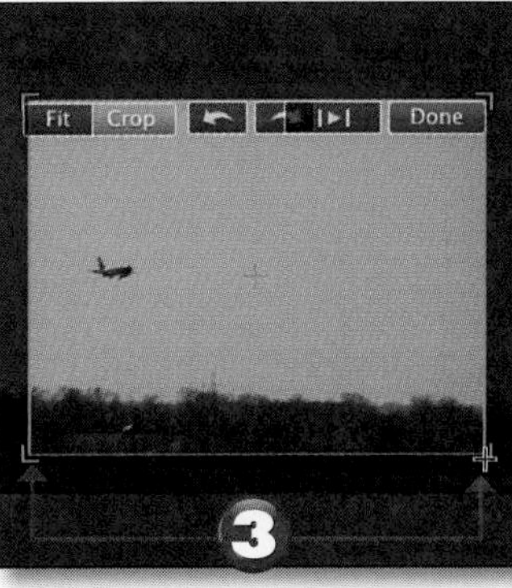

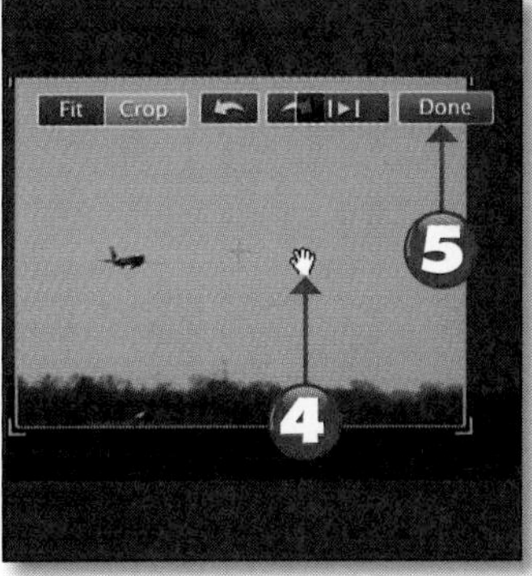

1. Select the clip you want to crop.
2. Open the clip's menu and choose **Cropping & Rotation**.
3. In the preview window, drag the corners of the green selection box so that it includes the part of the clip you want to keep.
4. Drag the selection box around so that the part of the image you want to keep is within the box.
5. Click **Done**. The clip is cropped.

End

TIP

Undo a Crop To restore the full clip again, click the **Fit** button. ■

TIP

Rotate a Clip To rotate a clip, open the **Cropping & Rotation** tool and click the curved left arrow to rotate it 90 degrees counterclockwise or the curved right arrow to rotate it 90 degrees clockwise. ■

ADJUSTING THE VIDEO QUALITY OF CLIPS IN A PROJECT

You can adjust the video quality of clips to improve their appearance. You do this with the Clip Inspector.

Start

1. Open the clip's menu and choose **Video Adjustments**.
2. Drag the **Levels** slider until you like what you see in the preview window.
3. Use the **Exposure**, **Brightness**, **Contrast**, and **Saturation** sliders to make changes to those aspects of the video.
4. Use the **White Point** wheel to set the white point for the video to help improve the appearance of whites and grays. Click **Done**.

End

TIP

Go Back! To remove any adjustments you've made, click the **Revert to Original** button on the Video tab of the Inspector. ■

TIP

Auto Adjustments To apply automatic adjustments to a clip, click **Auto** on the Video tab of the Inspector. This can often improve the overall quality of a clip, and it's very easy to do, so it should often be the first thing you do when you adjust a clip. ■

APPLYING SPECIAL EFFECTS TO A VIDEO CLIP

iMovie features a number of effects you can apply to clips to make your movies more interesting and fun. You can also make a clip play backward.

Start

1. Open the clip's menu and choose **Clip Adjustments**.
2. Click **Video Effect**.
3. Drag over the effects and see their impact on the clip in the preview window; click the effect you want to apply to the clip.
4. Drag the **Speed** slider to the left to slow the clip speed down or to the right to speed it up; to play it in reverse, check the **Reverse** check box.
5. Click **Done**.

End

NOTE

Stabilize If you have a clip that is "shaky" from the motion of the camera while you are filming, check the **Smooth Clip Motion** check box on the Clip tab. ■

TIP

Rewind To create a rewind effect, place a clip in a movie three times in a row. Select the middle clip, speed it up, and make it play in reverse. ■

ADDING iPHOTO PHOTOS TO A PROJECT

You can add photos from your iPhoto library to your movies. You can set how long a photo appears on the screen, and you can apply the Ken Burns effect to it to make it more dynamic.

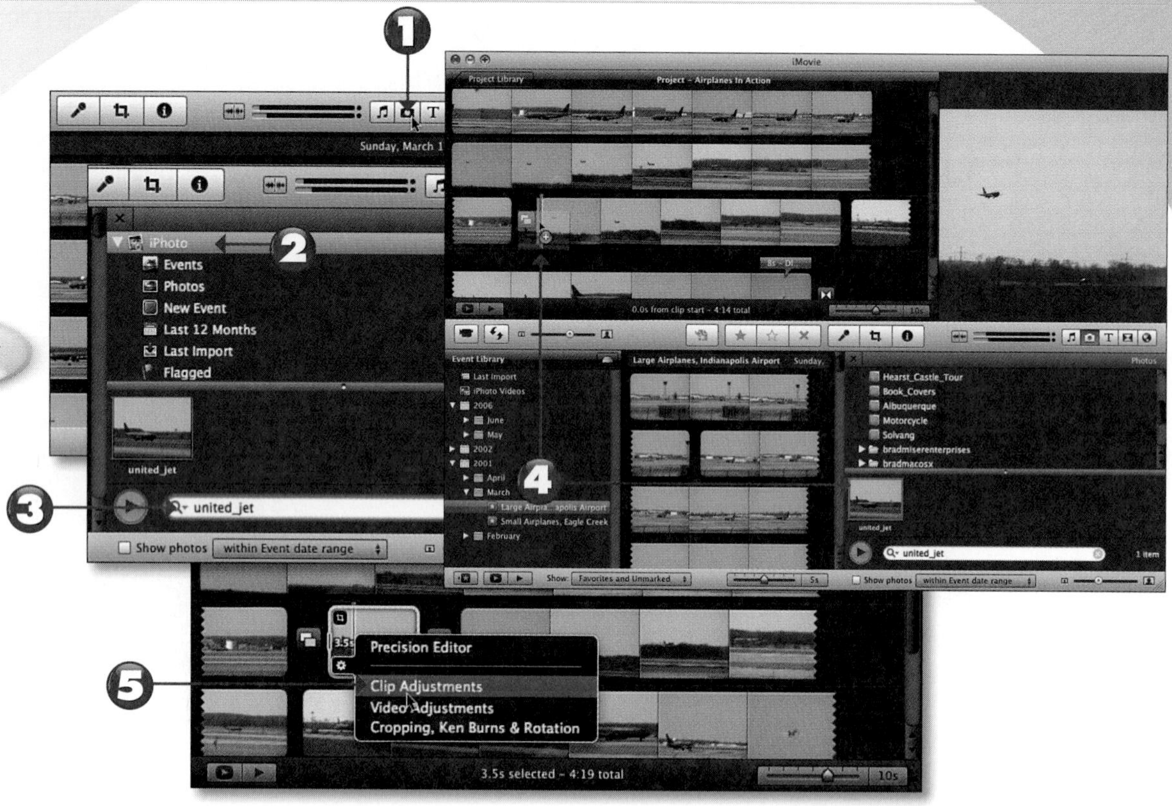

Start

1. Click the **Photos Browser** button.
2. Select the source containing the photo you want to add to the project.
3. Browse or search the source until you see the photo's thumbnail.
4. Drag the photo from the Photos Browser and drop it between the clips in the movie where you want it to appear.
5. Open the photo's menu and choose **Clip Adjustments**.

Continued

NOTE

Photo Duration A photo's duration determines how long it appears on the screen. A photo clip is in effect a one-frame video clip, and the duration of the clip determines how long the image appears on screen. ■

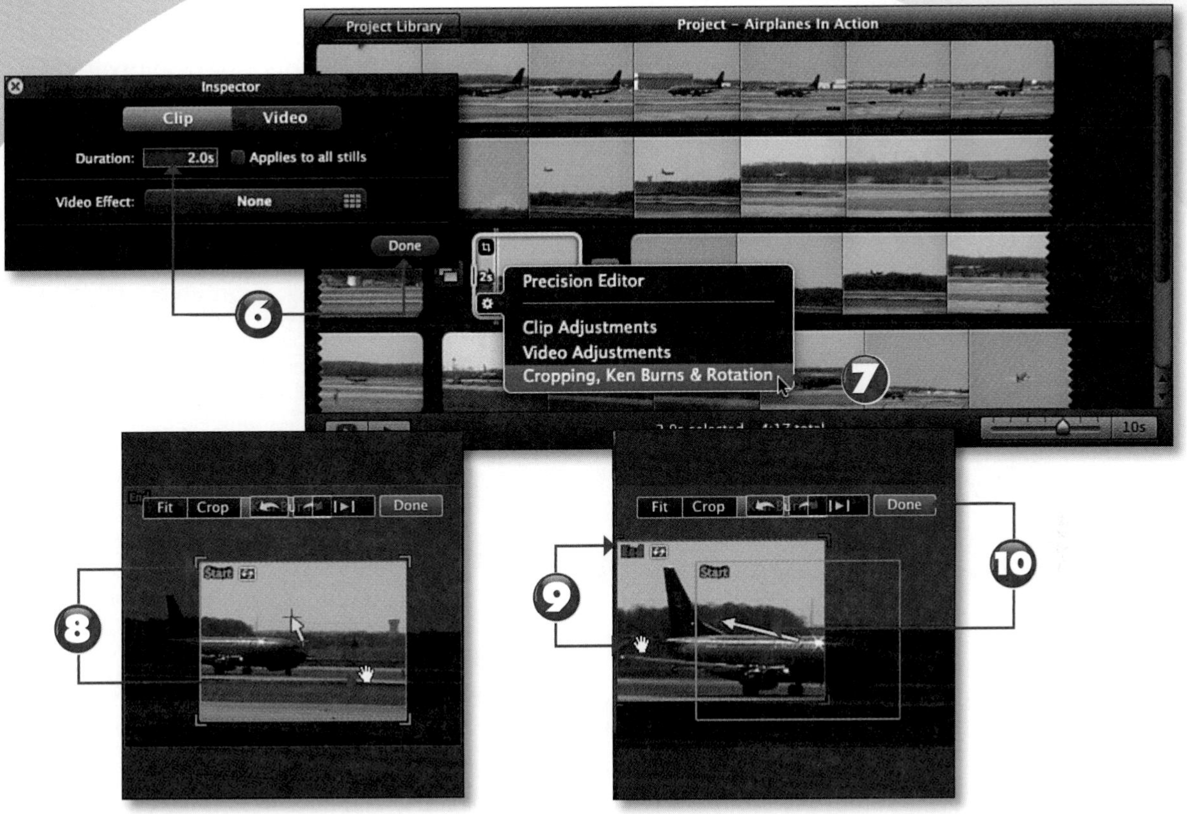

6. Enter the clip's duration in the Duration field and click **Done**.

7. Open the photo's menu and choose **Cropping, Ken Burns & Rotation**.

8. Size and place the green start box around the image so that it appears as you want it to at the beginning of the clip.

9. Size and place the red end box around the image so that it appears as you want it to be at the end of the clip.

10. Drag the two boxes so that the direction of the motion is what you want it to be (as indicated by the yellow arrow) and click **Done**.

End

TIP

Apply Video Effects You can use the Video Effect tool to apply effects to still images just as you can video clips. ■

TIP

Crop Photos You can crop a still image clip using the same cropping tool as you use for video clips. ■

ADDING TRANSITIONS BETWEEN VIDEO CLIPS IN A PROJECT

Transitions make a movie flow more smoothly by helping it transition between the clips of which it is made. iMovie features many kinds of transitions that you can use in your projects. You can also configure aspects of transitions to tailor them to your specific projects.

Start

1. Click the **Transitions Browser** button.
2. Drag over transitions to preview them within their thumbnails.
3. To add a transition to the project, drag it from the browser and drop it between two clips.
4. Place the pointer at the right end of the clip before the transition.
5. Press the **spacebar** to watch the transition in the preview window.

Continued

NOTE

Transitions and Themes Some themes include transitions in a project automatically. You can add additional transitions or edit existing transitions. To do so, you have to disable automatic transitions when prompted. ■

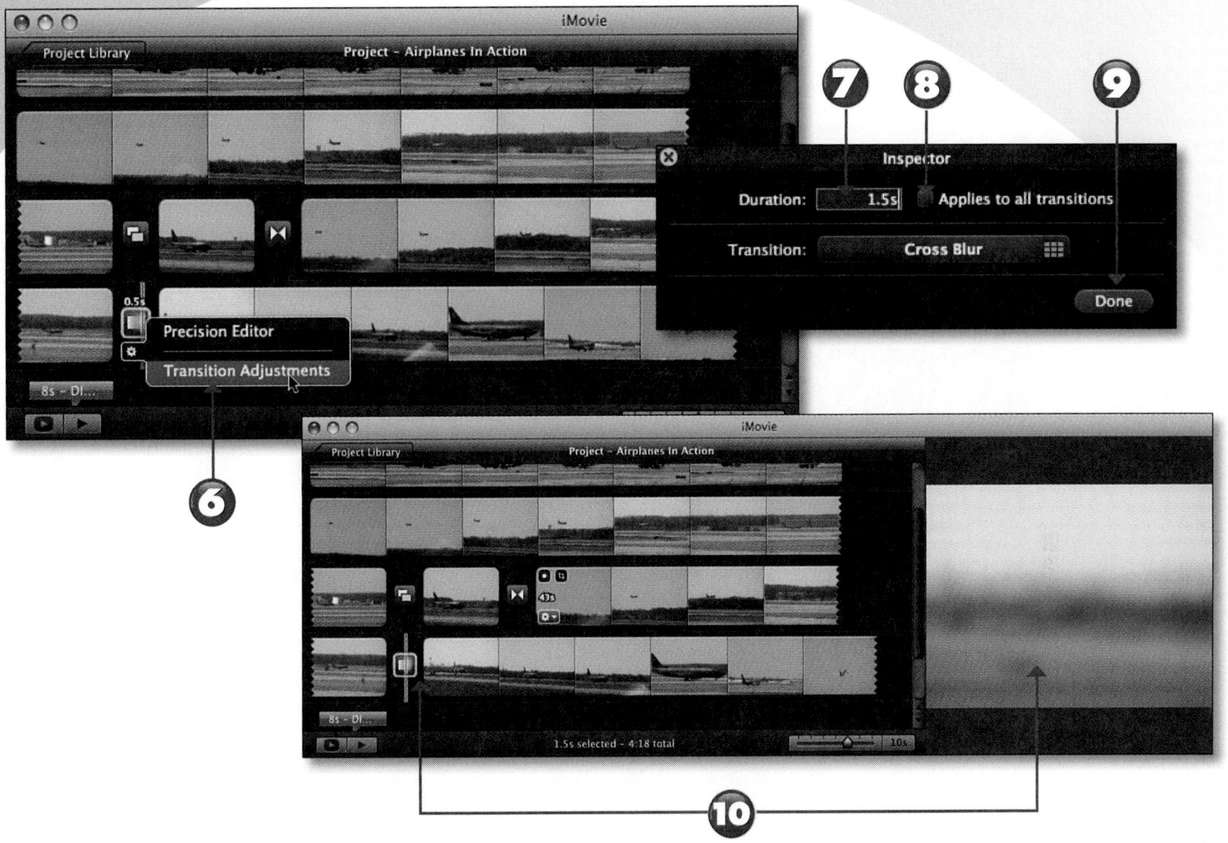

6. Open the transition's menu and choose **Transition Adjustments**.

7. Enter the duration of the transition effect in the Duration box.

8. If you don't want the same duration to be applied to all the transitions in the movie, uncheck the **Applies to All Transitions** check box.

9. Click **Done**.

10. Preview the transition again.

End

TIP

Changing Transitions To change a transition effect, click the **Transition** button on the Inspector and choose the new transition. ■

NOTE

Too Many Transitions Just because you can add a lot of interesting transitions to a movie doesn't mean you should. Transitions should make your movie more interesting and appealing, without being distracting. ■

ADDING AND EDITING TITLES

Titles are text that appears on the screen. Titles can be associated with clips, such as a caption, or the text can be the focal point of a specific part of a movie, such as closing credits. Some themes include text placeholders automatically. You can also add your own titles. You can edit the text in automatic titles and those you add manually.

Start

1. Click the **Titles Browser** button.
2. Drag over a title's thumbnail to preview it within the thumbnail.
3. To add a title to a project, drag it from the browser and drop it on top of a clip to have the text appear along with the clip or between, before, or after clips to have the title appear as its own clip.
4. If you place a title between, before, or after clips, point to backgrounds to preview the title in the preview window.
5. Click the background you want to apply to the title.

Continued

NOTE

Titles over Clips or Titles as Clips Some titles are designed to play "on top" of video clips, whereas others are like a video clip that takes up the entire frame. ■

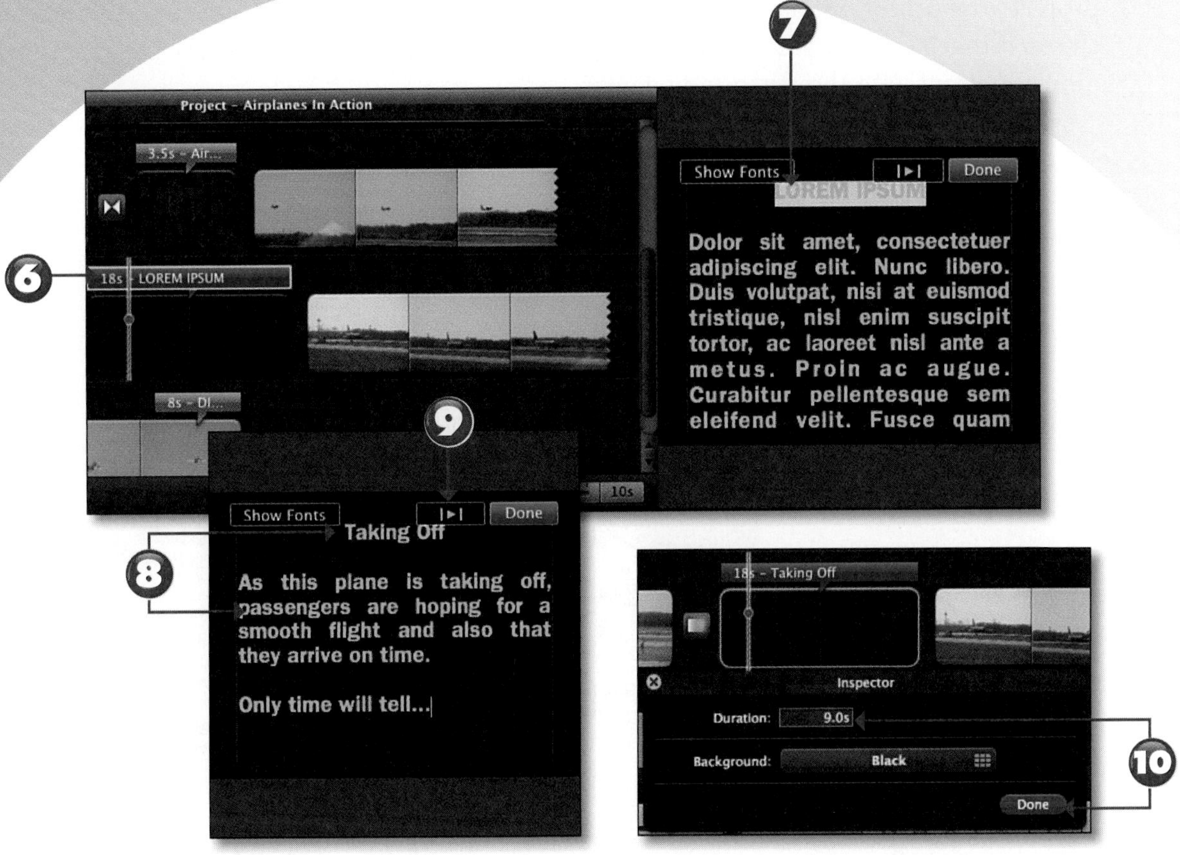

6 Select the text block associated with a title.

7 Select the title's text in the preview window.

8 Edit the title's text in the preview window.

9 Click the **Play** button and watch the title in the preview window and click **Done**.

10 If the title appears in its own clip, set its duration and click **Done**.

End

TIP

Copy and Paste Title Text You can write a title's text in another application and copy it. Then select the title text in iMovie and paste the copied text over it. ■

NOTE

Editing Automatic Titles Edit titles that are added automatically with a theme using the same steps; you just don't need to add the title, because it's added automatically. ■

EDITING CLIPS WITH THE PRECISION EDITOR

The Precision Editor does what its name implies: It enables you to more precisely edit a project. The editor enables you to precisely control when one clip ends and the next one starts. If there are transitions or titles between clips, you can also control how those elements interact with the surrounding clips.

Start

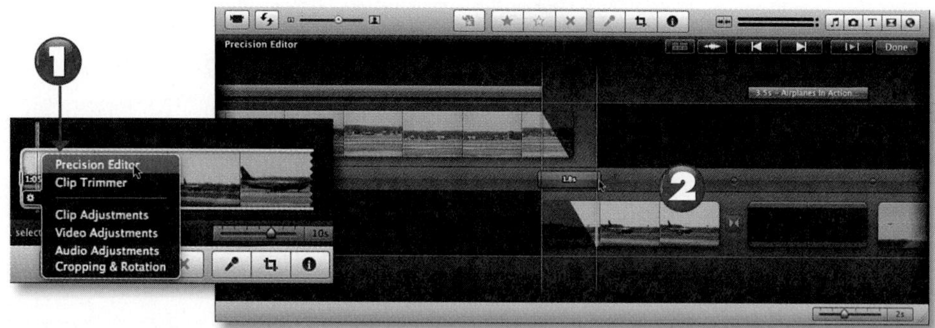

1. Open a clip's menu and choose **Precision Editor**.
2. If there is a transition between the clips, change the length of its bar to change its duration.
3. To change where a transition starts and stops, drag it to the left to have it start earlier in the top clip or drag it to the right to have it start later in the top clip.
4. Click the **Play** button to see the current edit in the preview window.
5. Click the **Next** button to move to the next edit point.

Continued

NOTE

Shading The parts of clips that are shaded indicate where the clip is not visible onscreen. When there is a transition between clips, the shaded line is diagonal, indicating that the clip is transitioning offscreen. ■

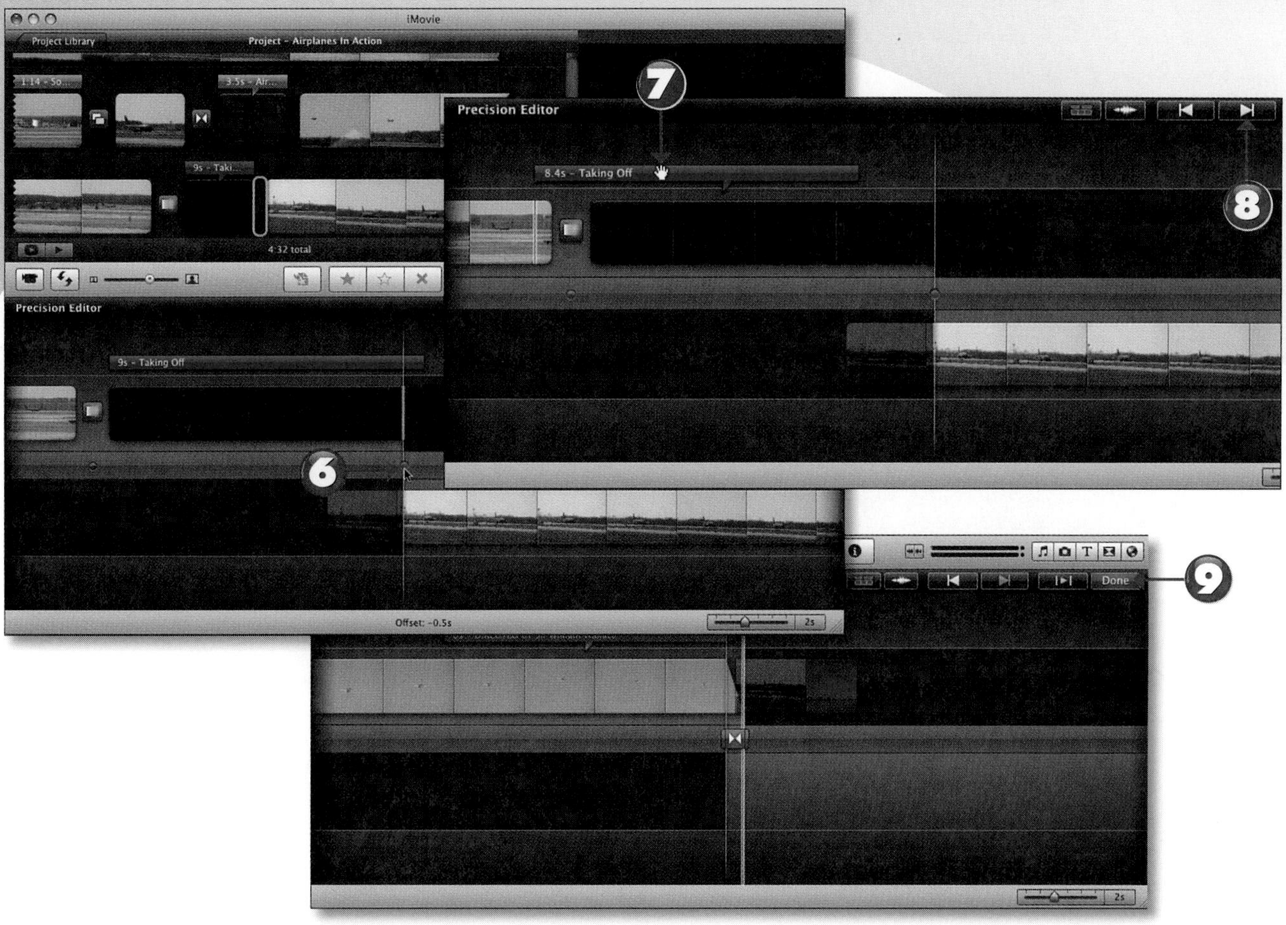

6 If two clips don't have a transition effect between them, drag the blue line to the left to end the top clip sooner or to the right to end it later.

7 To change when text appears, drag its bar to the left to have it start earlier or to the right to have it start later. (The red line indicates where the text starts.)

8 Click the **Next** button to move to the next edit.

9 When you've edited the entire project, click **Done**.

End

NOTE

Building a Movie Efficiently Because many elements you add to a movie impact others, you should add elements in a specific order to minimize rework. First, add all the video clips to a movie. Then add photos and transitions. Next, add title clips and titles over text. Finally, edit the entire movie with the Precision Editor. You'll then be ready for the soundtrack. ■

BUILDING A MOVIE'S SOUNDTRACK

If you've ever seen a movie, you know that hearing a movie is just about as important as seeing it. iMovie enables you to create soundtracks for your movie projects to enhance the visual experience with an auditory experience.

iMovie soundtracks can include the sound that was captured along with video when it was shot with a camcorder, sound effects, and music in your iTunes library.

As you add sound to your movie, you can edit and mix it to complete the sound "picture" that goes along with your movie.

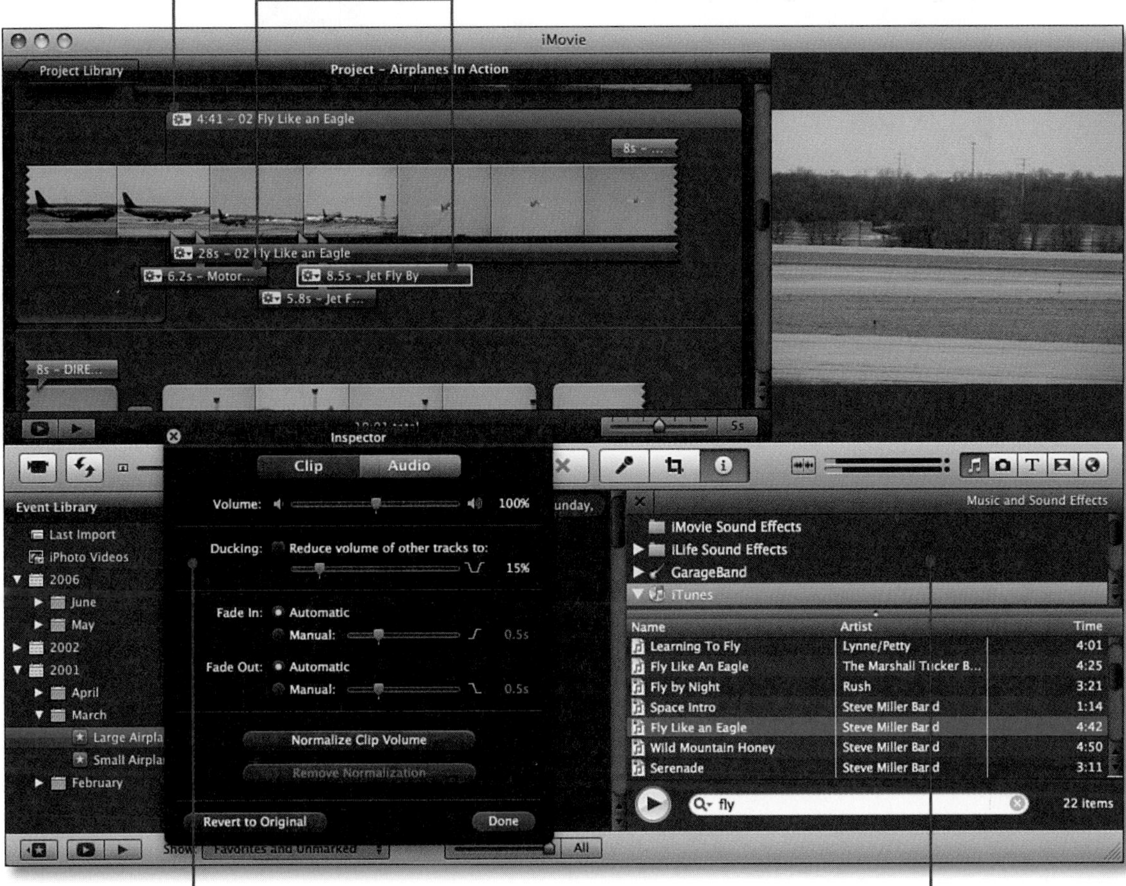
Background music
Sound effects
Tools to configure volume and other properties of audio
Music and Sound Effects Browser

ADJUSTING NATIVE AUDIO FOR VIDEO CLIPS IN A PROJECT

Video clips that you capture with a camera typically include audio, such as people talking, sounds from the activity happening in the video, and so on. This audio is sometimes called the native audio because it is naturally a part of the video. You can adjust the native audio for the video clips in a movie project to ensure it contributes to the overall experience.

1. Select the video clip whose audio you want to adjust.

2. Open the clip's menu and choose **Audio Adjustments**.

3. Set the relative volume level of the clip by dragging the **Volume** slider to the left or right.

4. If the audio is something you want viewers to hear above all the other audio tracks in the movie, check the **Ducking** check box.

5. If you enable ducking, use the slider to set the percentage of volume to which all other tracks will be reduced while this clip plays.

Continued

NOTE

Relative Volume When you set the volume level for a clip, you are setting the volume level relative to 100%, which is the "default" volume level of the clip. ■

6 To manually set the audio's fade in, click the **Fade In Manual** radio button and use the slider to set the amount of time over which the audio will fade in.

7 To manually set the audio's fade out, click the **Fade Out Manual** radio button and use the slider to set the amount of time over which the audio will fade out. Click **Done**.

8 To mute a clip so that it doesn't have any impact on the movie's soundtrack, select the clip.

9 Choose **Edit**, **Mute Clip**.

End

TIP

Setting a Consistent Volume Level To set the volume level for a group of clips so that it is consistent as each clip plays, select the clips whose volume you want to be similar. Then, open the Audio tab of the Inspector and click **Normalize Clip Volume**. ■

NOTE

Mix Last If you are going to add sound effects, music, and other audio to the movie, don't worry about setting relative volume levels until you are done with the soundtrack. After you have all the sound added to and placed in the movie, you can mix the relative volume levels to the appropriate levels. ■

ADDING SOUND EFFECTS TO A PROJECT

iMovie includes a number of sound effects that you can add to your movies to make them more enjoyable. You can place sound effects at any location in your movie. When that point is reached, the sound effect plays. You can even use multiple sound effects at the same time.

Start

1. Click the **Music and Sound Effects Browser** button.
2. Select the **iMovie Sound Effects** or **iLife Sound Effects** folder.
3. Browse the list of sounds. To hear a sound, double-click it.
4. To add a sound effect to a movie, drag its icon from the browser and drop it on the movie at the point at which you want it to play.

Continued

TIP

Pane Height To make the lower part of the browser taller so that you can see more sounds at once, drag the resize handle up. ■

TIP

iLife Sound Effects If you click the expansion triangle next to the iLife Sound Effects folder, you see subfolders that organize the sound effects by type, such as Animals. ■

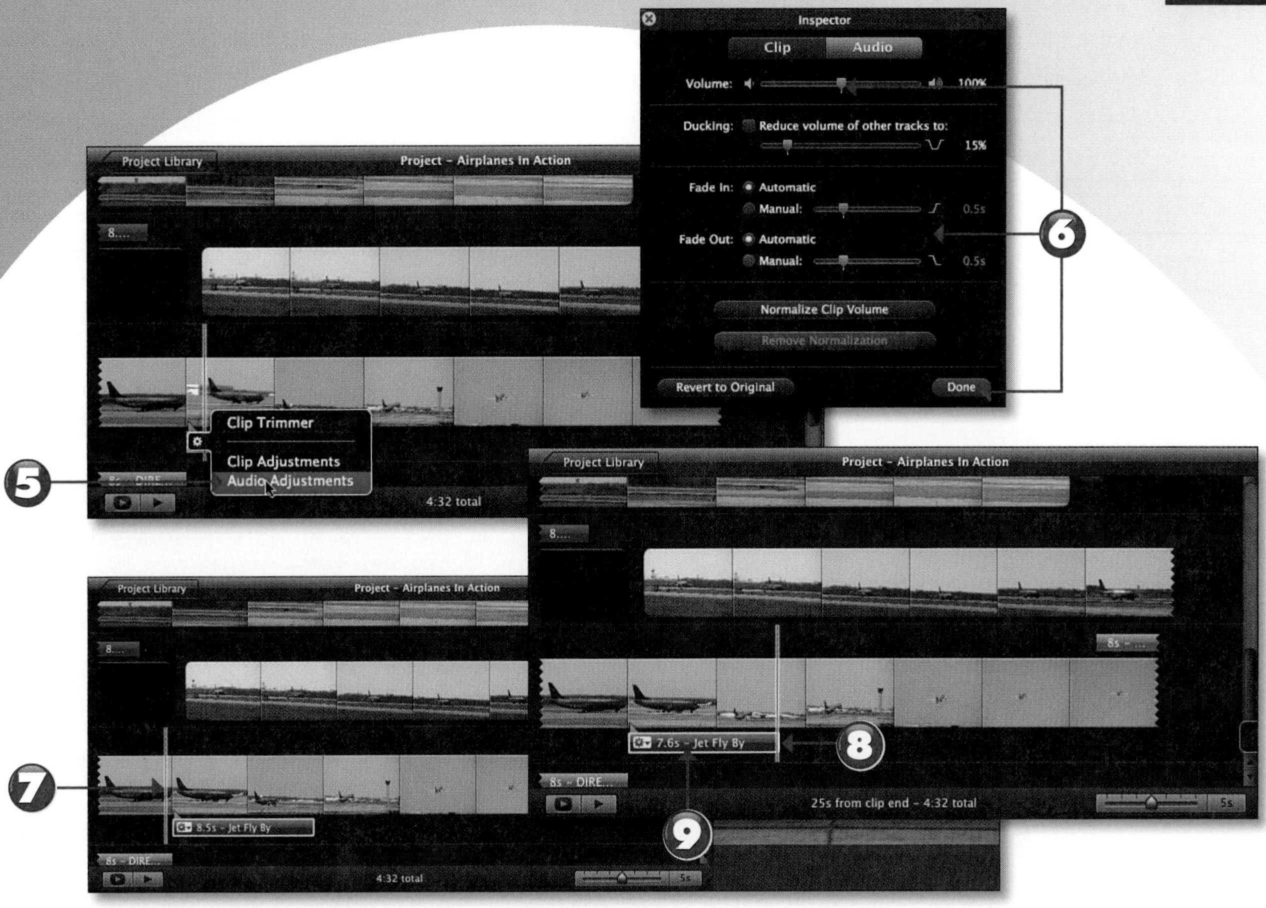

5 Open the sound effect's menu and choose **Audio Adjustments**.

6 Use the Audio tools to adjust the sound effect's volume and fade; then click **Done**.

7 Point to the left of the sound effect and press the **spacebar** to preview that section of the movie and hear the sound effect.

8 To shorten the sound effect, select it and drag the right edge of its box to the left until it is the length you want it to be.

9 To change when the sound effect plays, drag its box to the left or right.

End

TIP

Stacking Sound Effects You can stack sound effects so that they play at the same time. Just drag the effects to the same point in the movie, and when that part of the movie plays, all the sound effects play. ■

ADDING iTUNES AUDIO TO A PROJECT

What's a movie without music? Not much. You can add any music to a movie project. When you add music as background audio, it plays "behind" all the other audio (such as native audio and sound effects) throughout the movie's duration or as long as the music lasts.

Start

1. Click the **Music and Sound Effects Browser** button.

2. Select the **iTunes** source.

3. Browse the list of sounds or search for a song. To hear a song, double-click it.

4. To add the song as background to the movie, drag it from the browser onto the project window and release the mouse button when the window's background turns green.

Continued

TIP

iTunes Playlists You can select any of your playlists in iTunes to use the music they contain in your iMovie projects. ■

TIP

Adding iTunes Audio to Clips You can also drag iTunes audio next to a clip so that it plays with that clip instead of as background music. You do this just like adding sound effects. ■

5. Scroll up to the top of the project window so that you see the song you added.

6. Open its menu and choose **Audio Adjustments**.

7. Use the Audio tools to adjust the sound effect's volume and fade; then click **Done**.

8. To lock the start of background music to a specific clip, click its bar near its name. When you are in the right place, the music box turns purple.

9. Drag the bar so that the pin is at the point in the clip where you always want it to start.

End

TIP

Muting Sound To disable audio when you skim a movie, click the **Audio Skimming** button located to the left of the two audio monitor bars under the preview window. ■

NOTE

Pinning Your Clips When you pin background music to a clip, it always plays with that clip, even when you move the clip to a new location in the movie. ■

TRIMMING AN AUDIO TRACK

You can use the Clip Trimmer to more precisely trim an audio clip so that it is the exact length you want it to be.

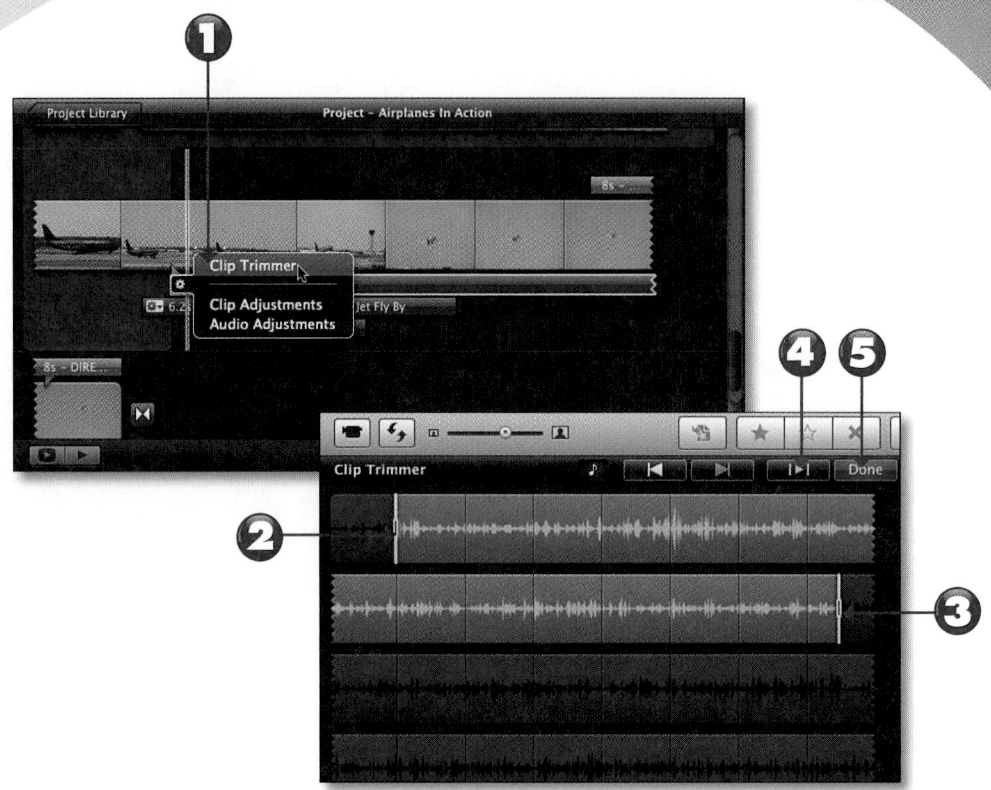

Start

1. Select the clip you want to trim, open its menu, and choose **Clip Trimmer**.
2. Drag the left selection bar to where you want the clip to start.
3. Drag the right selection bar to where you want the clip to stop.
4. Click the **Play** button to preview the project with the clipped sound.
5. Click **Done**.

End

NOTE

Light Part Plays The lighter part of the Clip Trimmer indicates the part of the audio that plays. ■

TIP

Clip Trimmer Works for Video You can use the Clip Trimmer to clip video, too. Open a video clip's menu and choose **Clip Trimmer**. ■

MIXING A PROJECT'S SOUNDTRACK

After you've added all the sound to your movie, including music, sound effects, and native audio, you need to mix the soundtrack so that the appropriate sounds have the right volume levels, occur at the right times, and play in the right order. You have most of the skills to do this already.

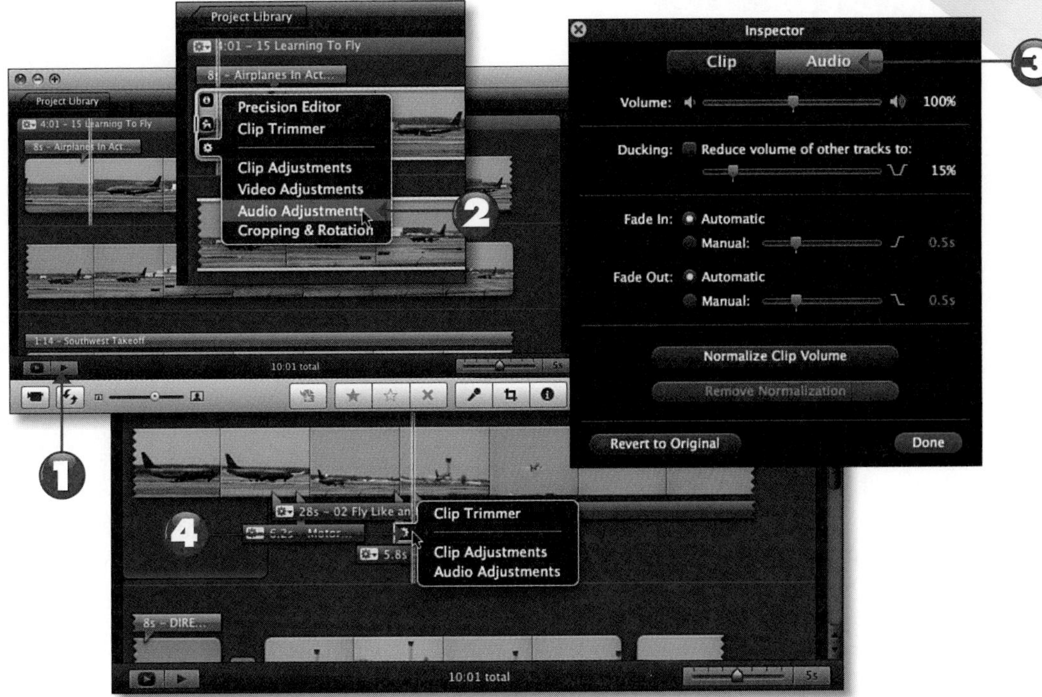

Start

1. Play your project and listen to the sounds that play.
2. When you discover a sound that is too loud, too soft, or that doesn't fade correctly, stop playback, open its menu, and choose **Audio Adjustments**.
3. Use the Audio tab of the Inspector to make any necessary changes to the sound.
4. Repeat steps 1 through 3 until the entire soundtrack sounds the way you want it to.

End

NOTE

Mixing Takes Time If a project has a lot of different audio, expect to spend a fair amount of time mixing the soundtrack, because you have to deal with each element individually. ■

TIP

Recording Narration You can record narration for clips by clicking the **Voiceover** button (microphone). Make adjustments to the sound-input settings. Click a clip and speak to record a narration track. ■

SHARING MOVIES WITH iMOVIE

Of course you can watch your movie projects within iMovie by selecting a project and clicking the **Full Screen** button. But, you'll make watching a movie even more convenient by putting it on a DVD that you can play in any standard DVD player, or on an iPhone or iPod so that you can watch it on the move.

You can also share your movies on the Web. There are many ways to do this, but some of the more useful are via MobileMe, by adding movie pages to your iWeb Web sites, and by making your movies really public by sending them to YouTube.

You can choose one or more of these methods to enjoy your movies. In fact, there's no reason not to give them all a try.

Put movies on a DVD you can play in any DVD player
Add your movies to your MobileMe gallery
iDVD Preview
MobileMe Gallery – Small_Planes
Small_Planes
Airplanes in Action
Put your movies on iWeb Web pages
Airplanes are fascinating...
... or at least they are to me. This movie contains footage I shot at local airports and s
variety of planes taking off, landing, and taxiing. I hope you enjoy it!
YouTube – Recitals
Recitals
Watch your movies on an iPhone
Send your movies to YouTube

PUTTING A MOVIE ON DVD

Putting a movie on DVD is one of the most convenient options because you can then watch the movie using any DVD player, such as the one in a home theater system or on a portable DVD player, a computer, and so on. Also, a DVD is a great way to store a movie over the long term. When you are done with an iMovie project, you can move it to DVD and eventually remove its files from your computer to free up space.

Start

1. Select the project you want to put on DVD.
2. Choose **Share**, **iDVD**. iMovie prepares the movie for DVD. When that is complete, iDVD launches, and the project is added to a new iDVD project.
3. Use iDVD to complete the DVD by customizing menus, adding more content, and burning your content to disc.

End

NOTE

More on iDVD You can do a lot more with iDVD than just put a movie on it. For example, you can put multiple movies and slideshows on the same DVD and design custom menus that include motion and sound effects. You learn how to create amazing DVD projects in Chapter 14, "Creating DVDs with iDVD." ■

TIP

Edit Well Before iDVD It can take a while for iMovie to prepare a movie for iDVD. If you find a mistake in a movie after you move it to iDVD, you have to prepare the movie again. Therefore, to limit the time spent preparing different versions of the movie, you should thoroughly edit your movies in iMovie before sharing. ■

PUBLISHING A PROJECT TO THE WEB USING MOBILEME

If you have a MobileMe account, you can easily share your movies by adding them to your MobileMe gallery. Once there, people can watch your movies from any computer with an Internet connection.

1. **Ctrl-click** or **right-click** the project you want to publish to your MobileMe gallery.
2. Choose **Publish to MobileMe Gallery**.
3. Select the size of the movie you want to publish by checking the check boxes.
4. Click **Publish**.
5. To see your movie on the Web, click **View**.

End

NOTE

Multiple Sizes If you select multiple sizes to publish, visitors to your Web site can choose the size of movie to view. ■

TIP

Securing a Movie If you want to share a movie on MobileMe but don't want just anyone to be able to view it, choose **Edit Names and Passwords** on the Viewable by pop-up menu. Create a username and password for the movie. ■

PUTTING A PROJECT ONTO AN iPHONE OR iPOD

Having a movie on your iPhone or iPod is a great way to enjoy your movie while you are moving about. You'll probably be amazed at the quality of your movies on these devices. To add a movie to an iPhone or iPod, it goes into iTunes and moves from there onto the device.

Start

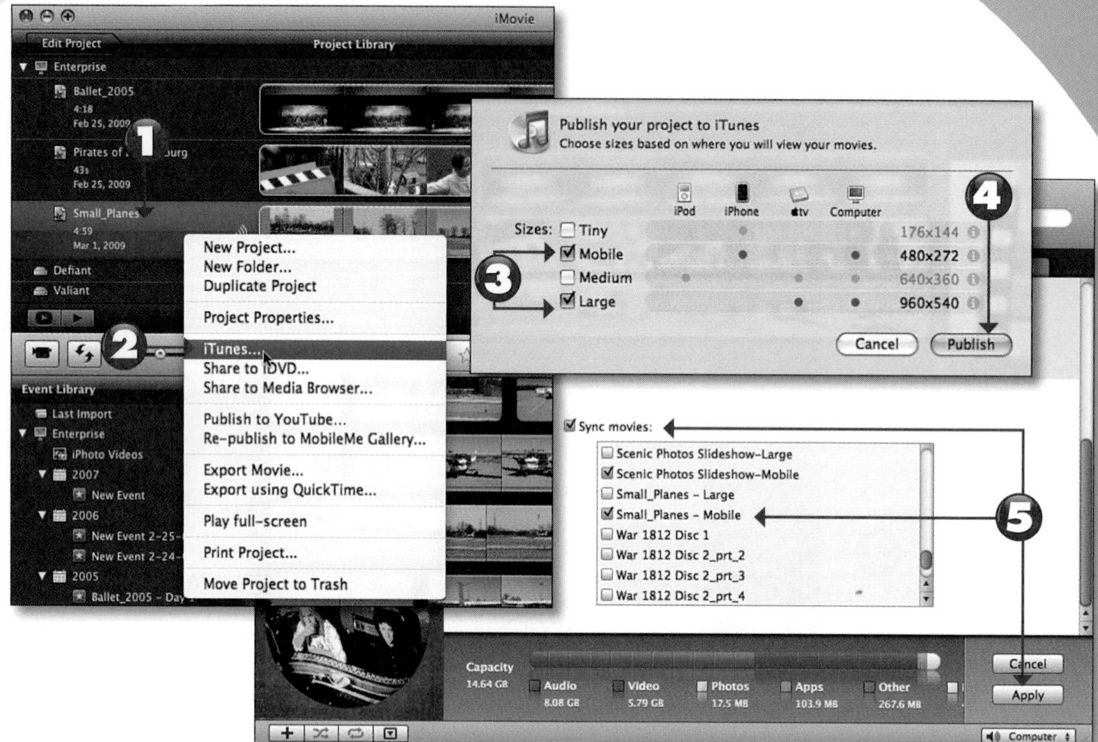

1. **Ctrl-click** or **right-click** the project you want to put on an iPhone or iPod.
2. Choose **iTunes**.
3. Select the sizes you want to be available in iTunes by checking their check boxes; include **Mobile** if you want to view the movie on an iPhone or **Medium** to view it on an iPod.
4. Click **Publish**. iMovie prepares the movie and sends it to the Movies folder in your iTunes library.
5. Configure iPhone or iPod synchronization so that the movie you added to iTunes is included. The next time you sync, the movie is added to the device.

End

NOTE

Movie Files Are Large Even with the compression and optimization that iMovie does when it saves movies for an iPhone or iPod, the files are still relatively large. You can manage a device's memory by excluding movie files from syncs. ■

PUBLISHING A PROJECT TO THE WEB USING iWEB

iWeb is a great application because it enables you to create sophisticated Web sites for many kinds of content, including your movies. You can add movie pages to your iWeb Web sites. Once your movies are published, people can watch them via any Web browser on a computer with an Internet connection. You can add movies to the Media Browser so that you can then use those movies in other iLife applications by opening the Media Browser in those applications.

1. Select the movie you want to add to an iWeb Web page.
2. Choose **Share**, **Media Browser**.
3. Select the sizes you want to be available for your iWeb pages.
4. Click **Publish**. The movie is added to the Media Browser and you see it there in other applications, such as iWeb.

End

NOTE

iWeb Revealed Use iWeb to add the movie to a page on your iWeb Web site. To learn more about iWeb, see Chapters 11 through 13 ("Getting Started with iWeb," "Building Up a Web Site," and "Publishing and Maintaining an iWeb Web Site," respectively). ■

PUBLISHING A PROJECT TO THE WEB USING YOUTUBE

YouTube is a global phenomenon. A huge number of videos are published to YouTube every day and are watched by an untold number of people located all over the world. If you have a YouTube account, you can add your movies to this massive video library.

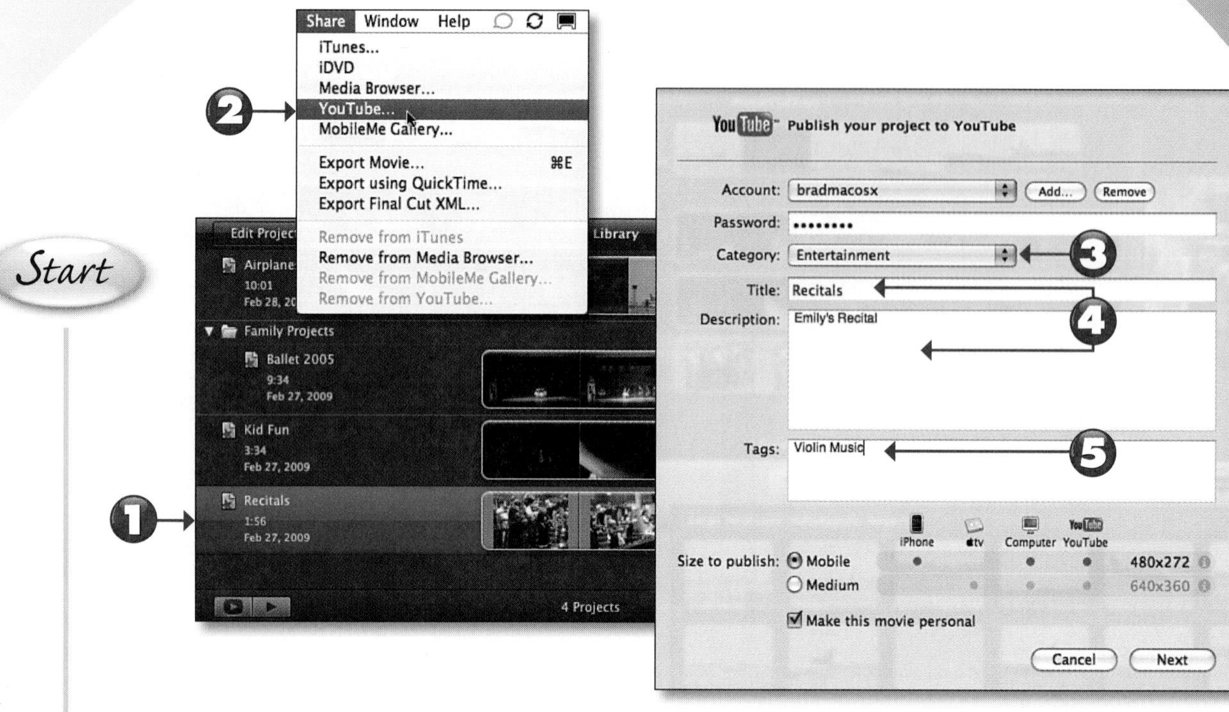

Start

1. Select the movie you want to share on YouTube.
2. Choose **Share**, **YouTube**.
3. Choose a category for the movie using the Category pop-up menu.
4. Enter a title and description for the movie.
5. Enter tags for the movie.

Continued

NOTE

Making Changes If you change a movie that you've published to YouTube and want the new version of the movie to be available there, you need to share it again. ■

TIP

Creating a YouTube Account If you don't already have a YouTube account, move to www.youtube.com and click the **Sign Up** link. Follow the onscreen instructions. ■

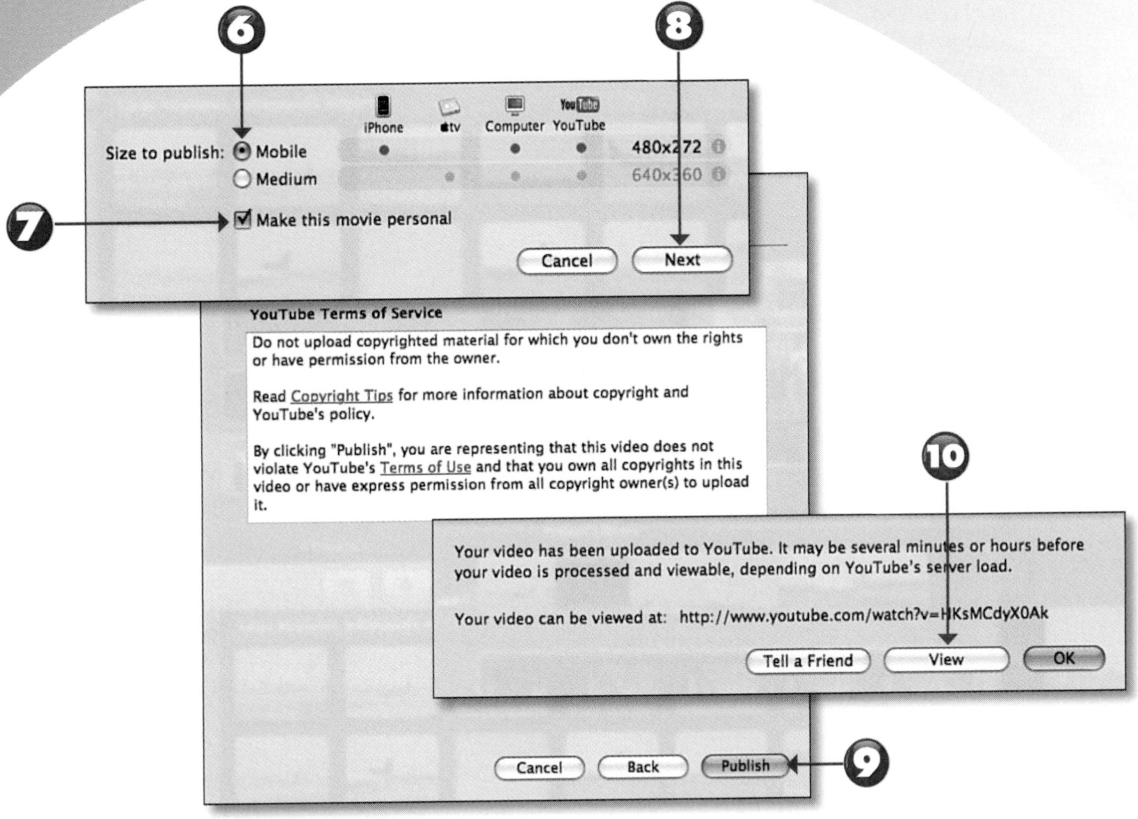

6. Select the size of the movie you want to publish.

7. If you want anyone to be able to view the movie, uncheck the **Make This Movie Personal** check box.

8. Click **Next**.

9. Click **Publish**.

10. To see your movie on YouTube, click **View**.

End

NOTE

Keep Movies to 10 Minutes or Less If you try to share a movie that is longer than 10 minutes, YouTube may reject it. ■

NOTE

Tags You can tag your movies with general descriptive terms so that when people search for those tags, your movies are found. ■

GETTING STARTED WITH iWEB

Imagine if you could build and publish your own Web pages as easily as you can build your own photo albums in iPhoto or movies in iMovie. With iWeb, you don't have to imagine this, because you can actually do it.

iWeb is an amazing application that you can use to create and publish your own Web sites. Instead of creating your Web pages starting with a "blank" screen, you can use iWeb's stylish and functional Web page templates as starting points. Then add your own content, resulting in great-looking Web pages that you can build quickly and easily.

With your MobileMe account, putting your sites on the Web requires just a few mouse clicks. iWeb and MobileMe take care of all the complexity of actually publishing the Web site, so you can spend your energy filling your Web sites with custom content and applying your creativity to make them look great.

Because iWeb is so easy to use, you might expect that the Web sites you build are limited, feature-wise. You'll be happy to know that your Web sites can include lots of great features, such as links within your sites and to external sites; Web widgets, including Google Maps; your own HTML code snippets; and so on.

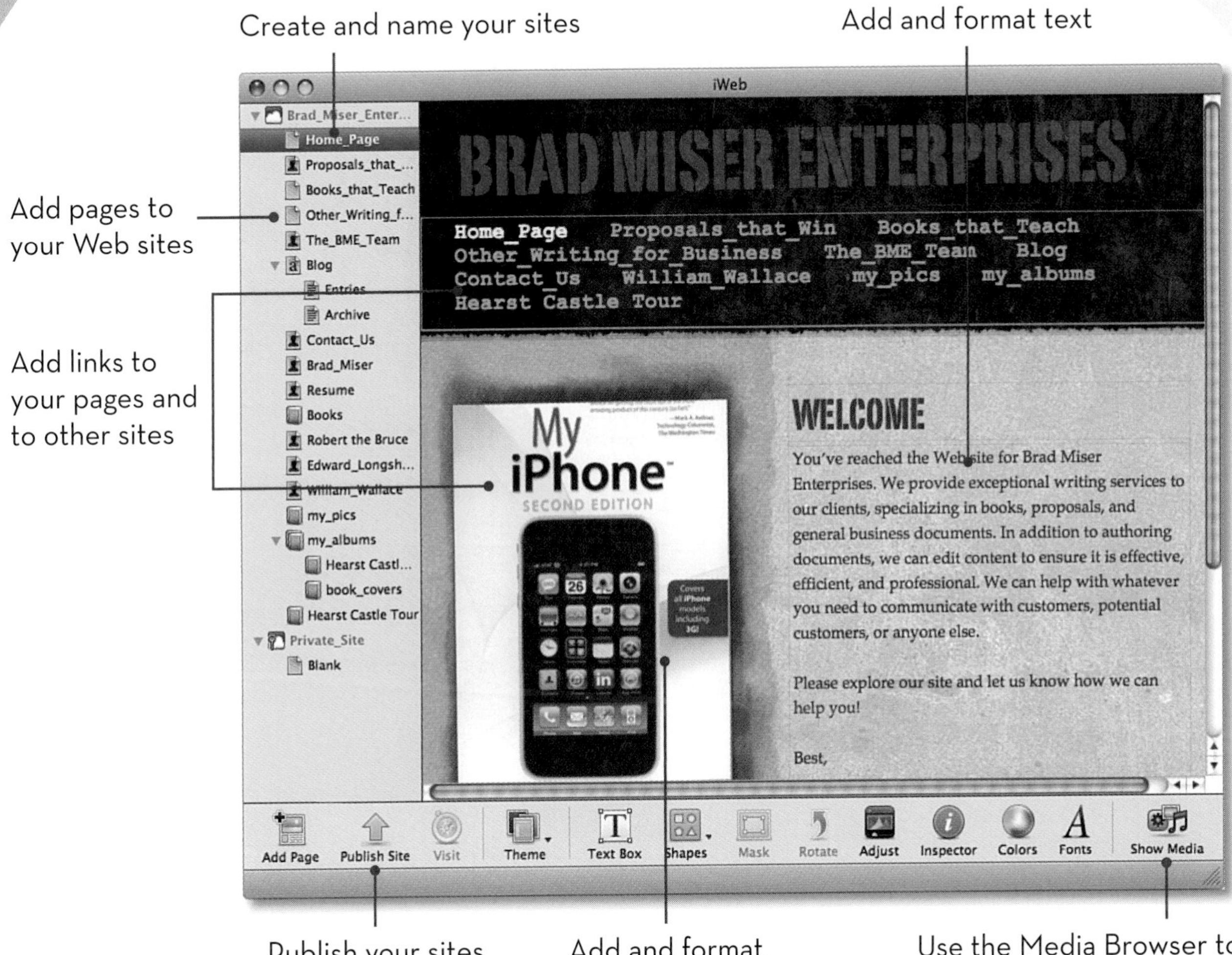
Create and name your sites
Add and format text
Add pages to your Web sites
Add links to your pages and to other sites
Publish your sites with a few clicks
Add and format graphics
Use the Media Browser to add your iLife content
iWeb
BRAD MISER ENTERPRISES
Home_Page Proposals_that_Win Books_that_Teach
Other_Writing_for_Business The_BME_Team Blog
Contact_Us William_Wallace my_pics my_albums
Hearst Castle Tour
WELCOME
You've reached the Website for Brad Miser Enterprises. We provide exceptional writing services to our clients, specializing in books, proposals, and general business documents. In addition to authoring documents, we can edit content to ensure it is effective, efficient, and professional. We can help with whatever you need to communicate with customers, potential customers, or anyone else.
Please explore our site and let us know how we can help you!
Best,
Home_Page
Proposals_that_...
Books_that_Teach
Other_Writing_f...
The_BME_Team
Blog
Entries
Archive
Contact_Us
Brad_Miser
Resume
Books
Robert the Bruce
Edward_Longsh...
William_Wallace
my_pics
my_albums
Hearst Castl...
book_covers
Hearst Castle Tour
Private_Site
Blank
My iPhone
SECOND EDITION
Add Page
Publish Site
Visit
Theme
Text Box
Shapes
Mask
Rotate
Adjust
Inspector
Colors
Fonts
Show Media

CREATING A WEB SITE

A Web site is a collection of Web pages. You can create and publish multiple Web sites in iWeb for various purposes, such as one dedicated to your business interests and another for your hobbies. You can add Web sites in iWeb for any purpose you'd like; and aside from the time it takes to create them, you are only limited by the amount of iDisk space you have and your own creativity.

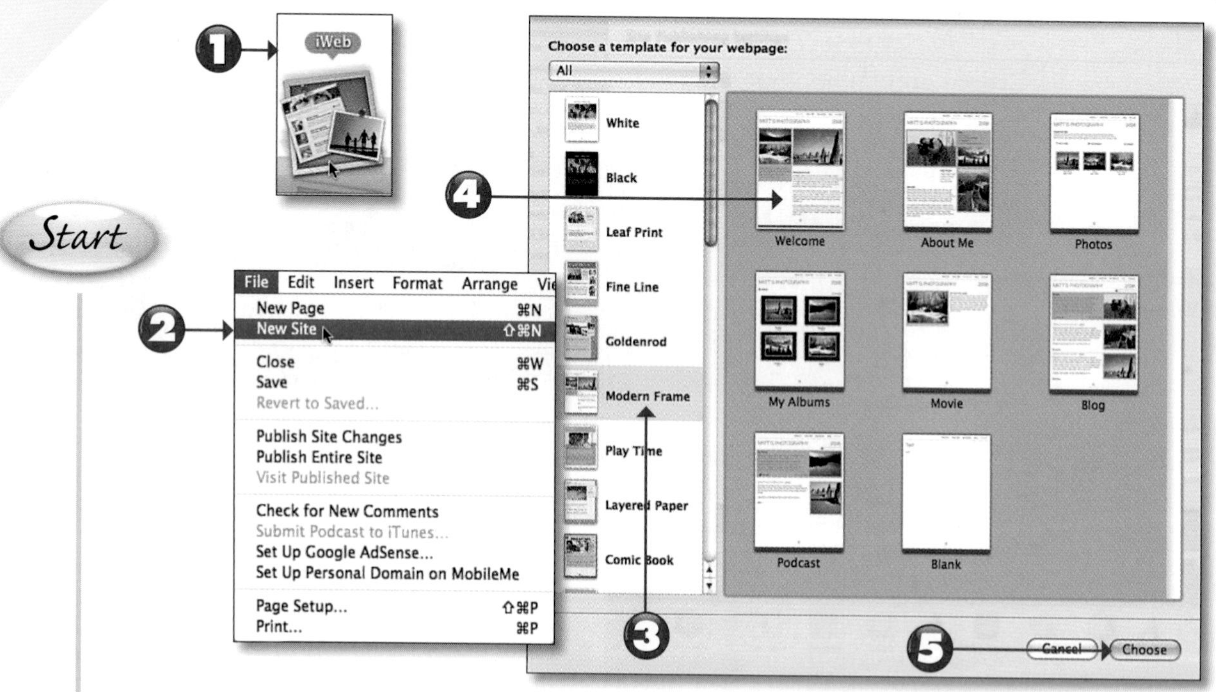

1. Click the **iWeb** icon on the Dock.
2. Choose **File**, **New Site**.
3. Click a theme.
4. Click a template.
5. Click **Choose**.

End

NOTE

Choosing a Template and Page An iWeb Web site has to include at least one page, which is why iWeb prompts you to select a page template when you create a site. iWeb creates the new site and adds one page to it based on the page template you select. ■

CONFIGURING A WEB SITE

After you create a site, you should configure it, which includes naming the site and setting its privacy policy. The name of a Web site helps you identify it when you work on it. More important, when someone visits your Web site, he sees the name of the site as the title of the Web browser window. You can also set an email address, privacy settings, and Facebook links for a site.

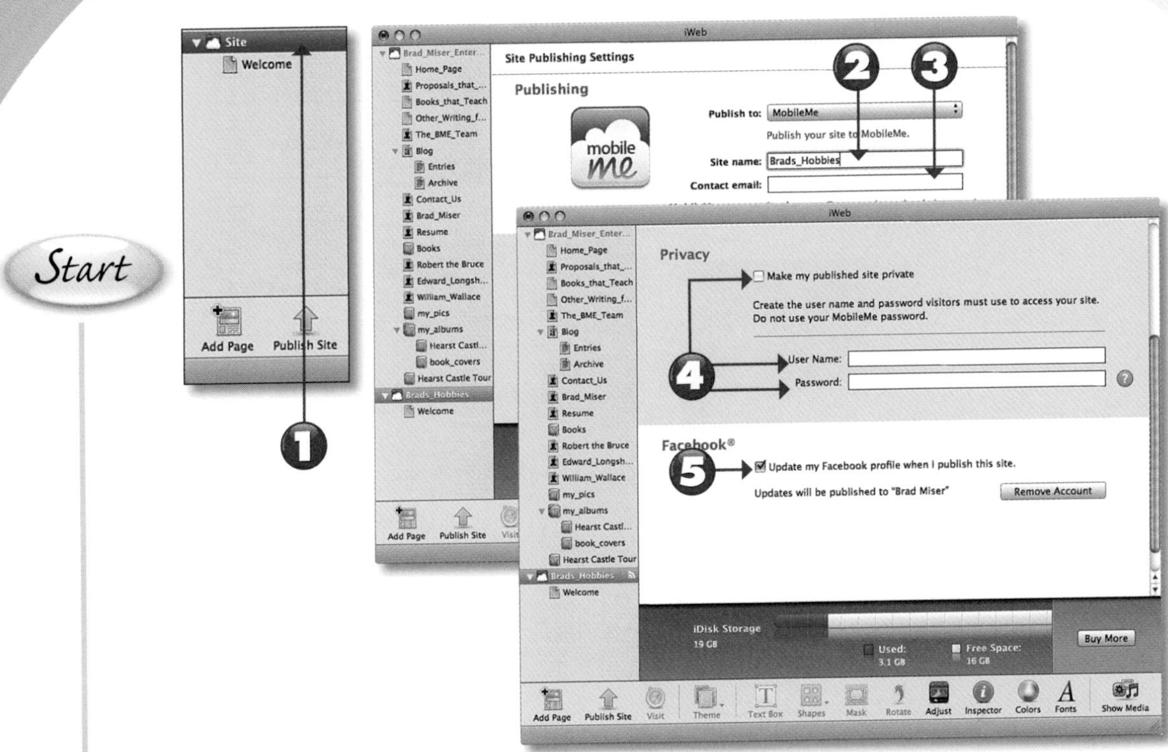

1. Click the site to select it.

2. Type the new name of the site.

3. If you want email contact information to be something other than your MobileMe email address, enter the email address you want to use.

4. To require a username and password for someone to view your site, check the **Make My Published Site Private** check box and enter the username and password.

5. To add the site information to your Facebook page, check the **Update My Facebook Profile When I Publish This Site** check box and log in to your Facebook account on the resulting sheet.

End

TIP

What Shouldn't be in a Name? Use only text or numbers (no spaces) in a site's name. ■

ADDING PAGES TO A WEB SITE

You build up a Web site by adding pages to it. Pages you add are based on templates for the pages that you choose. iWeb templates have two primary elements. The *theme* determines the overall style of the page, including its layout, the fonts used, colors, graphics, and so on. The *placeholders* are where you fill the page with the specific text, images, and other content that you want to include.

Start

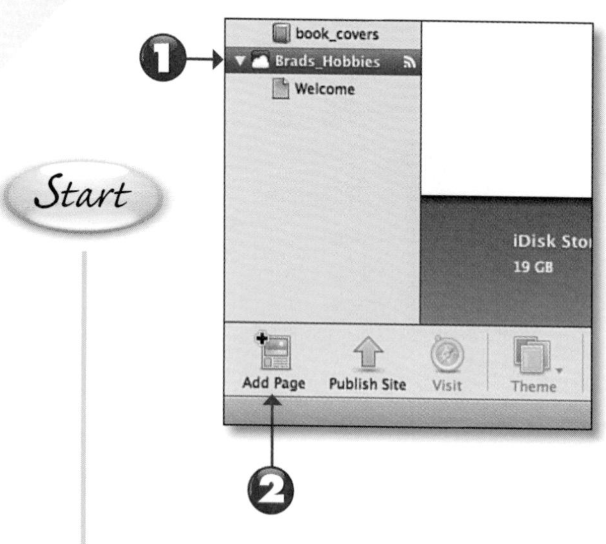

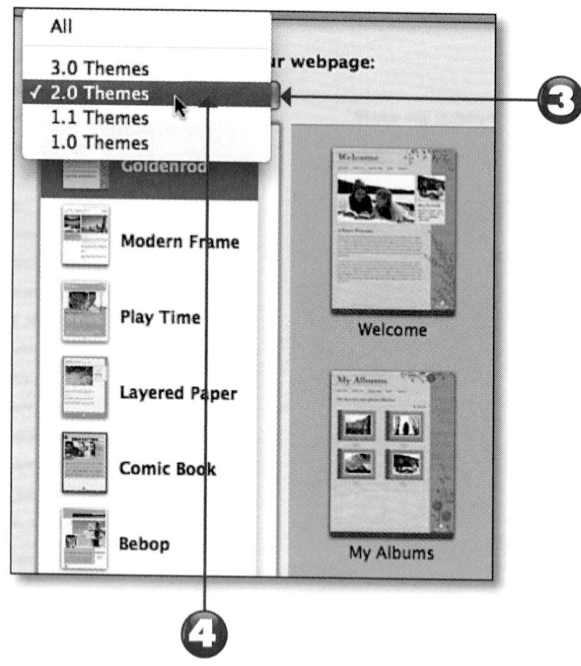

1. Click the Web site to which you want to add a page.
2. Click the **Add Page** button.
3. Open the Theme Collection menu.
4. Choose the collection of themes with which you want to work.

Continued

NOTE

Theme Collections On the Theme Collection menu, you see different groups of themes that are named according to the version of iWeb that they were first included in. Each collection includes different themes; each theme has a collection of templates within it. The same templates are part of each theme. Of course, they look quite different because they take their design from the theme in which they are contained. ■

5. Select the theme you want to use for the new page.

6. Click the template you want to use for the new page.

7. Click **Choose**. The new page is added to the site you selected in step 1.

8. Click the new page if it isn't selected already and press **Return**. The page's name becomes editable.

9. Type a name for the new page and press **Return**.

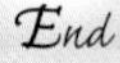

NOTE

On Themes As you build a Web site, you should avoid using multiple themes for the pages on the site if you want visitors to experience a smooth flow. ■

NOTE

On Themes 2 You see the example site in this and the next couple of chapters has more themes than should probably be used in one site. That's because I want to show several examples of themes. ■

ADDING TEXT CONTENT

Text is an important part of Web pages. Almost all of iWeb's page templates include placeholders for text. You'll see that text placeholders are formatted based on the purpose of the text, such as headings, body text, and bulleted lists. You can replace the contents of these text placeholders with your own text.

Start

1. Select the page on which you want to work.
2. Double-click a one-paragraph text placeholder whose text you want to replace. The text on which you double-clicked becomes highlighted, indicating you can replace it.
3. Type the new text.
4. Click within a multi-line text placeholder that has Latin text in it. All of its lines become highlighted, indicating you can replace them.

Continued

NOTE

Selecting Text When a text placeholder that you double-click includes multiple lines, only the line on which you double-click becomes highlighted. You must select each line individually to change its text. That is unless the text box has Latin text in it, in which case double-clicking it selects all the text in the text box. ■

5 Type the new text.

6 Double-click the first line of a multi-paragraph placeholder.

7 Type the text for the first line.

8 Click the next line of text.

9 Type the next text. Repeat steps 8 and 9 until you've replaced all the text on the page with your own.

End

TIP

Deleting Text Placeholders To remove a placeholder that you're not going to use, click it so it is selected, then press **Delete**. ■

TIP

Copy and Paste Text You can copy and paste text from other applications into a text placeholder. ■

FORMATTING TEXT ON A WEB PAGE

After text is on a Web page, you will want to format it to reflect your view of readability, aesthetics, and overall page design. iWeb has an extensive set of text tools you can use to format a number of aspects of your text, including font type, bold, spacing, lists, and so on. When you format text, you use the Format command, the Fonts panel, and the Text Inspector.

Start

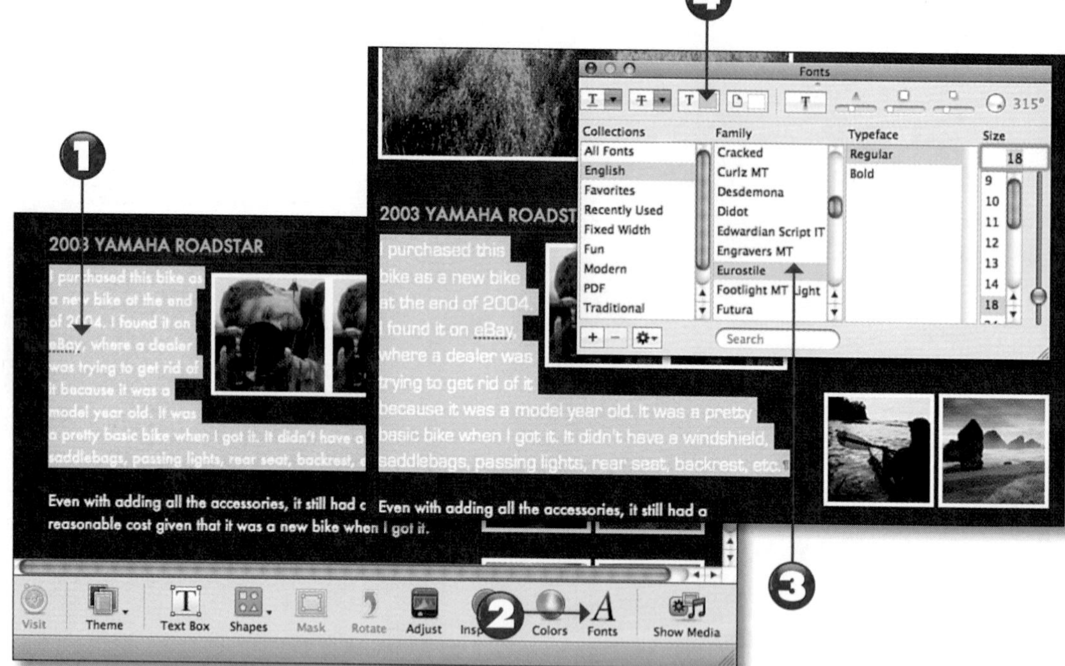

1. Select the text you want to format.
2. Click the **Fonts** button.
3. Apply the family, typeface, and size you want to use.
4. Use the buttons across the top to apply effects, such as strikethrough or drop shadows. Close the Fonts panel.

Continued

TIP

Formatting Efficiently To format more efficiently, select all the adjacent elements you want to format in the same way simultaneously. ■

TIP

Web-safe Fonts When formatting, it's a good idea to use only the fonts in the Web Collection to ensure that anyone who views your sites has the correct fonts on their computers. ■

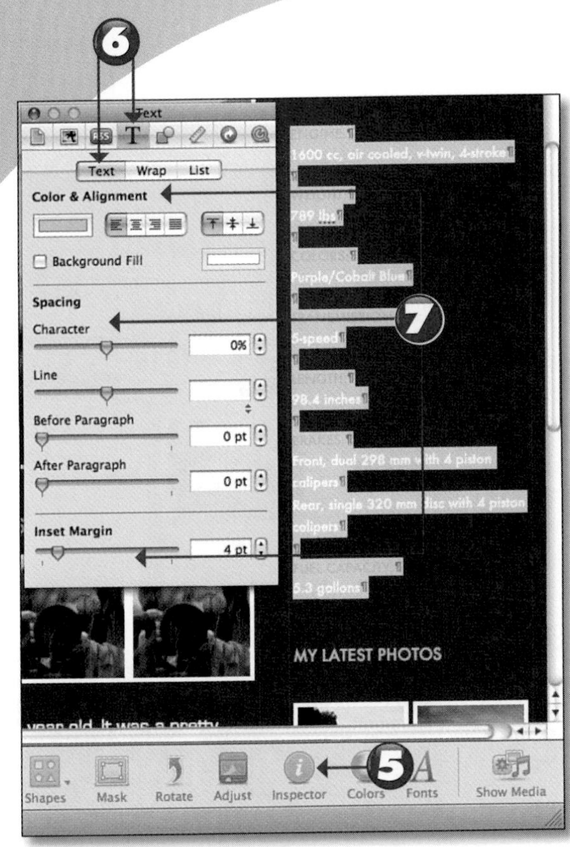

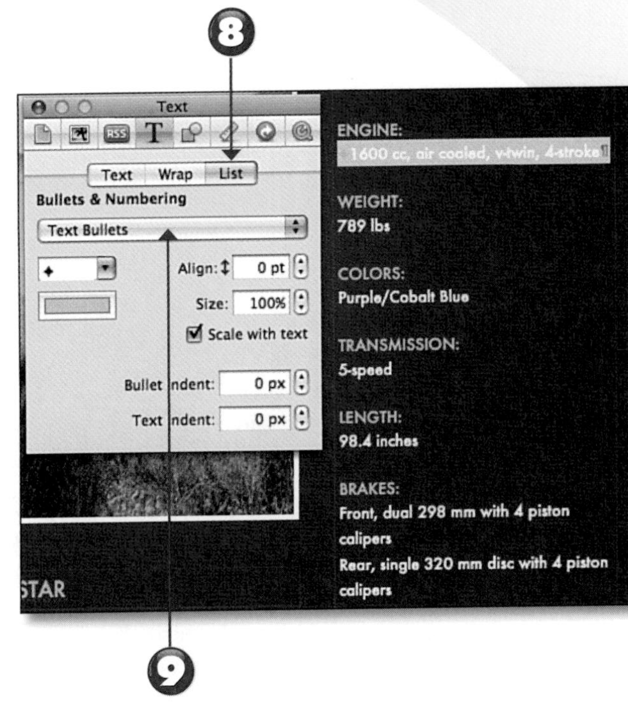

5. Click the **Inspector** button.

6. Click the **Text Inspector** tab, and then click **Text**.

7. Use the **Color & Alignment**, **Spacing**, and **Inset Margin** tools to format those aspects of the text.

8. Click **List**.

9. Use the **Bullets & Numbering** options to format a list.

End

TIP

Shortcuts To open the Fonts panel, press ⌘-**T**; press ⌘-**T** to close it again. To open or close the Inspector, press **Option-⌘-I**. ■

NOTE

Wrap This Up Use the **Wrap** pane of the Text Inspector to control how text wraps around a graphic that is embedded in a text placeholder. ■

REPLACING TEMPLATE GRAPHICS WITH DRAG AND DROP

Like text, most of the Web page templates in iWeb contain placeholders for graphics that you can replace with your own images. One way to replace the graphics in placeholders is by dragging files stored on your computer and dropping them onto a placeholder.

Start

1. Click the page on which you want to work.

2. Click the image you want to replace.

3. Click the **Finder** icon on the Dock to open a Finder window.

4. Select the folder in which the graphic you want to use is stored.

5. Drag the graphic from the Finder window onto the graphic placeholder in iWeb; when the + inside the green circle is over the placeholder, release the mouse button.

End

TIP

Another Way to Replace You can replace the graphic in a placeholder by selecting it and choosing **Insert**, **Choose**. Use the resulting window to select the graphic file you want to use. Click **Insert**. ■

REPLACING TEMPLATE GRAPHICS USING THE MEDIA BROWSER

Using iWeb's Media Browser, you can get to and use content you created or are storing in other applications, including iTunes, GarageBand, iPhoto, and iMovie, for your iWeb Web pages. Using the Photo tab of the Media Browser, you can use any image in your iPhoto Library to replace the contents of a graphics placeholder on a Web page.

Start

1. Click the page on which you want to work.
2. Click the **Show Media** button to open the Media Browser and click the **Photos** tab.
3. Click the **Photos** tab.
4. Select the source in which the image you want use to is stored, such as a photo album.
5. Drag the image from the Media Browser onto the image placeholder. When a thumbnail of the image appears in the placeholder, release the mouse button.

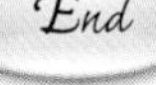

FORMATTING GRAPHICS

Adding a graphic to a Web page is just half the task. You also need to format your graphics so that they look the best they can. This task includes sizing a graphic, masking it, applying a frame, and so on. Each graphic has a mask that determines which part of the graphic is visible on the page. When you select a graphic, the Edit Mask tool appears. You can also use the Inspector to format various aspects of a graphic.

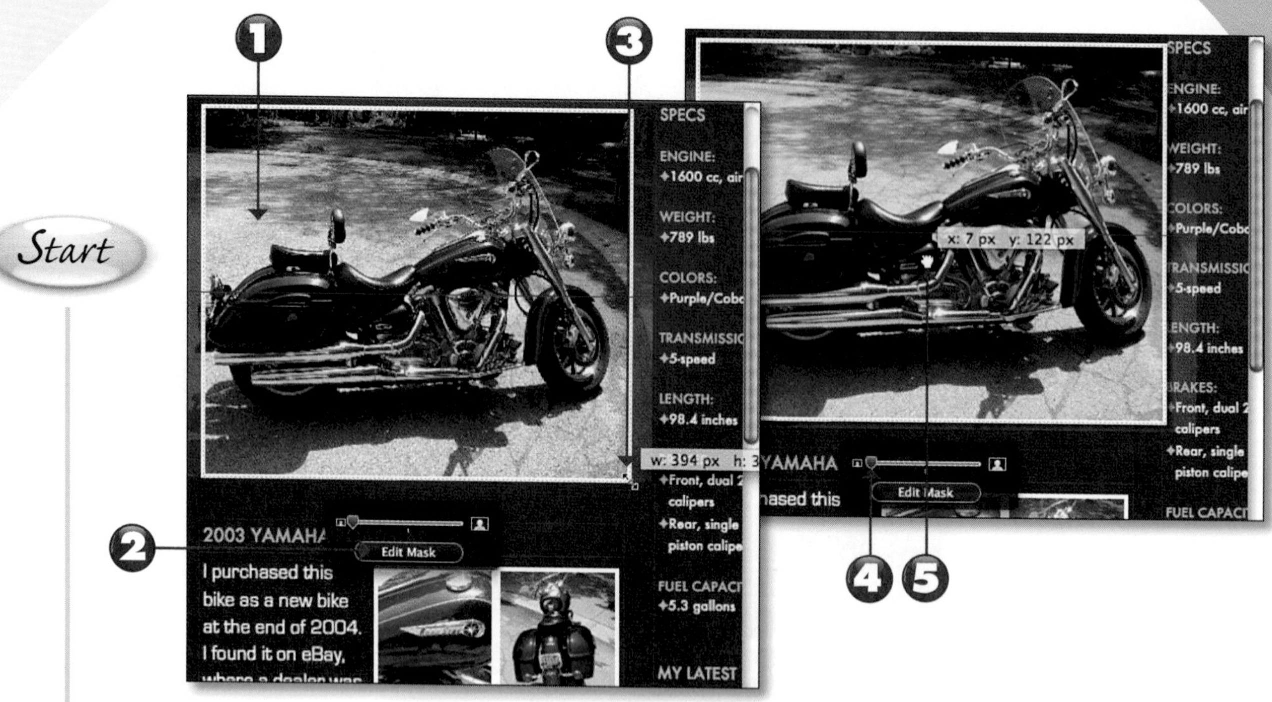

1. Click the graphic you want to format.

2. Click **Edit Mask**. You see the current mask shown by the brighter part of the image, while the part of the image that is outside of the mask (and won't appear on the page) is shaded.

3. Drag the corners of the mask box until it is the size you want the image to be on the page.

4. Drag the slider to resize the image until it is the size you want it to be on the Web page.

5. Drag the image within the mask until it is framed how you want it to appear on the Web.

Continued

TIP

Rotate a Mask If you hold the ⌘ key down while you are over a handle on a mask, the cursor changes to curved arrows. When you drag, you can rotate the mask 45 degrees to create a diamond-shaped mask. ■

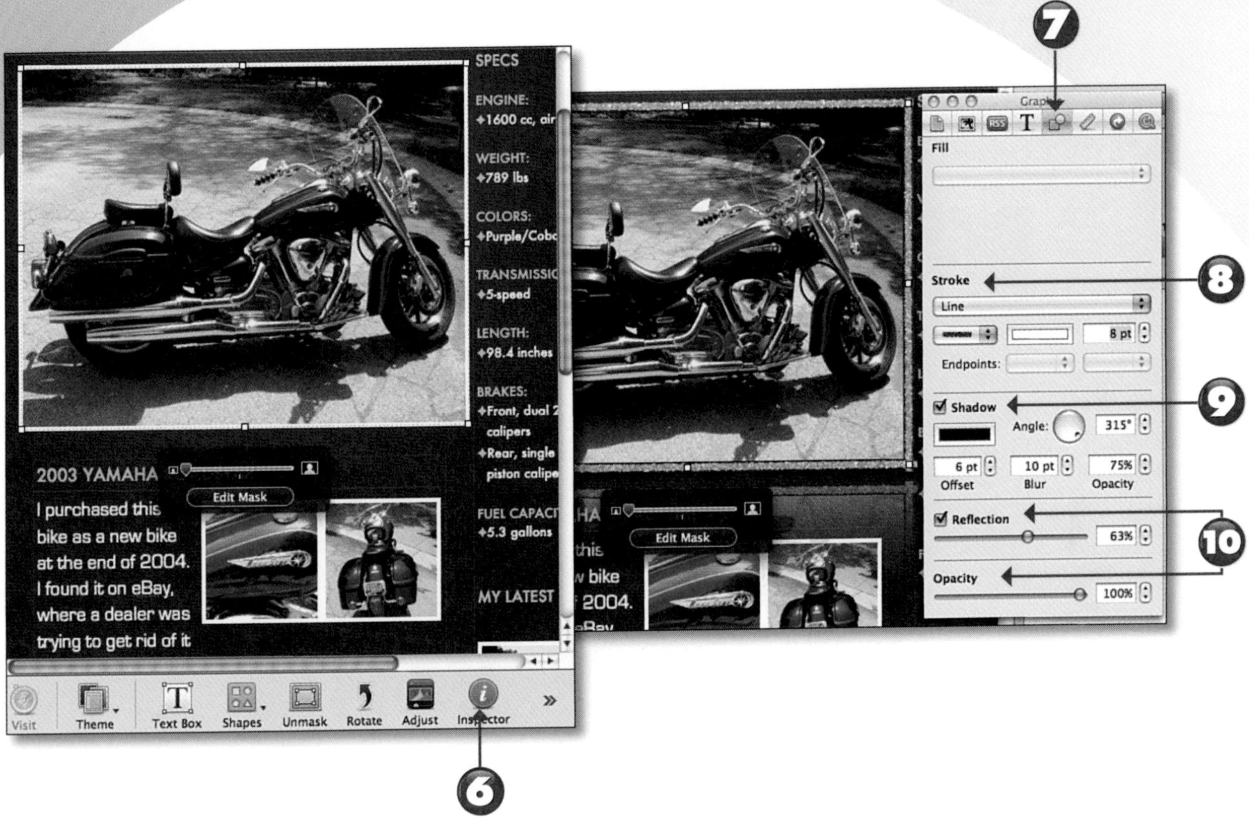

6. Click the **Inspector** button.

7. Click the **Graphic Inspector** tab.

8. Use the **Stroke** tools to apply and format a border, such as picture frame.

9. Use the **Shadow** tools to apply a drop shadow.

10. Use the **Reflection and Opacity** tools to include and size a reflection of the image and change its transparency.

End

TIP

Keeping Things in Proportion If you hold the **Shift** key down while you drag a mask's border, it remains at the same proportion as you change its size. ■

REPLACING AND FORMATTING PICTURES ON THE PHOTOS TEMPLATE

The Photos template is designed to display photos stored in your iPhoto library. This is a good choice for a page when your purpose is to display several photos individually. When you work with this template, you replace the images in the photo placeholders on the template with images from your iPhoto library. You can also format how photos appear on the page.

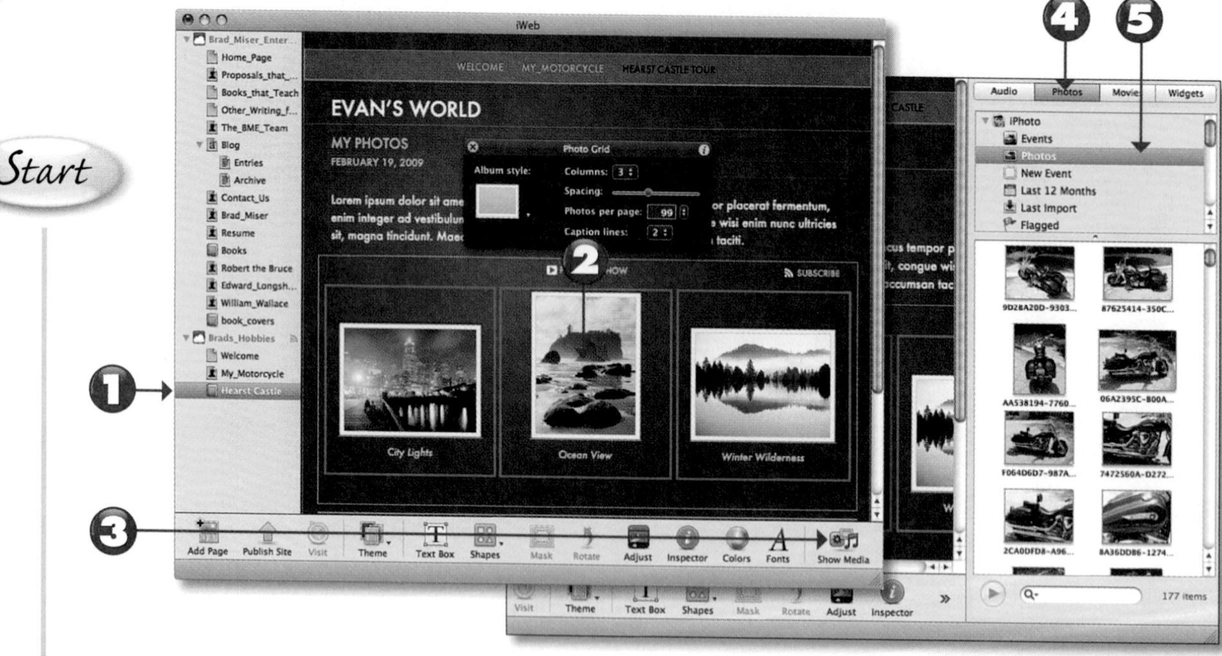

1. Click a Web page based on the Photos template.
2. Click the photos placeholder.
3. Click the **Show Media** button.
4. Click the **Photos** tab.
5. Click the source of photos you want to use, such as Photos to see all of your photos.

Continued

NOTE

How Many Pics? The photos placeholder contains only three images, but you can drag more or fewer images onto it. The images you drag replace the three photos in the placeholder, and it expands or contracts based on the number of photos you place there. ■

6. Select the images you want to move onto the Web page; hold the ⌘ key down while you click images to select multiple images at the same time.

7. Drag the images onto the photos placeholder. When the cursor becomes the + within a green circle, release the mouse button.

8. Select one of the photos.

9. Use the **Photo Grid** to format how the photos appear in the frame.

End

TIP

Searching for Photos You can search for photos in the source selected on the Photos tab of the Media Browser by using the **Search** tool located at the bottom of the browser. Click the **Magnifying Glass** icon to choose to search by all data, keywords, or rating. Then enter the information for which you want to search in the tool. The photos that meet your search appear in the center pane. ■

CONFIGURING SLIDESHOW AND DOWNLOAD OPTIONS FOR PHOTOS

Many of your Web pages will include photos. You can determine whether visitors to your sites can download photos, and you can control how slideshows are made available.

1. Click the page created using the Photos template you want to configure.
2. Click the **Inspector** button.
3. Click the **Photos Inspector** tab.
4. Click the **Photos** subtab.
5. Use the **Photo Sharing** options to configure how photos can be downloaded from your site.

Continued

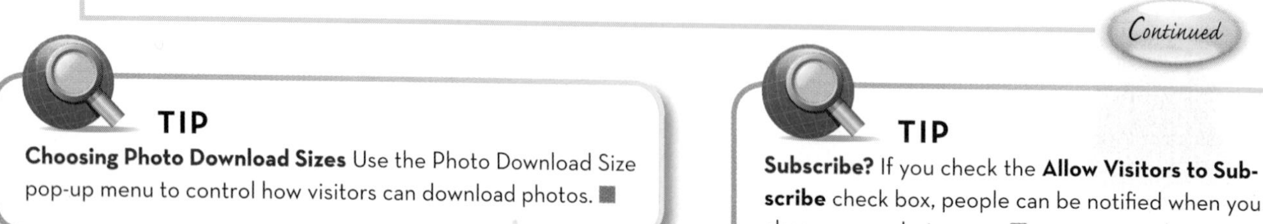

TIP

Choosing Photo Download Sizes Use the Photo Download Size pop-up menu to control how visitors can download photos. ■

TIP

Subscribe? If you check the **Allow Visitors to Subscribe** check box, people can be notified when you change your photo page. ■

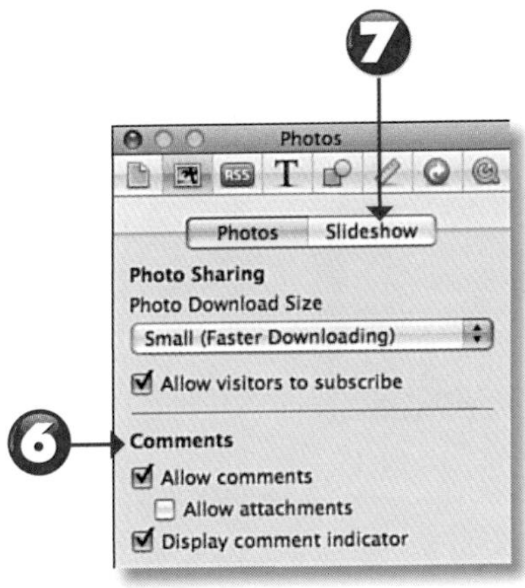

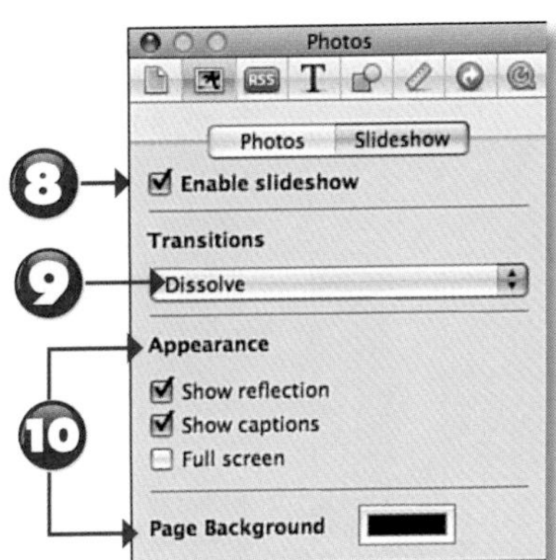

6. Use the **Comments** area to control how visitors can interact with your site.

7. Click the **Slideshow** subtab.

8. To enable visitors to see the photos in a slideshow, check the **Enable Slideshow** check box.

9. Use the Transitions menu to set the transitions between photos.

10. Use the **Appearance** and **Page Background** controls to format the screen during the slideshow.

End

NOTE

Leaving Comments If you check the **Allow Comments** check box, people can add comments to your photo page.

TIP

Seeing Detail To see a detailed version of a photo, double-click it. The image appears at a large size, and a thumbnail view of the other photos on the page appears above it.

ADDING AND FORMATTING ALBUMS ON THE MY ALBUMS TEMPLATE

The My Albums template is a great choice when you want to display photo albums in your iPhoto library on a Web page. You replace the albums in the template with albums from your iPhoto library.

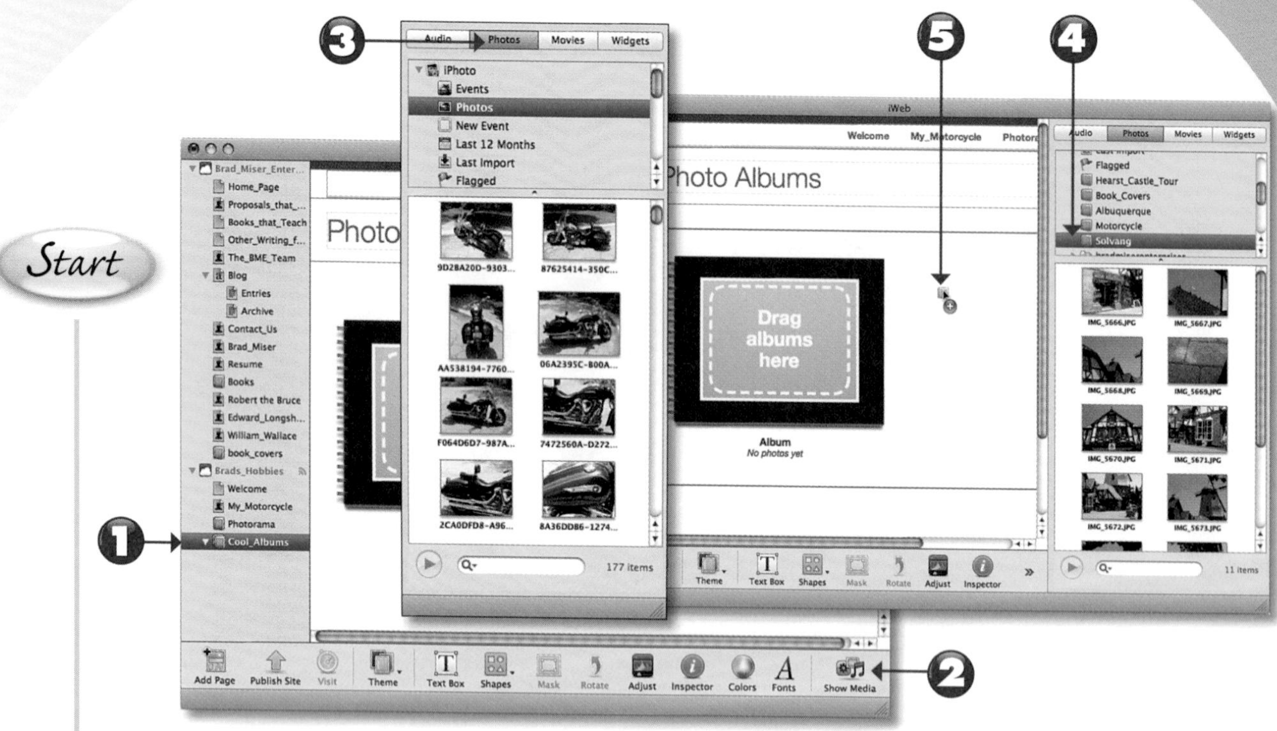

Start

1. Click a Web page based on the My Albums template.
2. Click the **Show Media** button.
3. Click the **Photos** tab.
4. Select a photo album you want to add to the page.
5. Drag the photo album onto the photo album placeholder. A new photos page is created under the album page and is displayed in the iWeb window.

Continued

TIP

Adding an Existing Photo Page to an Album Page You can add an existing photo page to an album page by dragging its icon on top of the album page's icon. ■

TIP

Opening Photo Pages To move to the photo page for an album, double-click it. ■

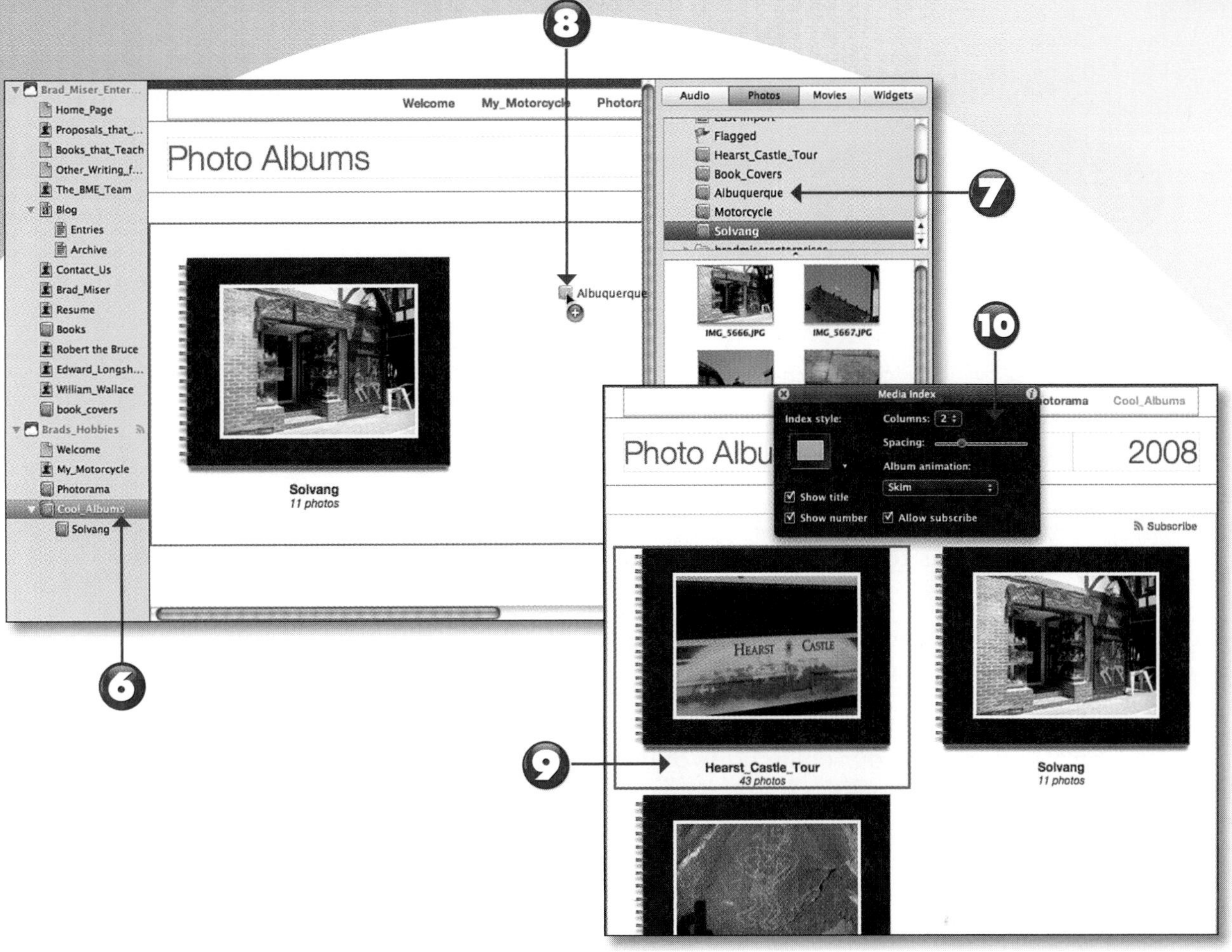

6 Click the album's page icon.

7 Select the next photo album you want to add to the page.

8 Drag the photo album onto the album page. As soon as the cursor becomes + within a green circle, release the mouse button. (Repeat steps 6–8 to add more albums to the page.)

9 Select an album.

10 Use the Media Index to format the page.

End

NOTE

Album Names Become Page Name The name of an album you drag onto an album's page becomes the name of the resulting photos page.

TIP

Formatting Album Pages You can drag albums around an album page to change their location.

BUILDING UP A WEB SITE

In Chapter 11, "Getting Started with iWeb," you learned how to create a Web site, add pages to it, replace content in text and graphics placeholders, and how to add photo and album pages. In this chapter, you learn how to build up your Web site by adding other elements to your pages, including text boxes, shapes, Web widgets, and movies.

Once you understand how to build up the content of your pages, you can focus on transforming your collections of pages into a Web site that flows. For example, you will be able to configure navigation and organization of pages within your site, links within your site, and links to sites outside of yours.

You'll also learn how to create multiple Web sites and do some fine-tuning by removing pages when they are no longer needed.

Add external and internal hyperlinks

Create multiple Web sites

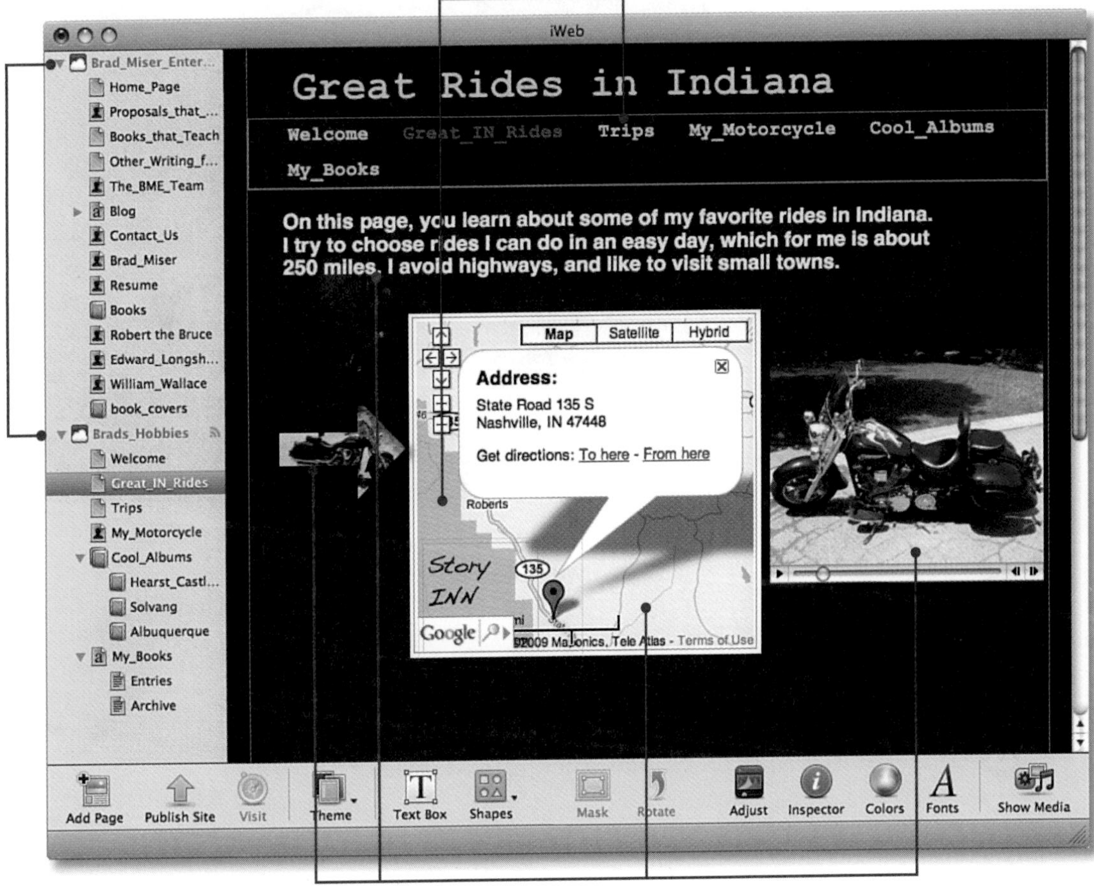

Add text, shapes, Web widgets, and movies to your pages

ADDING TEXT TO WEB PAGES

Most of the templates you use to create pages on your site include text placeholders whose text you can replace with your own. You can also add your own text to a site when the template you choose doesn't have placeholders for all the text that you want to include.

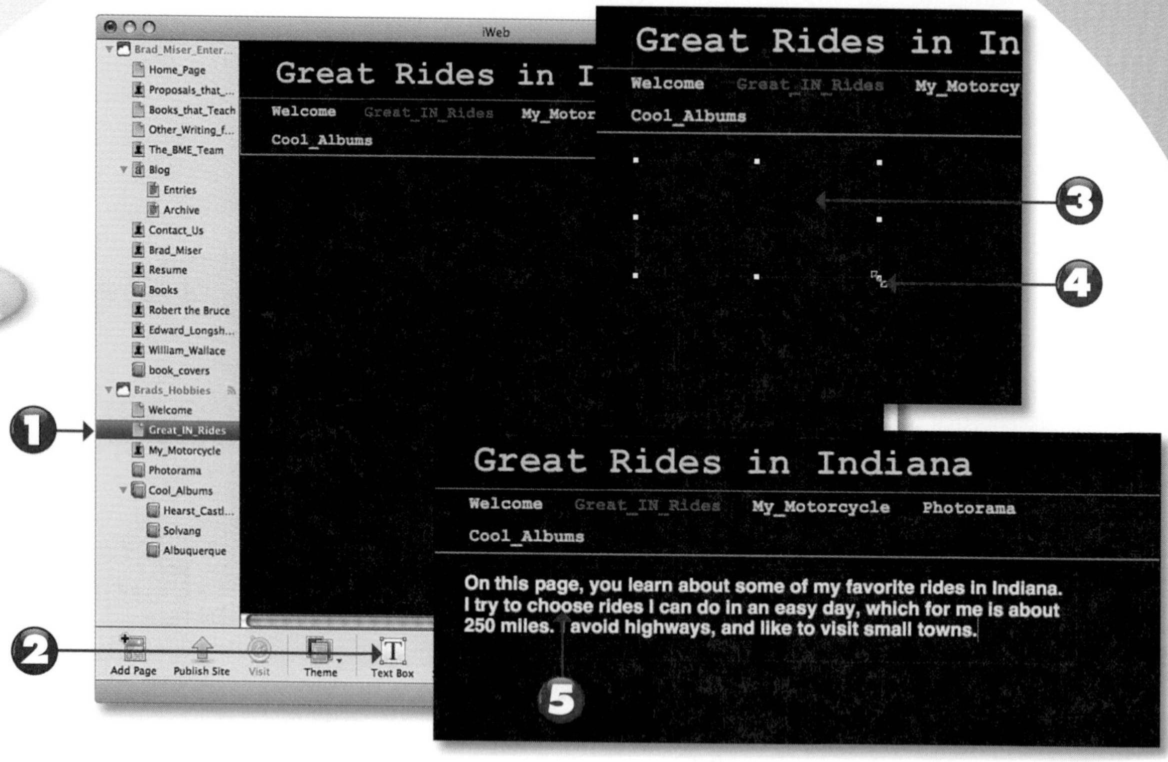

Start

1. Select the page to which you want to add text.
2. Click the **Text Box** button.
3. Drag the text box to its location on the page.
4. Resize the text box by dragging its handles.
5. Click inside the text box, type the text, and format it.

End

NOTE

Formatting Text Formatting text that you add to a page works just like formatting text that you replace in text placeholders. ■

TIP

Adding a Border to a Text Box To add a border around text, select the text box, open the Inspector, click the **Graphic Inspector** tab, and use the **Stroke** controls. ■

ADDING SHAPES TO WEB PAGES

iWeb's Shapes tool enables you to add basic shapes to your pages. These include lines, boxes, triangles, stars, and so on. You can use these elements to add visual interest to your pages. You can also link shapes to objects on your site or to other Web sites.

Start

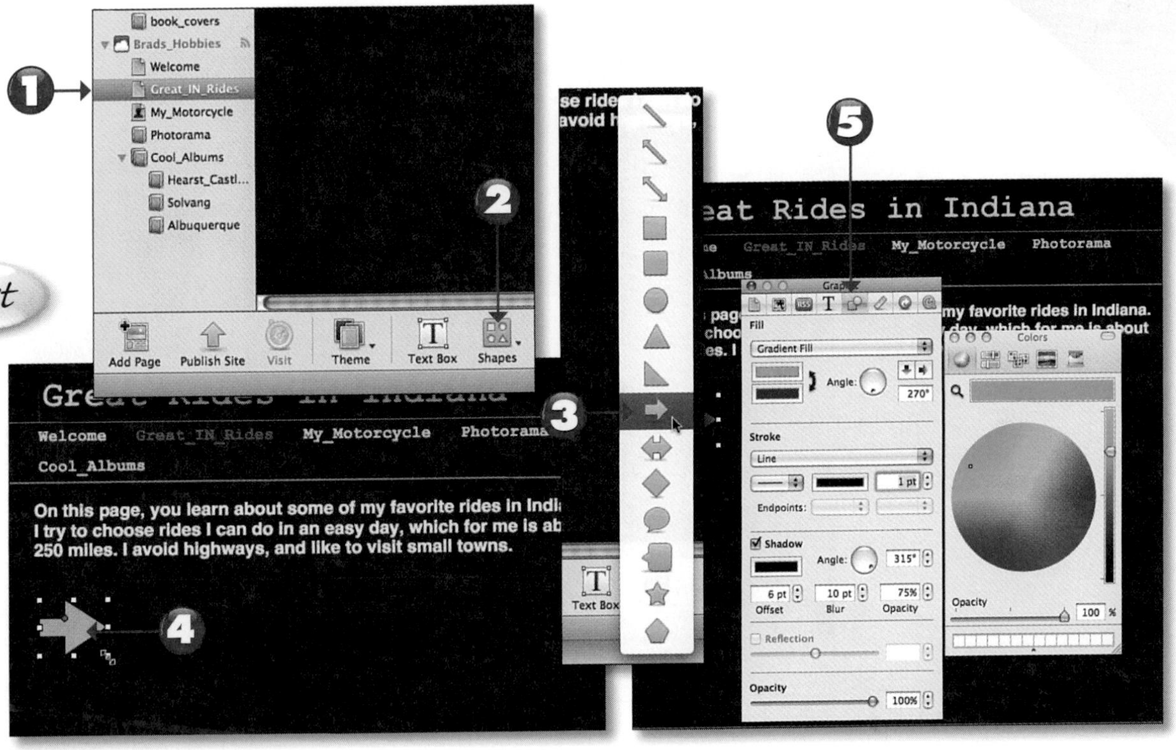

1. Select the page to which you want to add a shape.
2. Click the **Shapes** button.
3. Choose the shape you want to add.
4. Place and size the shape by dragging it to its location and using its resize handles.
5. Use the tools on the Graphic Inspector tab of the Inspector to format the shape.

End

TIP

Placing Photos Inside Shapes You can use a shape to mask a photo. Add and format the shape you want to use as a mask. Open the Media Browser and drag the photo you want to mask onto the shape. Use the **Edit Mask** button and slider to size the photo and drag it within the mask. ■

ADDING WEB WIDGETS TO WEB PAGES

Web widgets are mini-applications that you can add to your pages. There are a number of widgets included with iWeb, such as Google Maps, which you can use to add maps to your pages; YouTube, which adds YouTube videos; and so on. Although the details of configuring each widget are different, the general steps of adding one are similar.

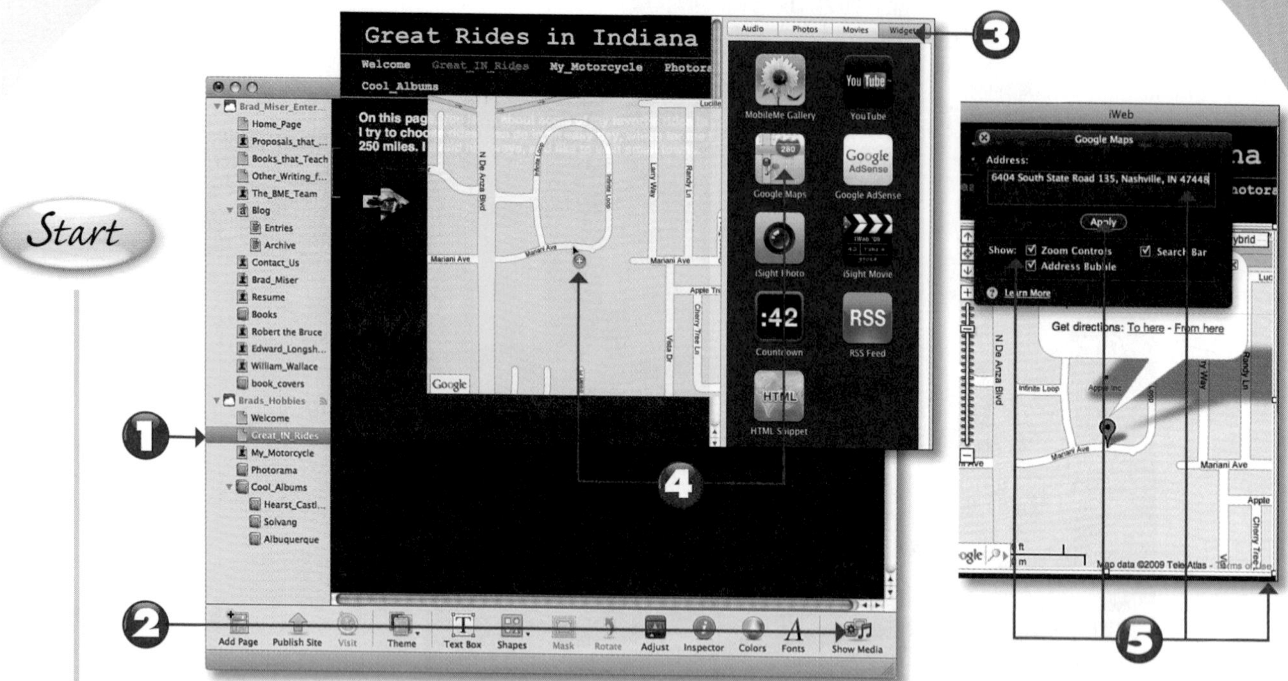

Start

1. Select the page to which you want to add a widget.
2. Click the **Show Media** button.
3. Click the **Widgets** tab.
4. Drag the widget onto the Web page.
5. Configure, size, and place the widget on the page.

End

NOTE

Configuring Web Widgets Each widget has its own controls to configure its content. ■

NOTE

HTML Snippet Widget? HTML is the code behind a lot of what you see on the Web. You can use the HTML Snippet widget to add blocks of HTML code to your Web pages. ■

ADDING MOVIES TO WEB PAGES

You can add movies to your Web pages. These can be movies you create yourself using iMovie or movies you download from the Web. Visitors to your pages can watch the movies you add.

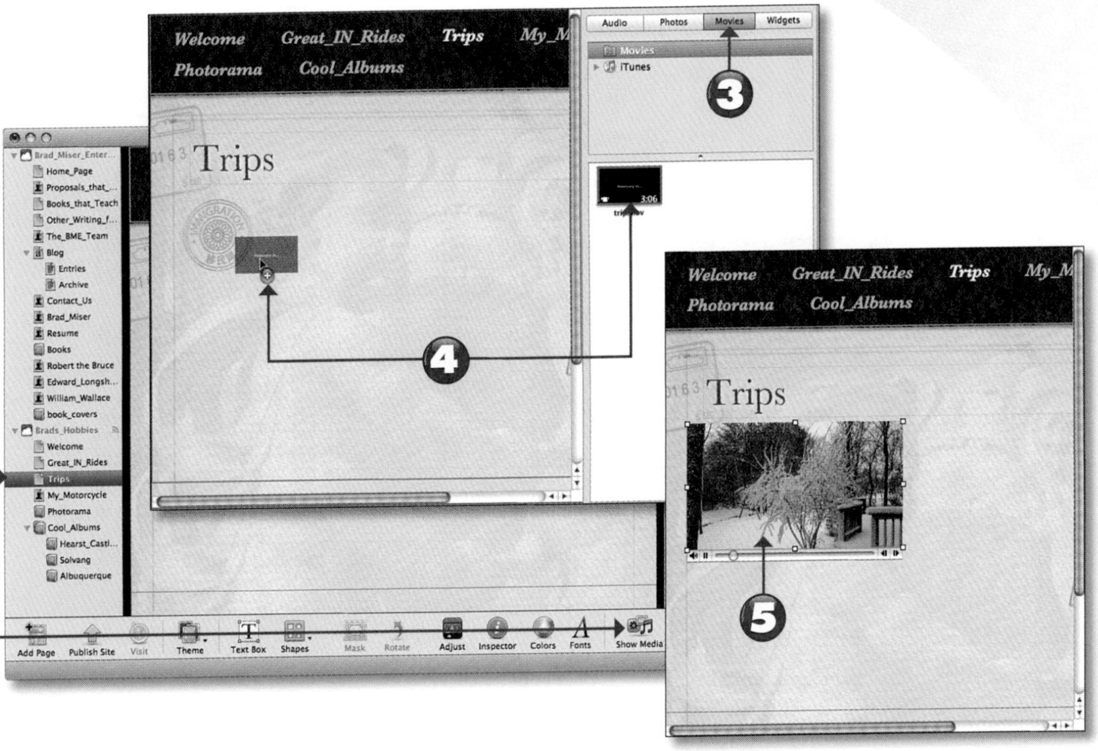

Start

1. Select the page to which you want to add a widget.
2. Click the **Show Media** button.
3. Click the **Movies** tab.
4. Drag a movie onto the Web page.
5. Drag the movie to its location and use its resize handles to resize it.

End

NOTE

Movie Page iWeb includes the Movie template page that is designed to display a single movie. You can use that template to create pages to display your movies or you can manually add a movie to any page. ■

NOTE

Movie Files Are Large Movie files tend to be very large, so you need to be mindful of the length and size of movies you add to your pages. ■

ADDING HYPERLINKS TO PAGES ON YOUR WEB SITE

Links between pages on your Web site enable a visitor to experience all the content you've added to your site by clicking its links. You can link text or graphics on any page to any other page on your site.

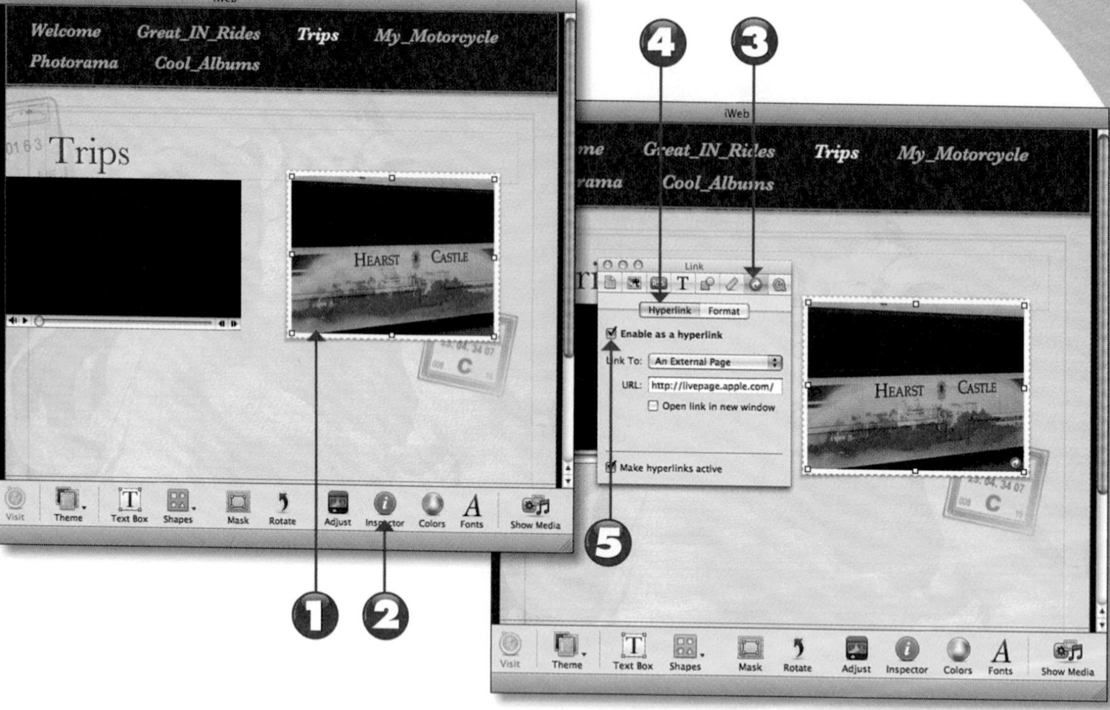

Start

1. Select the text or graphic that you want to become a link.
2. Click **Inspector**.
3. Click the **Link Inspector** tab.
4. Click **Hyperlink**.
5. Click the **Enable as a Hyperlink** check box.

Continued

TIP

Links Inactive The Make Hyperlinks Active check box enables or disables the links on your pages. When you are designing and building your pages, uncheck this check box so that you can select the linked objects without moving to where the link points. Before you publish you site, check this box so your links will work again. ■

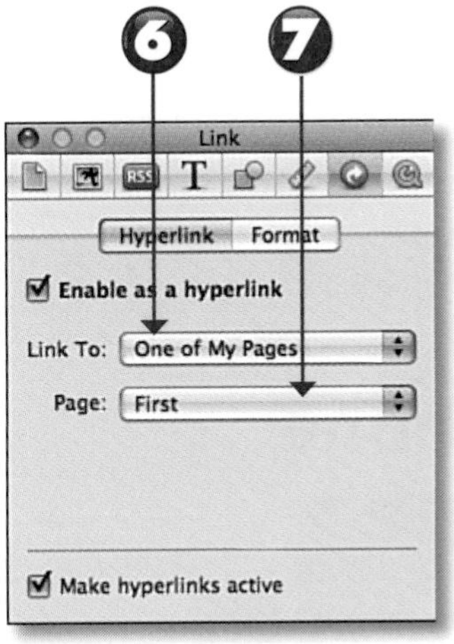

6 On the **Link To** pop-up menu, choose **One of My Pages**.

7 Open the **Page** pop-up menu.

8 Select the page to which you want the link to point.

9 Close the Inspector.

End

TIP

Text Links When you make text a link, use the Format tab on the Link Inspector to control the format of the linked text. You can format the text in four states: normal, rollover (when it is pointed to), visited, and disabled. Using consistent formatting conveys status information for visitors.

NOTE

Formatting and Browsers Some formatting selections you make can be overridden by Web browser settings, such as the color of visited links. But, most users don't configure such preferences and so will likely see the formatting options you apply.

ADDING HYPERLINKS TO OTHER WEB SITES

Links between Web pages are what makes the Web the Web. You can add links to other Web sites to elements of your page, including text and graphics. To add a link, you need the URL of the Web page to which you want to link. You then link that URL to your Web page.

1. Open a Web browser and move to the page to which you want to link.
2. Select the URL.
3. Choose **Edit**, **Copy**.
4. Switch back to iWeb.
5. Select the page that contains the object or text that you want to set as a link.

Continued

NOTE

Things Are Changing Some Web pages, such as those on news Web sites, have dynamic content, meaning that the content changes over time. If you link to one of these pages, when the visitor clicks the link, she may or may not see what you intended. ■

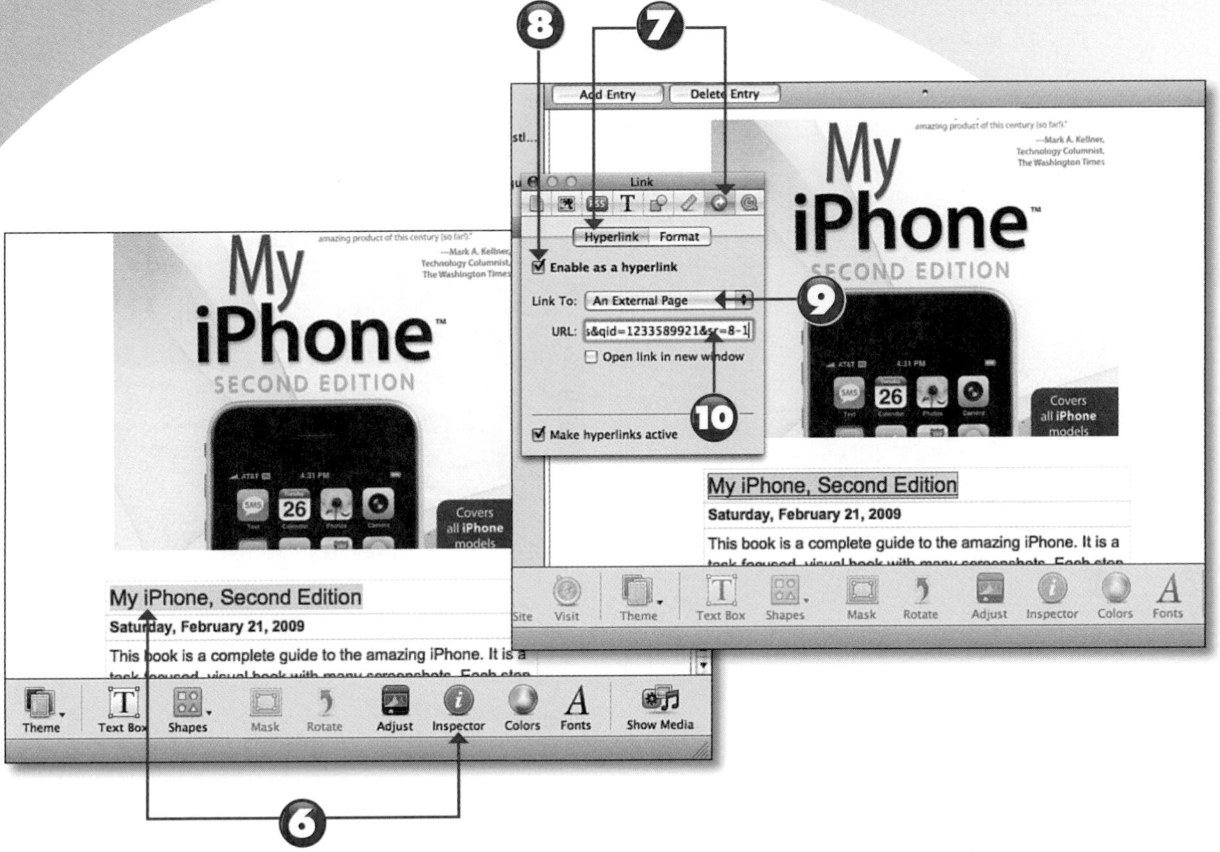

6 Select the text or graphic that you want to become a link and open the Inspector.

7 Click the **Link Inspector** tab, and then click **Hyperlink**.

8 Click the **Enable as a Hyperlink** check box.

9 On the **Link To** pop-up menu, choose **An External Page**.

10 Select the **URL** in the URL field and press ⌘**-V**. The URL you copied is pasted into the field.

End

TIP

Bring 'em Back A good way to make it easy for visitors to return to your site is by checking the **Open Link in New Window** check box. When a link is clicked, it opens in a new Web browser window, while your site remains open in the previous window. ■

CONFIGURING A WEB PAGE

You can configure a Web page by choosing whether it is included in the navigation menu that appears at the top of each page, setting whether the navigation menu is included at the top of a page, and defining the page's layout.

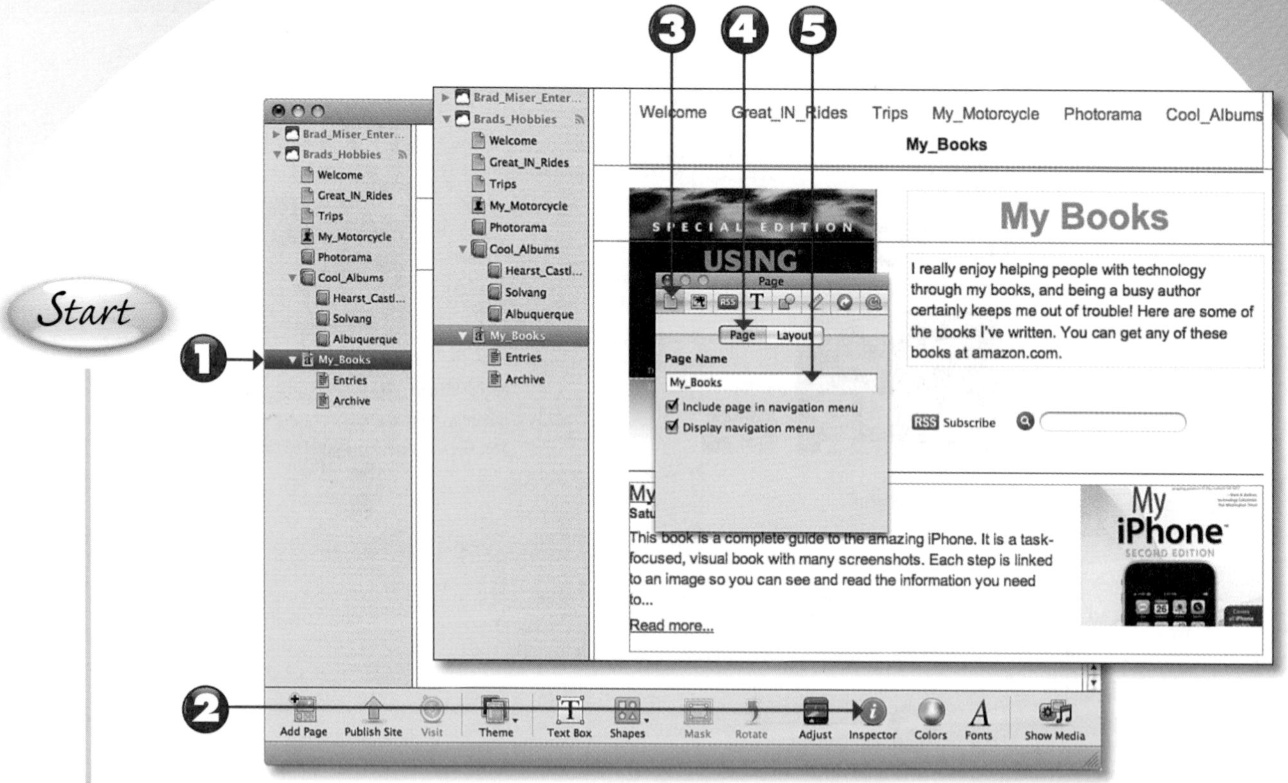

Start

1. Click the page you want to configure.
2. Click **Inspector**.
3. Click the **Page Inspector** tab.
4. Click **Page**.
5. Update the page's name.

Continued

NOTE

Navigation Menu By default, the site navigation menu appears at the top of each page in your site. On this menu, you see the names of each page you have created. ■

TIP

Hierarchical Web Pages, Part 1 To make your site hierarchical, so that some pages are beneath others, uncheck the **Include Page in Navigation Menu** check box for the nested pages. ■

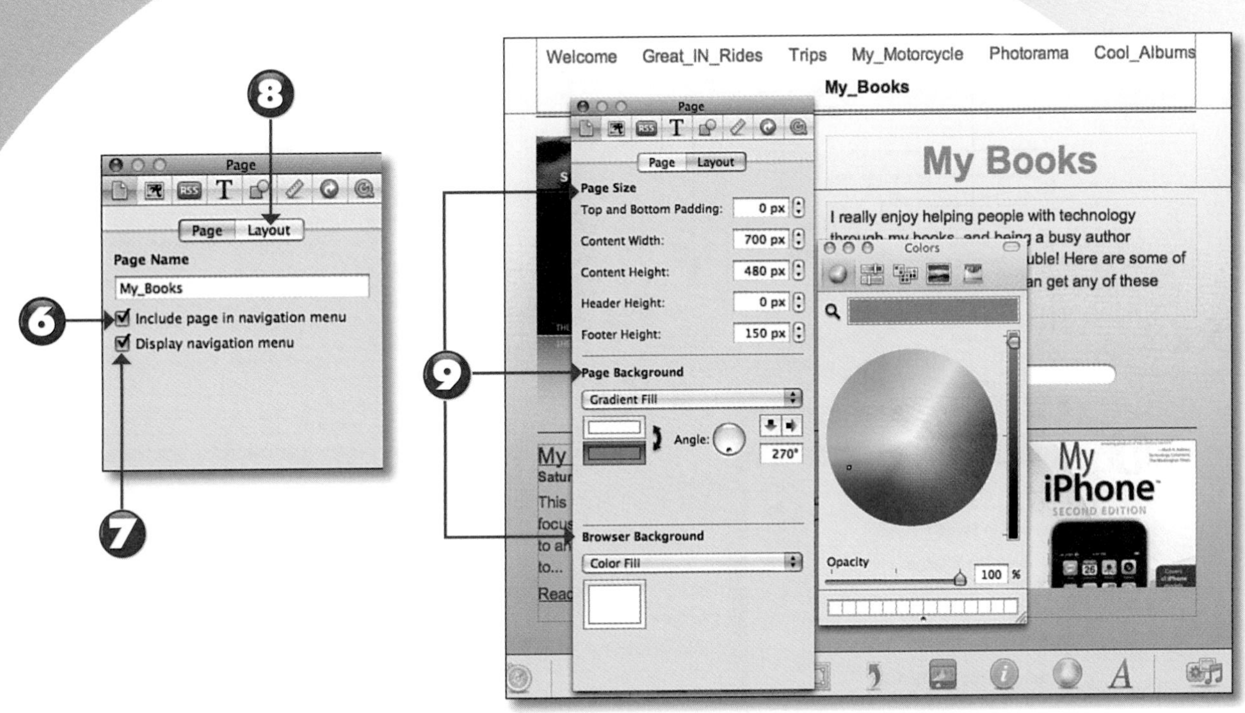

6. To have the page appear on the site's navigation menu, enable the **Include Page in Navigation Menu** check box.

7. To show the site navigation menu on the page, enable the **Display Navigation Menu** check box.

8. Click **Layout**.

9. Use the **Layout** tools to configure page size, page background, and browser background.

End

TIP

Hierarchical Web Pages, Part 2 To create the site structure, include links from the higher-level pages to the lower-level pages and from the lower-level pages only back to the higher-level pages by hiding the navigation menu on those pages. This enables you to build a more structured site with multiple levels. If you leave all pages on the navigation menu, your site will be flat (in structure, not content). ■

ADDING MORE SITES TO A WEB SITE

Using iWeb, you can create and publish multiple Web sites. You might create one site for your business-related interests, and another for personal interests. When you publish your sites, they are independent; so how you've designed one site has no impact on the others.

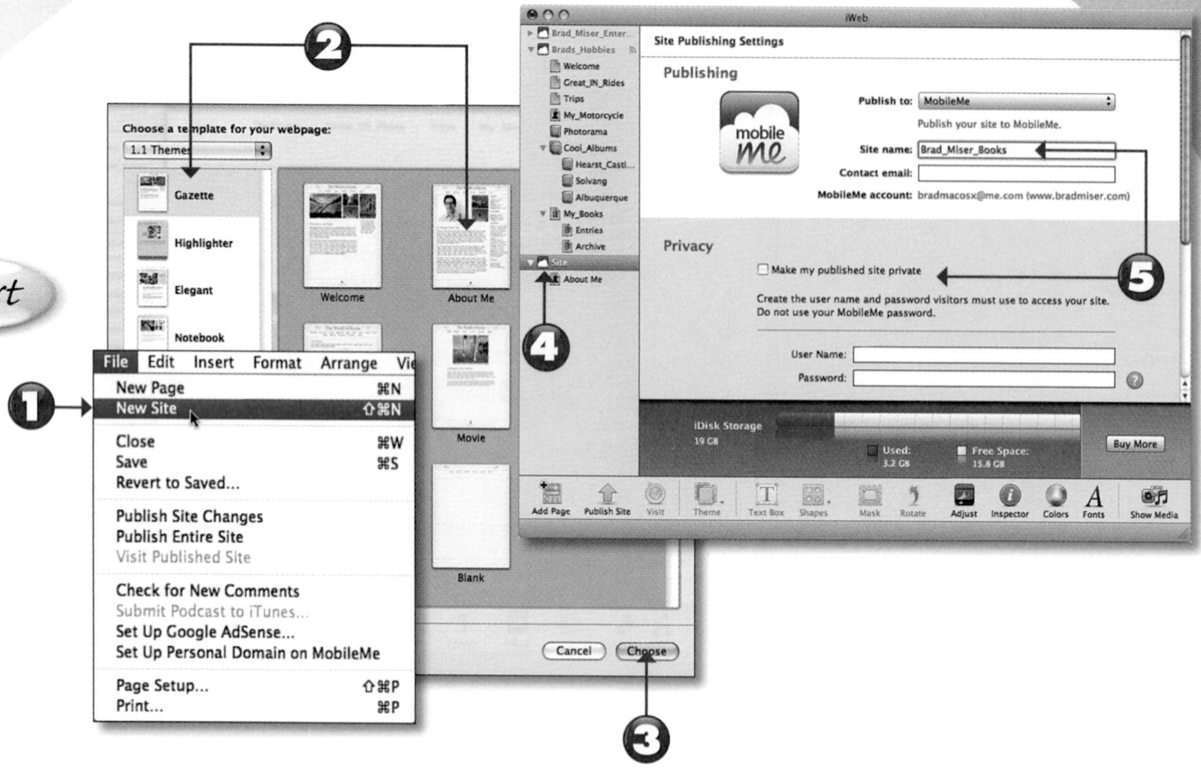

Start

1. Choose **File**, **New Site**.
2. Select a theme and template for the first page on the new site.
3. Click **Choose**.
4. Select the new site.
5. Configure the new site and add pages to it.

End

TIP

Privacy Please You can protect a site by requiring that a username and password be provided in order for someone to visit that site. ■

TIP

Linking Sites To make it easy for visitors to one of your sites to visit the other sites, create a link from a page on one site to a page on the other, and vice versa. ■

REMOVING CONTENT FROM A WEB SITE

As you build your site, if you discover content or even whole pages that don't live up to your expectations, you can remove the content you don't want from your site.

Start

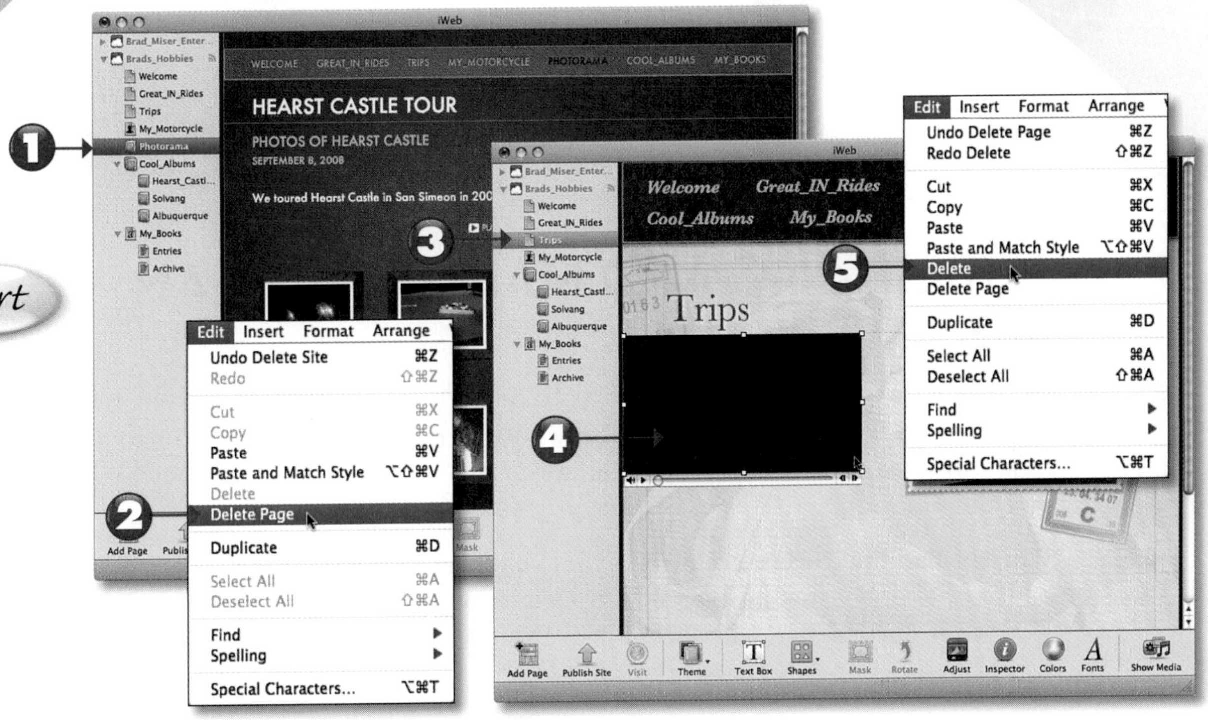

1. Select a page you want to delete.
2. Choose **Edit**, **Delete Page**.
3. Select a page containing text or graphics you want to ditch.
4. Select the content you want to delete.
5. Choose **Edit**, **Delete**.

End

TIP

Holding Pen You can create a site to hold pages you are considering deleting. Add the site and make it private so that only you can access it. Drag pages you are considering deleting onto this site's icon. ■

PUBLISHING AND MAINTAINING AN iWEB WEB SITE

Here's where your work in iWeb starts to pay off in a big way. One of the best things about iWeb is that it is amazingly easy to publish your Web sites to get them online so that other people can enjoy the work you have done by exploring your sites.

You'll notice that this is a relatively short chapter. The reason for that is because iWeb manages the technical details of publishing a Web site for you, so from your perspective, there's not a lot to do. (Of course, iWeb does a lot of work for you, but that's not your concern.)

After your sites are online, you should test them to make sure they work and look the way you intend. Optionally, you can register your own domain name so that the URL site is completely unique to you. And, your Web sites are living things that you should maintain and update over time.

iWeb makes putting your Web sites online simple!

PUBLISHING WEB SITES USING MOBILEME

When you're ready, you can publish your Web sites to the Internet. Once this is done, your sites are available for other people to view. If you have a MobileMe account, you can easily publish your Web sites using that account.

Start

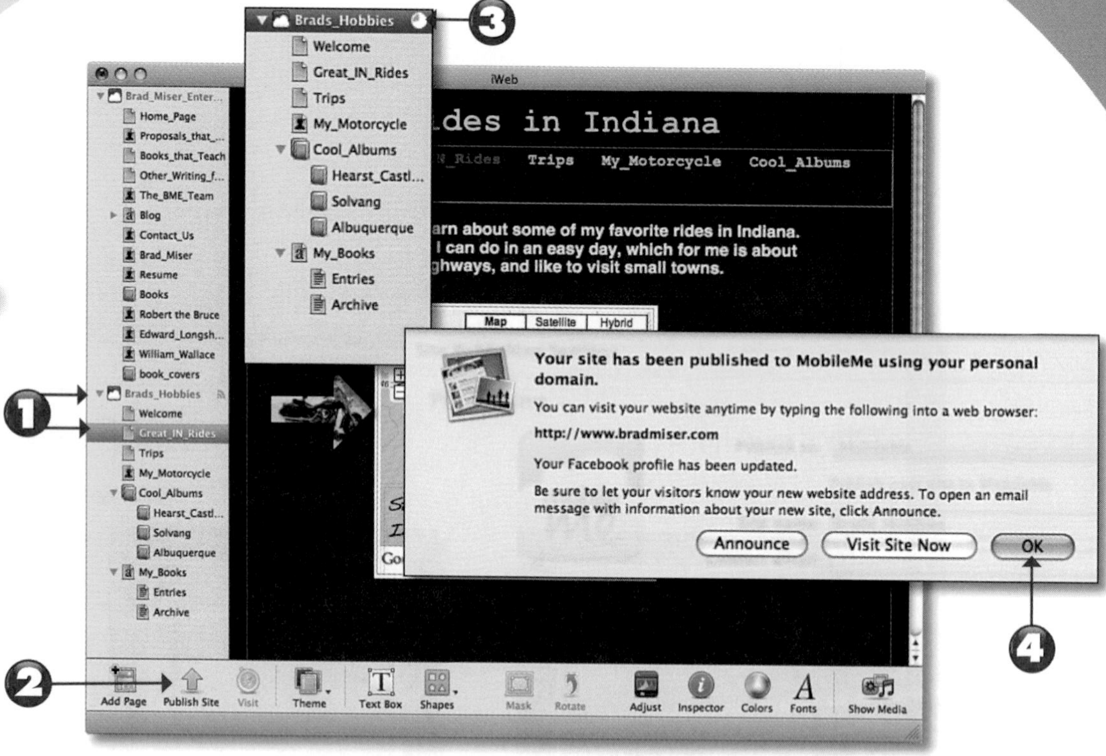

1. Select a page on the Web site or the Web site itself that you want to publish.
2. Click **Publish Site**. iWeb prepares your pages and publishes them to the Web.
3. As the process happens, watch the Publish Status icon to the right of the site name. When done, this icon goes away, and the site's icons turn blue.
4. When the process is complete, click **OK**.

End

NOTE

Colors and Publishing Status When the current version of a Web site or page is published, its icon on the left pane of the iWeb window is blue. If you change or add pages, their icons become red until you publish the updates, at which point their icons become blue again. ■

NOTE

URL The URL for your Web sites is http://web.me.com/*membername*/*sitename*, where *membername* is your MobileMe member name, and *sitename* is the name of the site you want to visit. If you leave *sitename* out of the URL, you move to your default Web site. ■

TESTING WEB SITES

Sometimes the representations of your sites in iWeb's window don't exactly match how your sites and pages look in a Web browser on the Internet. After you have published your sites, you should use a Web browser application to visit your sites to test how they look and work.

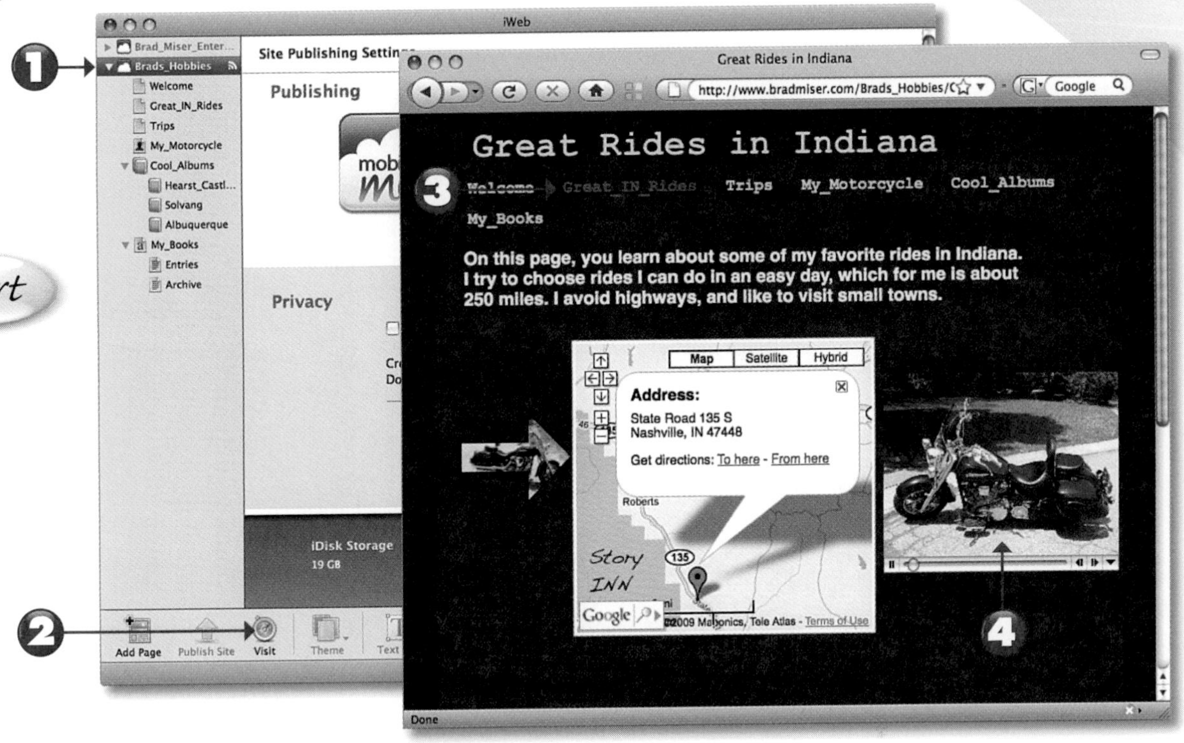

Start

1. Select the published site.
2. Click **Visit**. Your default Web browser opens and you move to the published Web site.
3. Click links to move around your site.
4. Click the **Play** buttons for movies or slideshows, and experiment with your Web widgets.

End

TIP

Test with Multiple Web Browsers If you can, you should visit your published sites in a variety of Web browser applications on Mac and Windows computers. Ideally, you'll test your site in Safari and Firefox on Macs, and Internet Explorer, Firefox, Safari, and Chrome on Windows PCs. Testing with these browsers will cover the applications with which the vast majority of users browse the Web. ■

TIP

Straight to the Site If you click the **Visit Site Now** button in the Publish Confirmation window, your default browser opens and you move to the published site. ■

MAINTAINING AND UPDATING WEB SITES

The results of your testing might reveal problems that you need to fix. And, you should update your Web site over time to change existing information, add new pages, update information on existing pages, and so on. Web sites aren't supposed to be static, and visitors to your site will expect it to change as time passes. You can use iWeb to make updates to your sites as needed.

Start

1. Select a page you want to change.
2. Use iWeb's tools to make changes to the page.
3. Choose **File**, **Publish Site Changes**. iWeb prepares and publishes your changes.
4. Click **Visit Site Now** to see your updated site.

End

TIP

Inviting People to Your Sites If you click the **Announce** button in the Publish Confirmation window, an email containing a link to your site is created in your default email application. You can send this to other people so that they can visit your sites. ■

TIP

Sites Aren't Linked by Default When you publish multiple Web sites, those sites aren't connected automatically. If you want visitors to be able to access all of your sites from any of them, you need to include hyperlinks to the other sites on each of your published sites. ■

SETTING A DEFAULT WEB SITE

When someone moves to http://web.me.com/*membername*/, he or she moves to your default Web site. You should make this site the one you want people to be the most likely to come across or the one you want them to see first when they don't use a specific site name in the URL.

Start

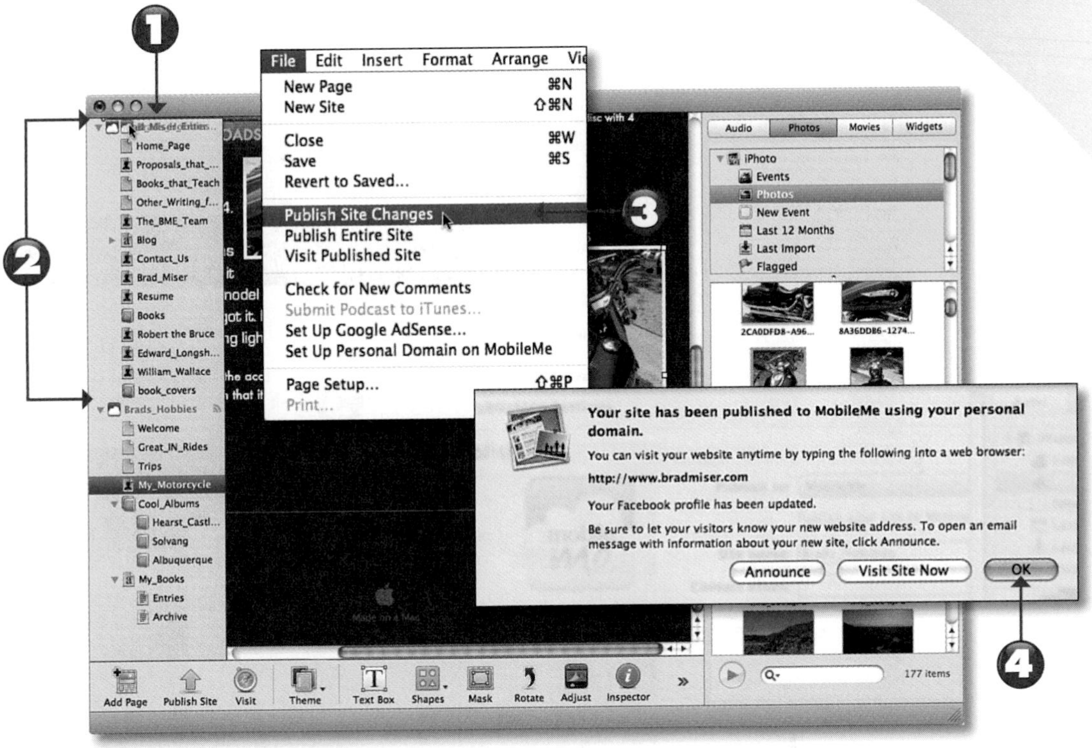

1. Move to the iWeb site list. The current default site is at the top of the list.
2. Drag the site you want to be the default to the top of the list.
3. Choose **File**, **Publish Site Changes**.
4. Click **OK**.

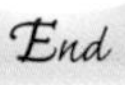

NOTE

The Importance of a Default Site Setting a default Web site is even more important when you publish your sites under a personal domain, especially if it is an obvious one, like your name. With an obvious URL, people are much more likely to just enter that URL and move directly to your default Web site. ■

TIP

Inviting People to Your Sites, Part 2 You can invite people to your site at any time by moving to it in a Web browser, copying the site's address (or an individual page's address for that matter), and pasting that URL into an email. ■

USING YOUR OWN WEB SITE ADDRESS WITH MOBILEME

If you prefer, you can publish a MobileMe Web site under your own domain name so that your URL is something like www.bradmiser.com rather than web.me.com/bradmacosx. There are two steps to this. First, you must register your domain name (for which you must pay a fee). Second, you configure iWeb to publish your sites under that domain name.

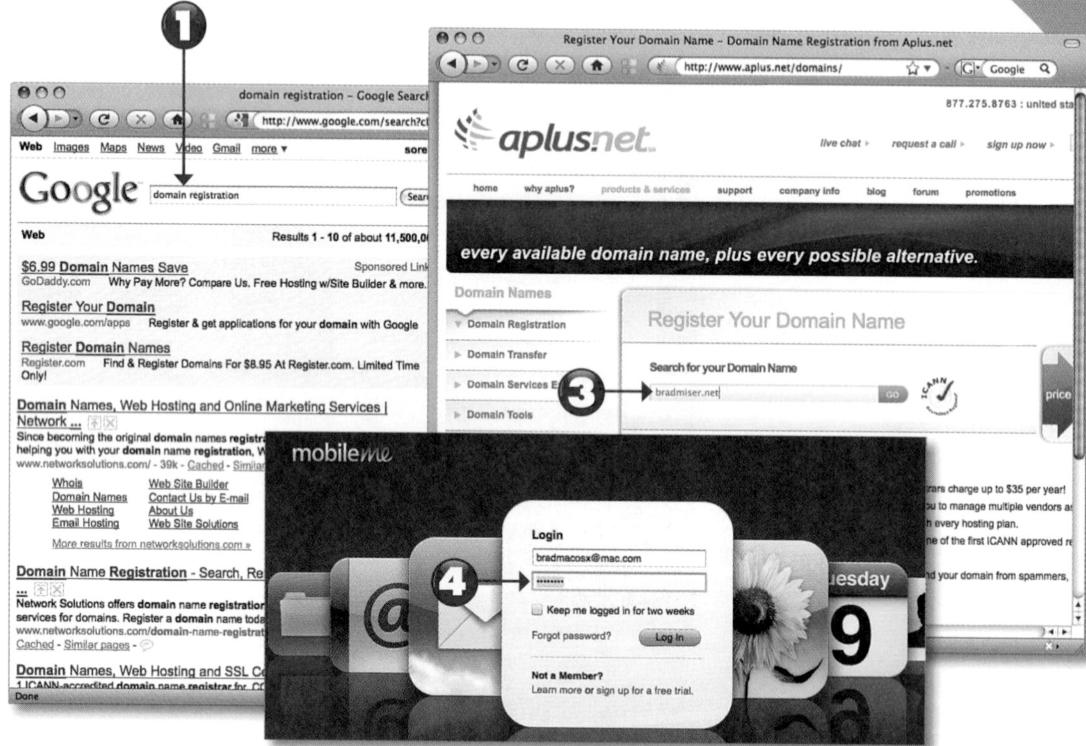

1. Do a Web search for domain registration services.
2. Explore the results of the search until you find a service you want to use.
3. Move to that service's Web site and start the domain registration process, usually by searching for the domain you want to use. Follow the onscreen instructions until you've registered your domain name.
4. Move to me.com and log in to your MobileMe account.

Continued

TIP

CNAME When you register your domain's account, you need to set its CNAME (canonical name) to be web.me.com. Check the help information for the service you choose to get the details on how to do that. ■

NOTE

Which Registration Service Is for You? There are many domain registration services available to you, and they all perform the same basic function, which is to provide you with your own domain. There are significant differences in cost, features, and ease of use between them, so you should use these factors to choose the right service for you. ■

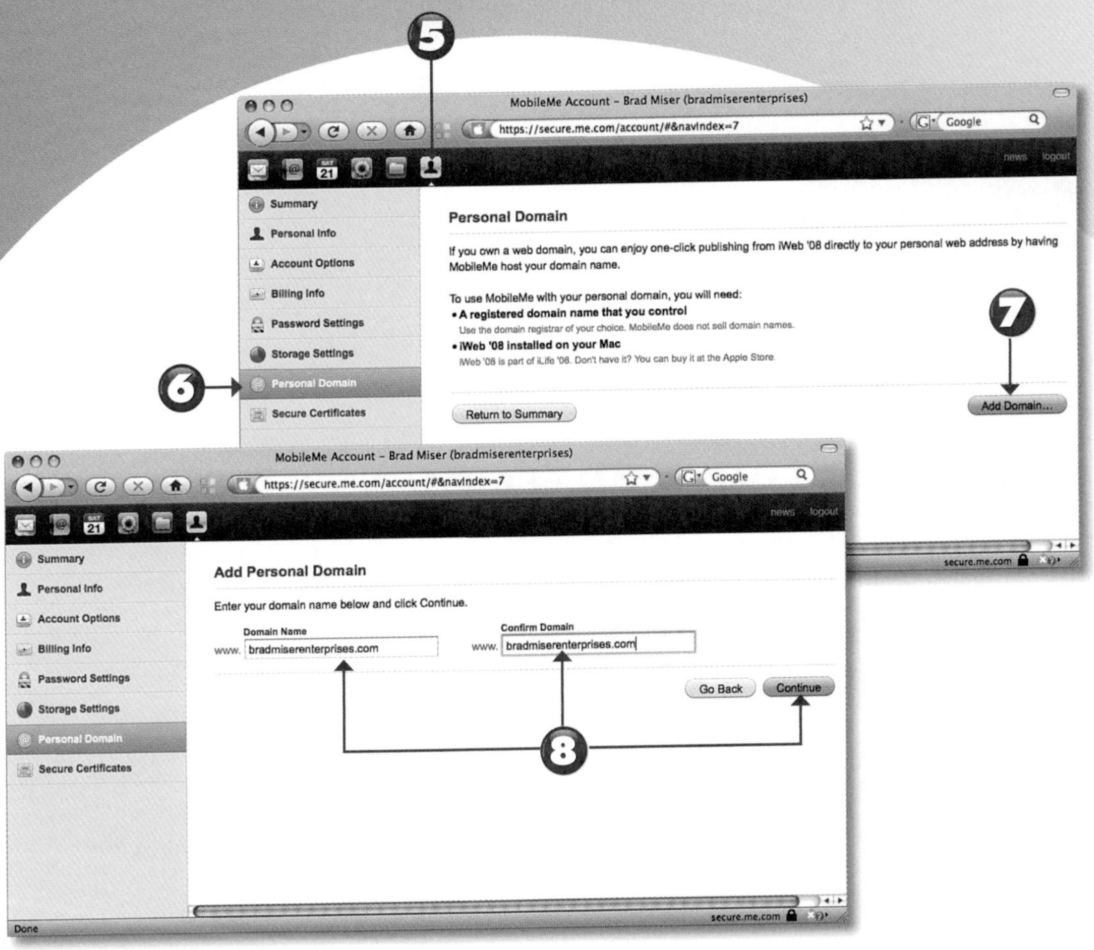

5 Click the **Account** button. (Confirm your account password if necessary.)

6 Click **Personal Domain**.

7 Click **Add Domain**.

8 Enter your domain name in both places and click **Continue**.

End

TIP

No MobileMe? You can use other hosting services to publish an iWeb Web site if you don't have or want to use MobileMe. Select the site you want to publish with another service and choose **FTP Server** on the Publish To pop-up menu. Enter your account information for the service you use to publish the site. ■

NOTE

All Domains Are Unique A domain must be unique. When you request a specific domain, the service checks to see whether it is available. If it hasn't been used, you can select and use it. If it is already being used, you must choose something else. ■

CREATING DVDS WITH iDVD

A DVD is great way to enjoy and share movies you create with iMovie and slideshows based on photos you have in iPhoto. Because DVD players are everywhere, having your iLife projects on DVD makes them easily accessible.

With iDVD, you can go way beyond just putting your content on a disc. You can create very sophisticated menus that have motion and audio. In fact, with not much effort on your part, you can create menus that rival those on professionally produced DVDs.

Start by creating a new project in iDVD. Then add content to it, and design its menus. When it is done, preview it in iDVD, and then burn it to disc.

Drop zones contain static images or movies or slideshows that play

Themes determine the look and feel of a disc's menus

Buttons can lead to movies or slideshows or other menus

Menus can have interesting motion and sound effects

DVDs can have multiple menus and submenus that you can view on a map

You can simulate a DVD before you burn it by previewing it

CREATING A NEW iDVD PROJECT

The first step in creating a DVD is to create an iDVD project. If you've used iDVD before, when you open it, it automatically opens the most recent project you've worked on, but you can create a new project to start a new DVD. If you've never used iDVD before, you're prompted to open a project or create a new one. Once you have saved at least one iDVD project, you use the same steps to create new projects.

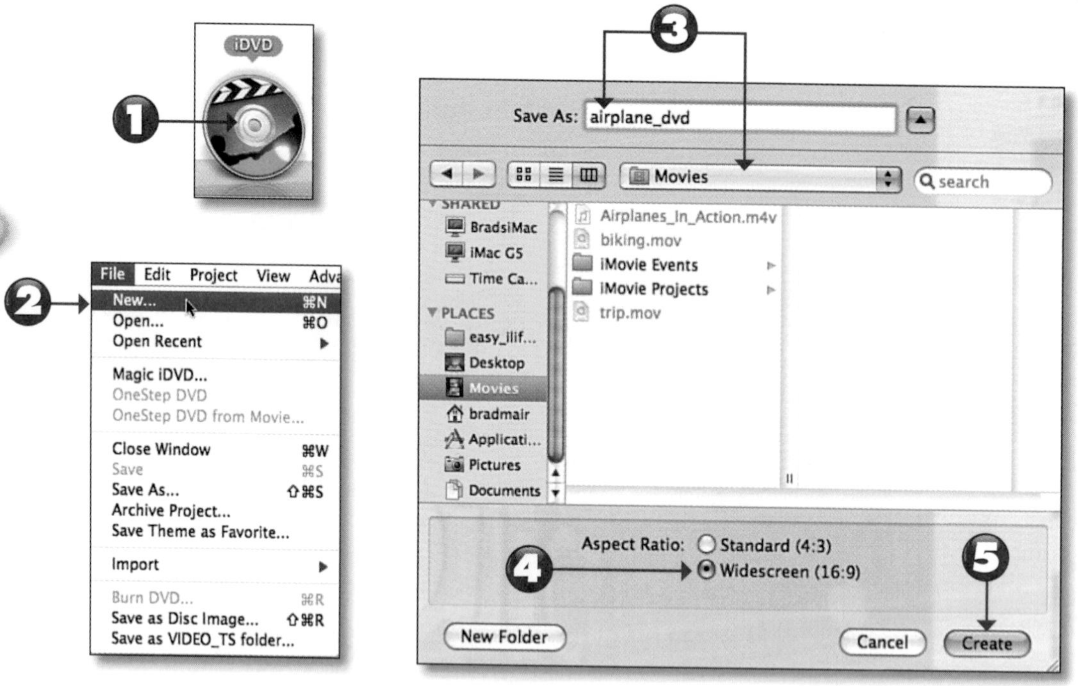

1. Click the **iDVD** icon on the Dock.
2. If you've used iDVD before, choose **File**, **New**; if you haven't created a project before, click the **Create a New Project** button at the prompt.
3. Name the new project and choose a location in which to save it.
4. Select an aspect ratio for the DVD.
5. Click **Create**.

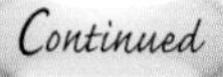

NOTE

Creating iDVD Projects from iMovie or iPhoto You can send content, such as a movie, to iDVD from another iLife application. ■

6 Choose the set of themes you want to browse.

7 Browse the available themes.

8 Click the expansion triangle next to a theme to collapse or expand it so that you see the styles of submenus for that theme.

9 Click the theme you want to use for the DVD.

End

NOTE

No SuperDrive? If you open iDVD on a Mac without an internal SuperDrive, you see a warning that you can work on a project but won't be able to burn it until you have access to a compatible drive. ■

NOTE

Menus By default, some themes include different designs for various menus, including the main menu, chapter menus, and extras menus. When you select a theme, new menus you add automatically get their designs from the theme you applied to the project. ■

ADDING MOVIES TO A DVD PROJECT

You can add movies, such as those you've created with iMovie, to a DVD by adding them to a project. You can add a movie to the main menu or you can create additional menus and add movies to those. When you add a movie to a menu, a button is created for that movie. When a viewer clicks the button, the movie plays.

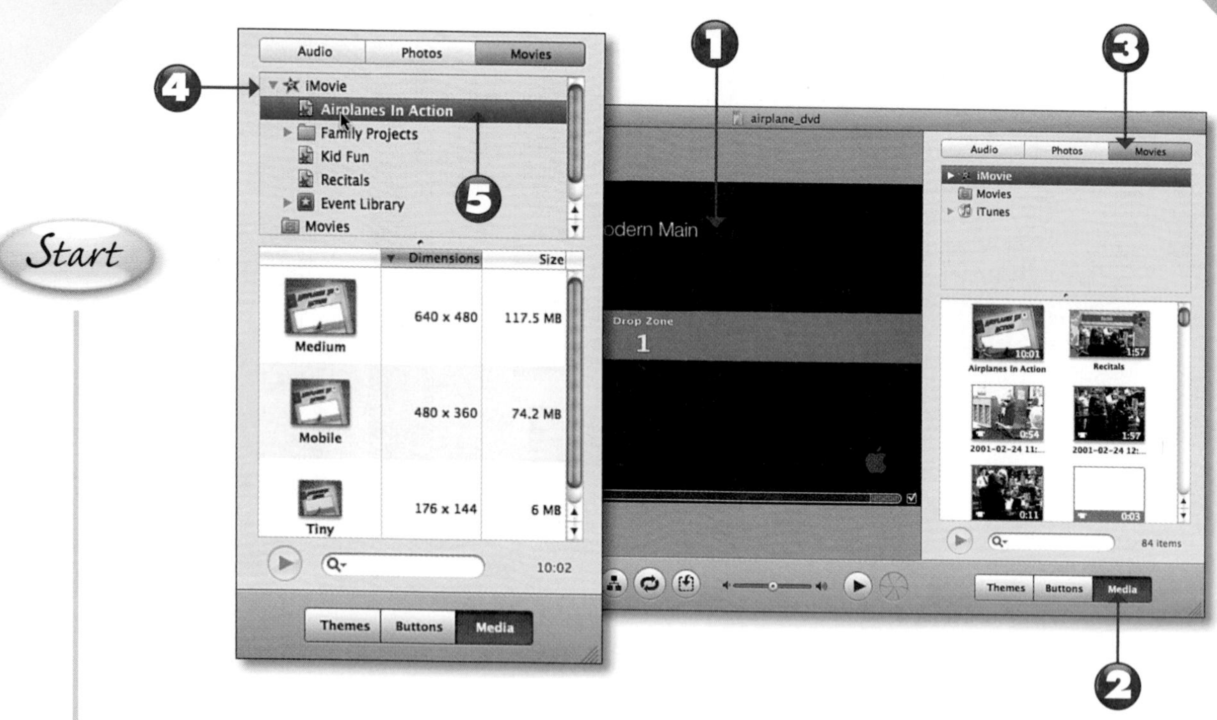

Start

1. View the menu on which you want to place a movie; if you haven't added any menus to the project, you view the main menu.
2. Click **Media**.
3. Click **Movies**.
4. Select and expand the source of movies containing the movie you want to add to the menu.
5. Select the movie you want to add to the menu.

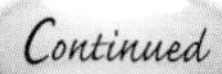
Continued

NOTE

Movie Sources On the Movies pane of the Media Browser, you see various sources of content, such as iMovie and iTunes. ■

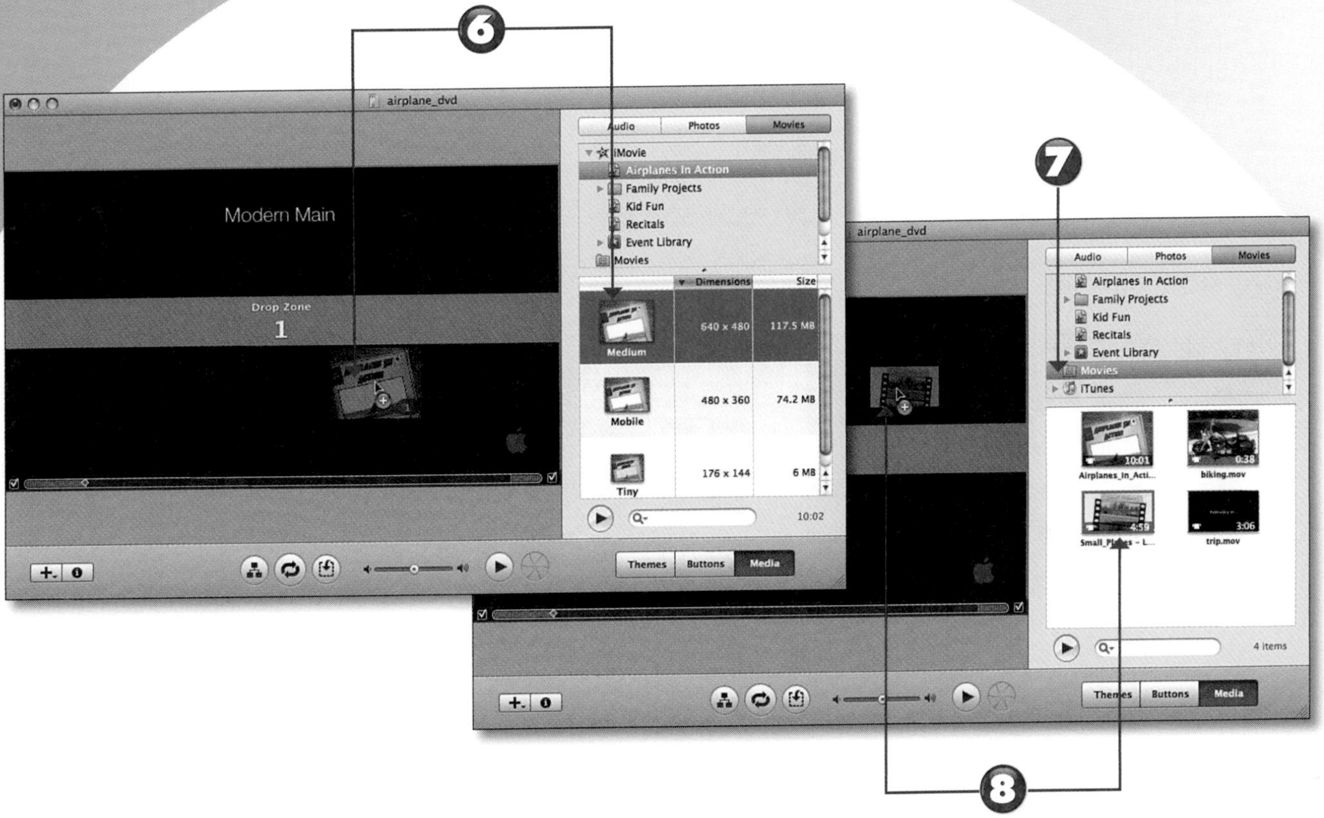

6 Drag the size of the movie you want to add from the Media Browser onto the menu. When you release the mouse button, a button for the movie is created according to the theme you selected.

7 Select another source of movies.

8 Drag a movie from the source onto the menu. Repeat steps 7 and 8 until you've added all the movies to the menu that you want to include there.

End

TIP

Size Usually Doesn't Matter Unlike other devices where memory can become an issue (and so you need to consider size), when you create a DVD, you should always choose the largest size available so that you get the best quality. ■

NOTE

Button Names By default, the name of a movie's button is the name of the movie in the source from which it came. As you learn in a later task, you can rename buttons to have any label you'd like. You can also format their text and other options. ■

ADDING SLIDESHOWS TO A DVD PROJECT

You can create slideshows on a DVD from images on your computer. The most common case is to create a slideshow based on images in your iPhoto library. You can choose the images you want to include in a slideshow and then configure how it plays on the DVD.

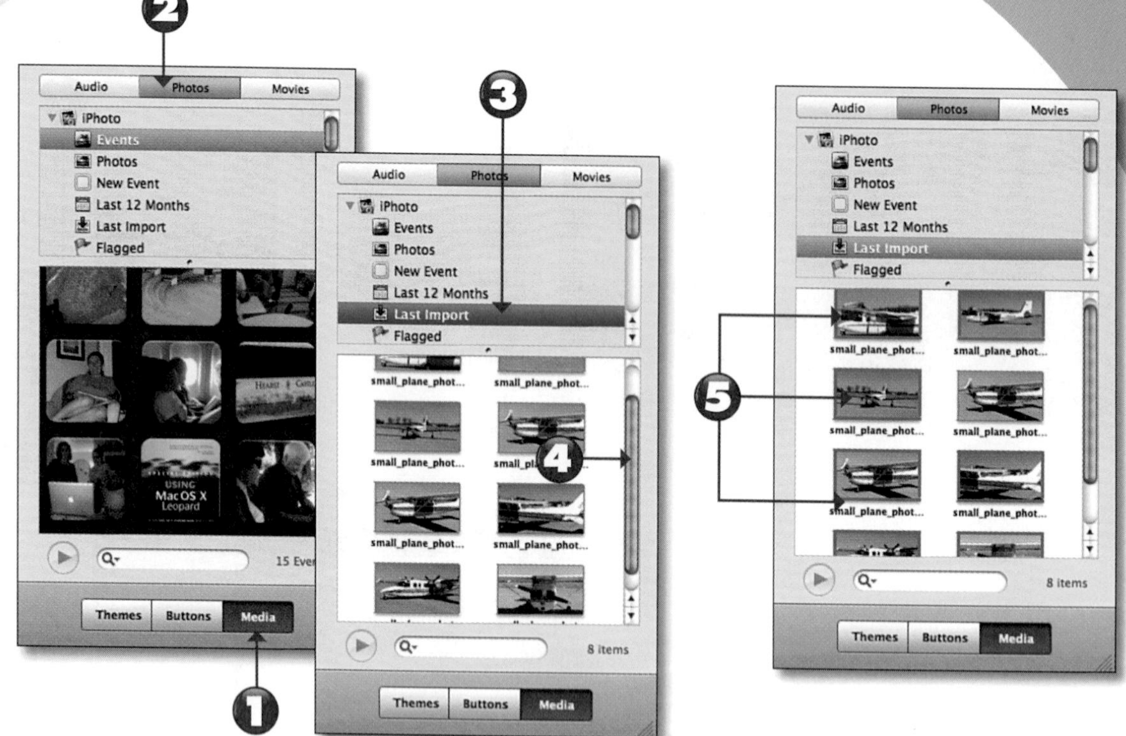

Start

1. Click **Media**.
2. Click **Photos**.
3. Select the source of photos you want to include in a slideshow.
4. Browse the selected source.
5. Select the photos you want to include in the slideshow.

Continued

TIP

Adding iPhoto Slideshows to a Project You can create slideshow projects in iPhoto that are more sophisticated than those you create in iDVD (see Chapter 6). To add a slideshow to a DVD, in iDVD open the menu to which you want to add the slideshow. In iPhoto, select the slideshow, and choose **Share**, **Send to iDVD**. ■

6 Drag the photos onto the DVD menu.

7 Double-click the **My Slideshow** button.

8 Drag the photos around the window to set the order in which they appear, starting with the upper-left corner and moving right.

9 Use the Slide Duration and Transition pop-up menus to set the time each slide appears onscreen and the transition effect between slides.

10 Click **Audio** and drag music or other sounds into the slideshow window to have those sounds play with the slideshow.

End

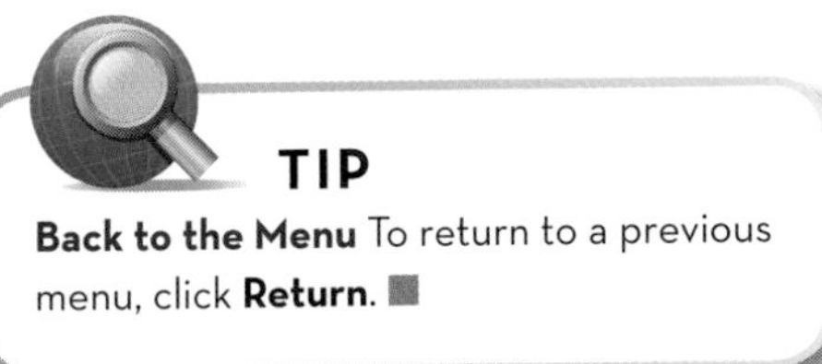

TIP

Back to the Menu To return to a previous menu, click **Return**.

NOTE

Settings Click the **Settings** button to access additional controls for a slideshow.

DESIGNING MENUS

Menus are a major part of any DVD project. In addition to organizing the content on a DVD, they provide visual and audio interest to a DVD. You can design many aspects of a menu. In this section, you learn how to configure some of the more basic elements of a menu, such as its title and buttons. In subsequent sections, you learn how to apply motion and other effects.

1. To apply a different theme to a menu, browse the available themes and click the theme you want to apply.
2. To change a menu's name, double-click it.
3. Type the new name of the menu.
4. Use the Font, Typeface, and Size pop-up menus to format the title; click outside the title when you're done.
5. Click a button for content on the menu, pause, and click again.

Continued

NOTE

Themes Themes include designs for titles, buttons, and other elements, but you can override any of these options with your own choices. ■

TIP

Click Too Fast If you click a button a second time so that a double-click is registered, you play any content linked to that button instead of making its name editable. ■

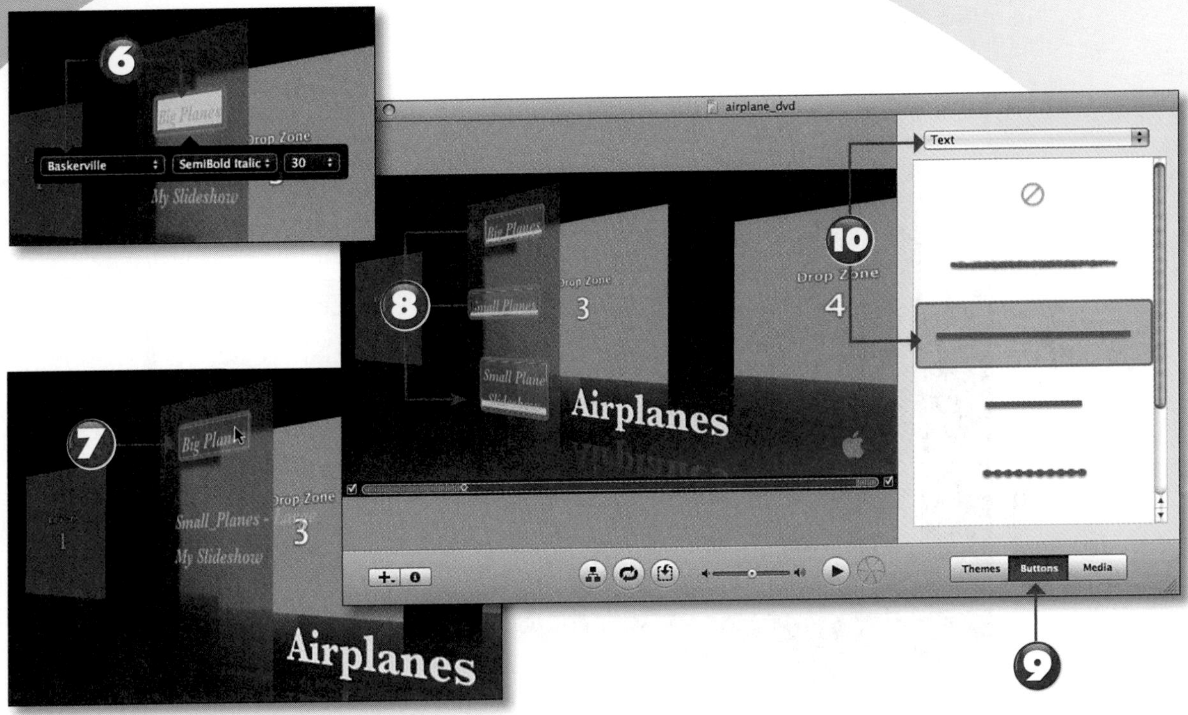

6 Type a name for the button and format it just like the menu's title.

7 Click outside the button and then click it again; then drag the button to its menu location.

8 Select buttons you want to format.

9 Click **Buttons**.

10 Choose a button type on the menu and select a format option.

End

NOTE

Button Styles If you open the pop-up menu at the top of the Buttons pane, you see many different types of buttons you can use. Select a type to see the options you have for that type. ■

CONFIGURING DROP ZONES ON A MENU

Drop zones are areas on a menu where you place images, slideshows, or movies that appear within the zone. Many menus feature drop zones with motion, which means they move around the screen to make them even more interesting. Unlike buttons, drop zones aren't linked to content; they are only for the appearance of the menus on which they are placed.

Start

1. Click the **Edit Drop Zone** button.
2. Click the drop zone you want to configure.
3. Click **Media**.
4. To add a photo to the drop zone, click **Photos**.
5. Find and drag the photo you want to add from the browser and drop it onto the drop zone.

Continued

NOTE

Number of Drop Zones Each theme has a specific number of drop zones for various menu types. Make sure you add content to each of them. ■

TIP

Motion Menus Many themes have dynamic menus where drop zones move around the screen. You can't edit these while motion is on. To turn motion off, click the Start/Stop Motion button. ■

6. Hold the ⌘ key down and drag an image within a drop zone to set the part of the image that appears.
7. Select the next drop zone you want to configure.
8. To add a movie to the drop zone, click **Movies**.
9. Find and drag a movie onto the drop zone.
10. Select the movie in the preview section at the top of the window and use the sliders to determine when the movie starts and ends.

End

CONFIGURING MENUS

You can place images, video, or audio in a menu's background so that content appears or plays while the menu appears on the screen. You can also configure the menu's motion effects.

Start

1. Click the **Inspector** button.

2. To place an image or movie as the menu's background, drag it from the Media Browser onto the center image well at the top of the Inspector.

3. If the menu has motion and you don't want the intro motion to play, uncheck the **Intro** check box.

4. If the menu has motion and you don't want the exit motion to play, uncheck the **Outro** check box.

5. Drag the **Loop Duration** slider to set the amount of time the menu's motion loop plays.

Continued

TIP

Removing Background To remove a background image or movie, drag it out of the center image well at the top of the Inspector. ■

TIP

No Free Advertising Please If you don't want the Apple logo to appear on menus, open the General pane of the iDVD Preferences dialog box and uncheck the **Show Apple Logo Watermark** check box. ■

6. To add an audio background to the menu, click **Audio**.

7. Drag the audio you want to use from the browser onto the Inspector's Audio well.

8. Set the relative volume level for the background audio using the **Menu Volume** slider.

9. Use the Buttons radio buttons and Highlight menu to determine whether buttons can be freely positioned on the screen and to set the color of highlighted buttons.

10. To hide drop zones, uncheck the **Show Drop Zones and Related Graphics** check box.

End

TIP

Setting Menu Motion You can also turn off the Intro or Outro motion effects by unchecking the check boxes located at the left and right end of the scrubber bar. ■

NOTE

Button Inspector If you select one or more buttons while the Inspector is open, it becomes the Button Inspector that you can use to configure the buttons. ■

ADDING MENUS TO A DVD

You can add more menus to a DVD project to expand its contents. For example, you might want to organize movies and slideshows on the disc by topics or by timeframe. You can create a menu for each category and then add content to, design, and configure each menu.

1. Click the **Add** pop-up menu.
2. Choose **Add Submenu**.
3. Add and format a title for the menu's button.
4. Click off the button, and then double-click it.
5. Add content to, design, and configure the menu.

End

TIP

Add Button You can use the Add pop-up menu to add empty placeholders for movies or slideshows. Choose **Add Movie** or **Add Slideshow** to create an empty button for each. ■

TIP

Change Theme and Type To change the theme and type of any menu, open the Themes pane of the browser and click the theme and type you want to use. ■

MAPPING A DVD

As you add menus to a disc, you should check its flow to make sure the viewer can navigate around the disc as you intend and that there aren't navigation problems, such as can happen if you delete a menu accidentally.

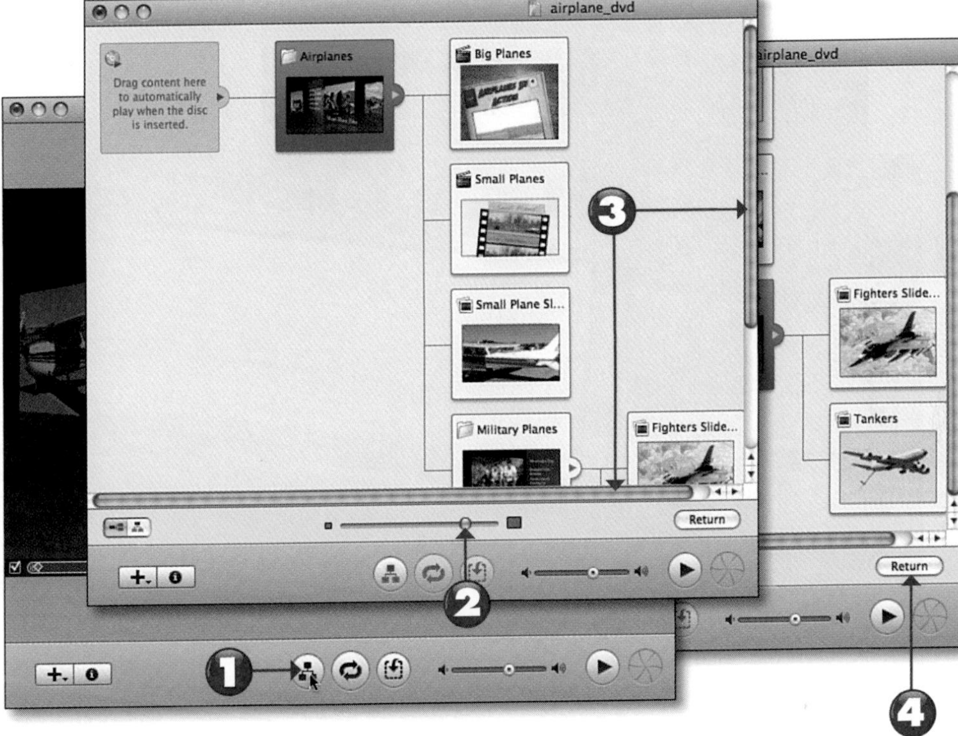

Start

1. Click the **DVD Map** button.
2. Drag the slider to the left to see more of the DVD map.
3. Use the scrollbars to browse the map.
4. To return to the menu view, click **Return**.

End

NOTE

Errors If there are errors on the disc, such as an orphaned menu, iDVD flags those problems to warn you about them. Fix them before you burn the disc. ■

TIP

Autoplay If you want a movie or slideshow to play automatically when the DVD is inserted into a player, drag that content to the first box on the DVD map. ■

PREVIEWING A DVD

You can preview a DVD to see how it will work once it is burned. It's a good idea to do this before you burn a disc so that you don't waste time and discs burning a disc that has mistakes on it. When you preview a DVD, you use the onscreen remote to control it.

Start

1. Click the **Play** button.
2. Click buttons on the DVD to view its content and to move to submenus.
3. Use the onscreen remote to control playback of movies and slideshows.
4. When you are done previewing, click **Exit**.

End

NOTE

No Coasters Please Make sure you spend an appropriate amount of time checking a DVD project by previewing it before you burn it to a disc. When you use a DVD-R disc, you can burn it only once. If the resulting DVD has mistakes, the disc becomes no more than a coaster. More significant is the time it takes to burn a disc, which is also wasted if the project has problems when you burn it. ■

BURNING A DVD

Burning a DVD is somewhat anticlimactic because it is so easy. Once you start the process, you don't need to do anything while it burns, which is good because burning a disc can take a long time. Start the burn process and go about your business while it is burning. Eventually, it will be done, and you can use the resulting disc.

Start

1. Click the **Burn** button.
2. Insert a blank disc.
3. Periodically check in on the burn process; an estimate of the remaining time displays at the bottom of the progress window. When the process is done, remove the disc.

End

NOTE

Erasable Discs If you insert an erasable disc that has content on it, iDVD will prompt you about erasing the content on the disc before the burn process begins. ■

TIP

Minimize Other Activity For best results in the shortest time, minimize other activities on the Mac while the disc is burning. Any processor or disk activity can slow the burn process. Ideally, you will close all other applications while iDVD is burning a disc. ■

CREATING A SIMPLE SOUNDTRACK IN GARAGEBAND

With GarageBand, you can make your own music and soundtracks that can include multiple instruments, narration, special effects, and other audio elements. Even better, if you have limited musical talent or knowledge, you can still be creative with GarageBand because it can assist you in creating music.

You can record music that you play with real instruments that are connected to your Mac, and you can use GarageBand's soft instruments to play and record music based on many different types and styles.

You can mix the tracks until you achieve just the sound you are looking for. You can then use those tracks in your iLife projects, or even just listen to them.

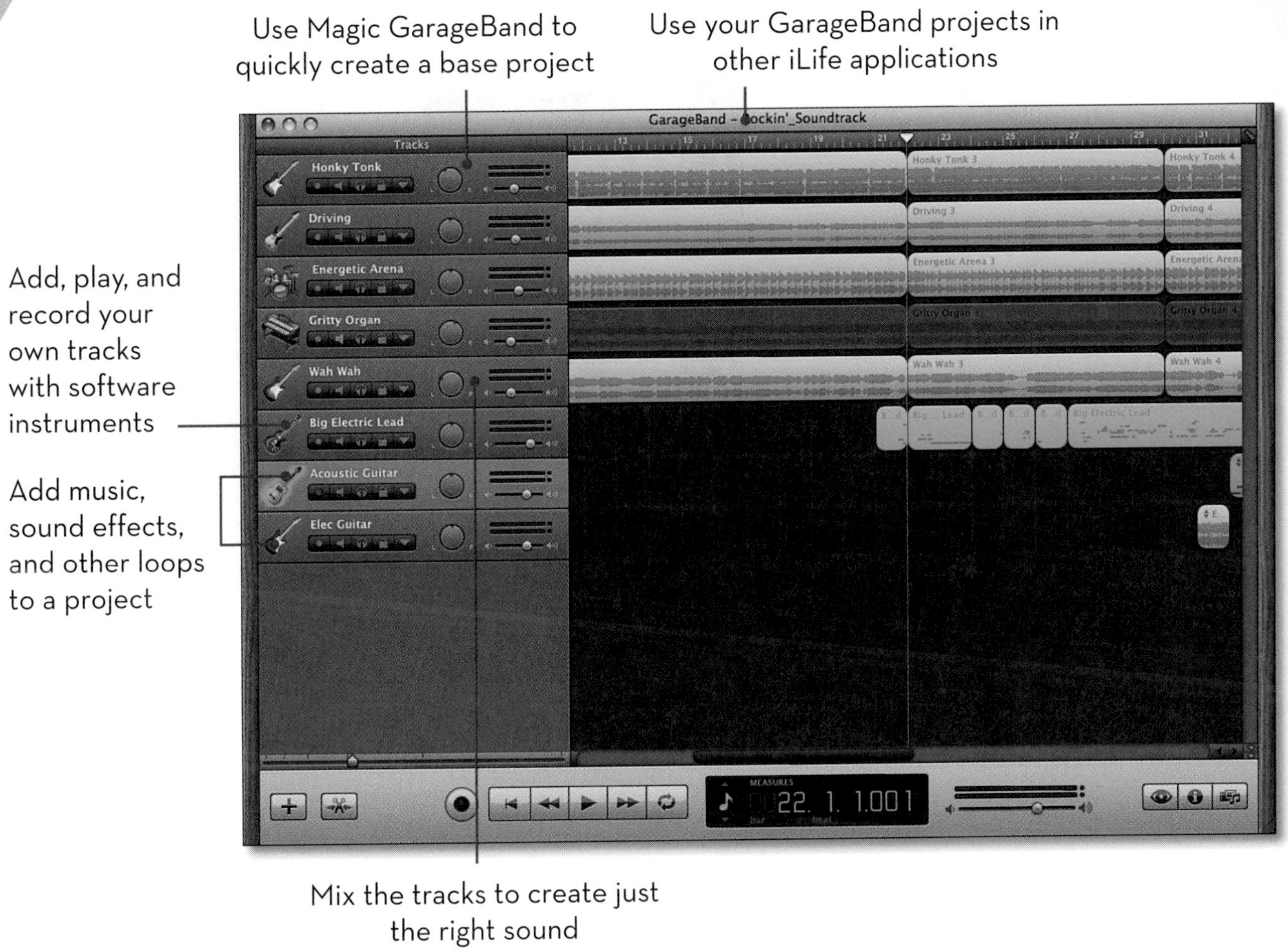
Use Magic GarageBand to quickly create a base project
Use your GarageBand projects in other iLife applications
Add, play, and record your own tracks with software instruments
Add music, sound effects, and other loops to a project
Mix the tracks to create just the right sound
GarageBand – Rockin'_Soundtrack
Tracks
Honky Tonk
Driving
Energetic Arena
Gritty Organ
Wah Wah
Big Electric Lead
Acoustic Guitar
Elec Guitar
Honky Tonk 3
Honky Tonk 4
Driving 3
Driving 4
Energetic Arena 3
Gritty Organ 3
Gritty Organ 4
Wah Wah 3
Wah Wah 4
Big Electric Lead
MEASURES
22. 1. 1.001

CREATING A NEW PROJECT WITH MAGIC GARAGEBAND

Magic GarageBand creates a complete song that includes multiple instruments played according to the musical genre you select. You can then tweak the song to customize it for your purposes, such as to create a soundtrack for one of your projects. Magic GarageBand is a great time saver, but it is especially useful if you don't play an instrument or don't have much musical knowledge.

Start

1. Launch **GarageBand**.
2. Click **Magic GarageBand**.
3. Click the music genre you want to use, such as Rock.
4. Click **Choose**.
5. Click the **Play** button to hear the song GarageBand created.

Continued

NOTE

Don't Believe in Magic? If you don't want an assist from Magic GarageBand, you can click **New Project** and build a project from scratch. ■

TIP

Preview a Genre When you point to the bottom of a genre's box, the Preview tool appears. Click the **Play** button to hear a sample of that genre; click the **Stop** button to stop the preview. ■

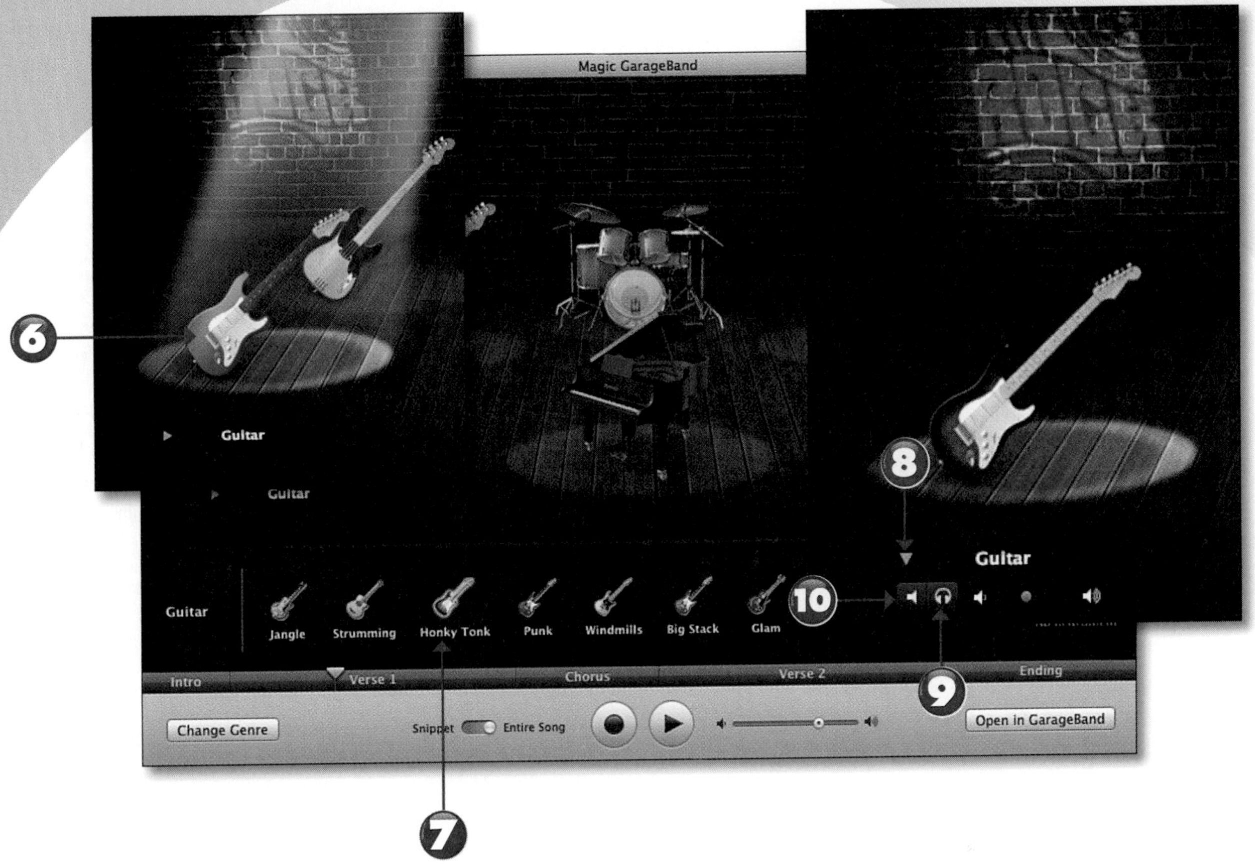

6. Select an instrument that you want to change.

7. Choose a new style for the instrument and play the song to hear it with the new instrument.

8. Expand the instrument's toolbar.

9. To hear only the instrument, click the **Headphones** button; click the **Headphones** button to hear all the instruments again.

10. To mute the instrument so that it isn't included in the song, click the **Mute** button.

Continued

NOTE

Spotlight When an instrument is included in the song, its spotlight shines on it; the spotlight is the brightest on the instrument you have selected. When you mute an instrument, it goes dark. ■

TIP

Change Genre If you want to restyle the song into a different genre, click the **Change Genre** button. ■

11 To set its relative volume, drag the slider to the left to make the instrument quieter or to the right to make it louder.

12 Select another instrument.

13 Configure the instrument.

14 Repeat steps 12 and 13 until you've configured all the instruments used in the song.

15 Click **Open in GarageBand**.

End

TIP

Control Music with the Spacebar In any section of GarageBand, you can control music playback by pressing the **spacebar**. ■

TIP

Playing a Snippet Songs are divided into parts. You can select part of a song to play by clicking it, such as Verse 1. To return to the entire song, move the switch at the bottom of the window to **Entire Song**. ■

SAVING AND NAMING A PROJECT

After you've created a project, you should save it with a name that you'll recognize when you want to work with it later.

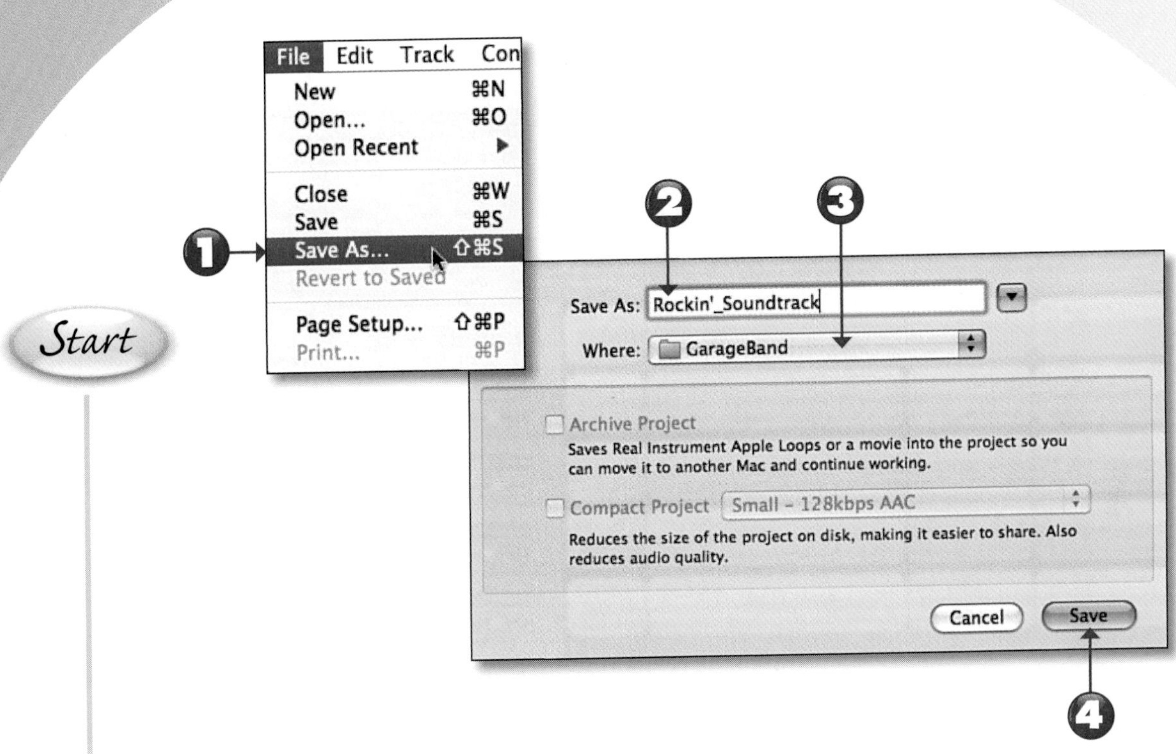

Start

1. Choose **File**, **Save As**.
2. Name the project.
3. Choose a save location.
4. Click **Save**.

End

NOTE

GarageBand Folder By default, GarageBand projects are stored within the GarageBand folder within your Music folder in your Home folder. This is a good location for your Garage-Band projects; you'll always know where they are. However, you can save them anywhere you'd like. ■

SELECTING A TRACK'S INSTRUMENT

When you are working in the GarageBand window, you can change the instrument associated with a track. If you used Magic GarageBand to create a project, one track is for your instrument, meaning that you can use that track to play and record to add your own music to the song that Magic GarageBand created.

Start

1. Double-click the track whose instrument you want to change (the bottom track if you used Magic GarageBand to create the song).
2. Click the category you want to use for the instrument.
3. Click the instrument you want to use for the track.
4. Choose **Track**, **Hide Track Info** to close that pane.

End

NOTE

Change Existing Instruments You can use the same steps to change any of the instruments that Magic GarageBand included in the song. ■

TIP

Getting Track Info You can also open or close the Track Info pane by selecting a track and pressing **⌘-I**. ■

PLAYING AN INSTRUMENT WITH THE KEYBOARD

You can play your instrument using an onscreen keyboard on which you click the keys you want to play. You can also record what you play to add that music to a project. The keyboard displays four octaves of keys, and you can select the set of octaves you want to display and play.

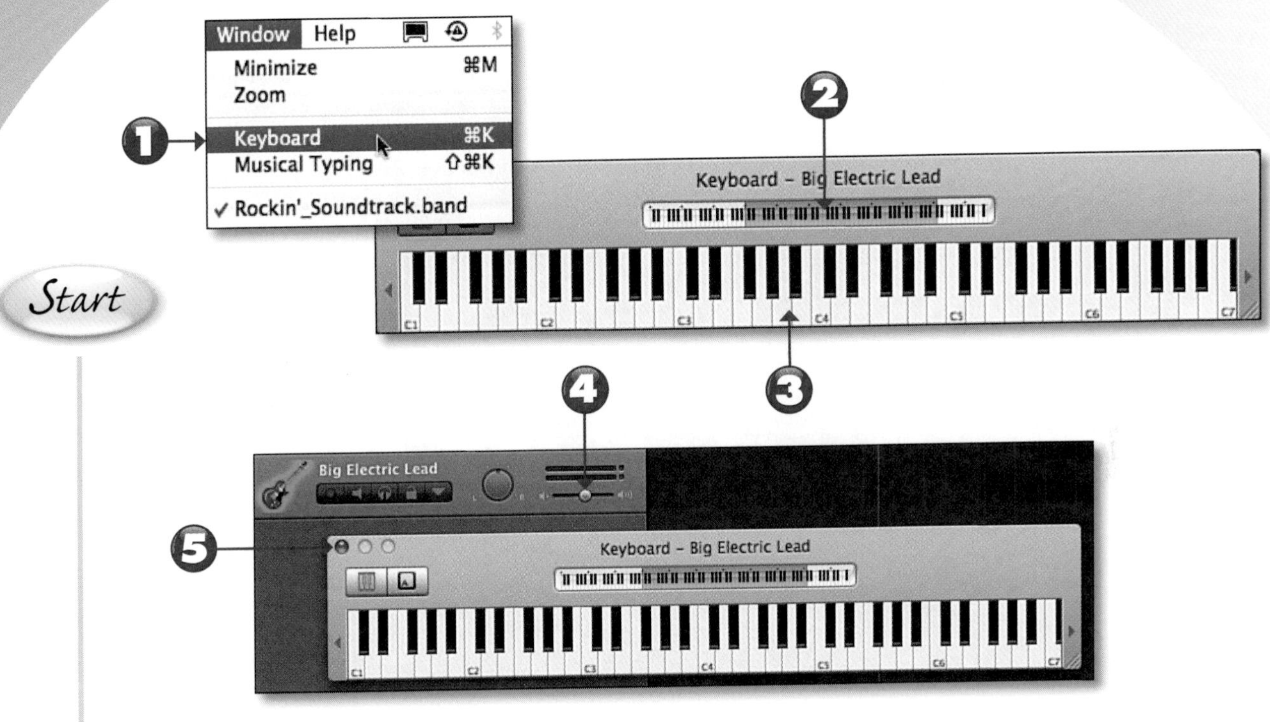

1. Select the bottom track and choose **Window**, **Keyboard**.
2. Click the octave range you want to display on the keyboard.
3. Click the keys you want to play.
4. Drag the instrument's **Volume** slider to the left to make it quieter or to the right to make it louder.
5. When you're done playing, close the keyboard.

End

NOTE

Taking Lessons You can take guitar or keyboard lessons in GarageBand. To get started, choose **File**, **New**. Then click **Learn to Play**. ■

TIP

Displaying and Playing More You can make the keyboard larger to display more keys by dragging its resize handle located in the lower-right corner of the Keyboard window. ■

PLAYING AN INSTRUMENT WITH MUSICAL TYPING

You can play your instrument by pressing keys on your Mac's keyboard. You can select an octave range to play in. And, you can choose various notes and sounds that are activated by specific keys. You can then play music or sounds by pressing those keys.

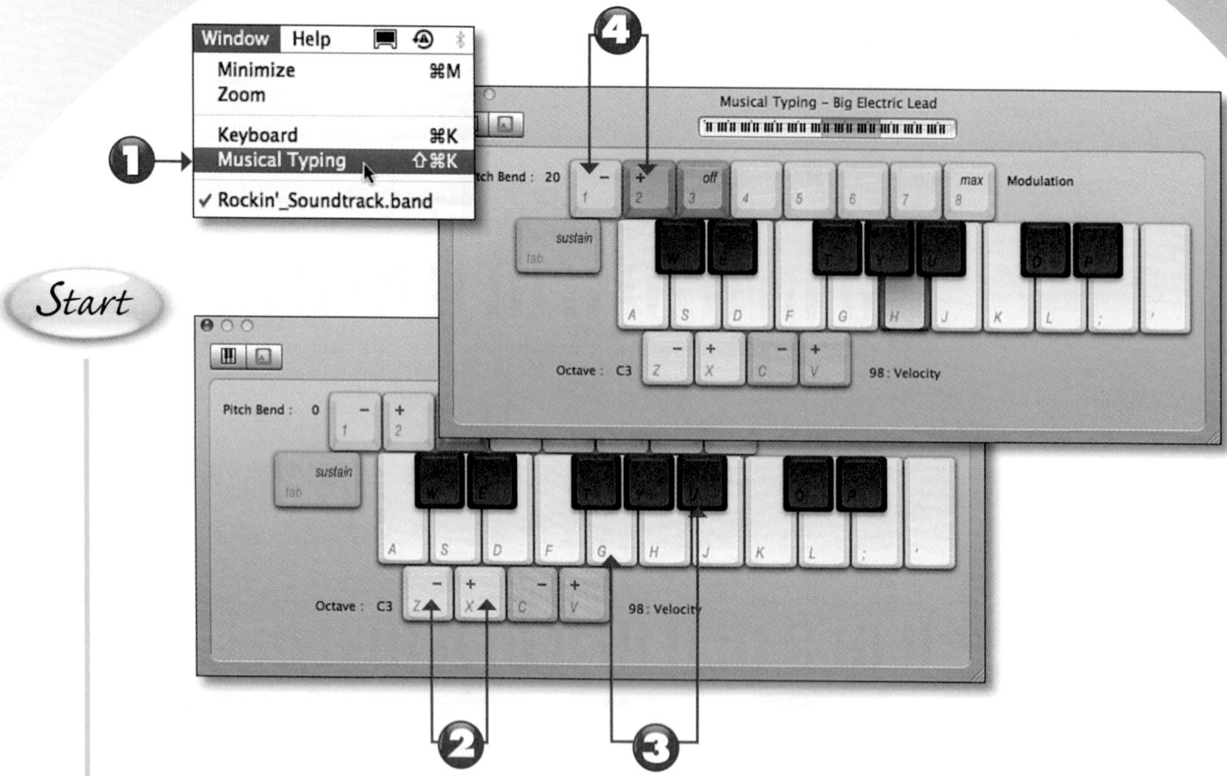

Start

1. Select the bottom track and choose **Window**, **Musical Typing**.
2. Press the **Z** or **X** key to set the range of octaves you want to display.
3. Press the keys on the Mac's keyboard corresponding to the notes you want to play on the instrument.
4. As you are pressing a note key, press **1** to decrease the pitch bend or **2** to increase it.

Continued

NOTE

Pitch Bend Pitch bend simulates the effect of dragging a guitar string up or down on the neck while you play that string. The Pitch Bend keys bend the pitch as long as you hold them down. ■

NOTE

Sustain As you hold a key down, the note plays and starts to fade. If you hold the key down long enough, the note stops. Sustain "stretches" the duration of the note. ■

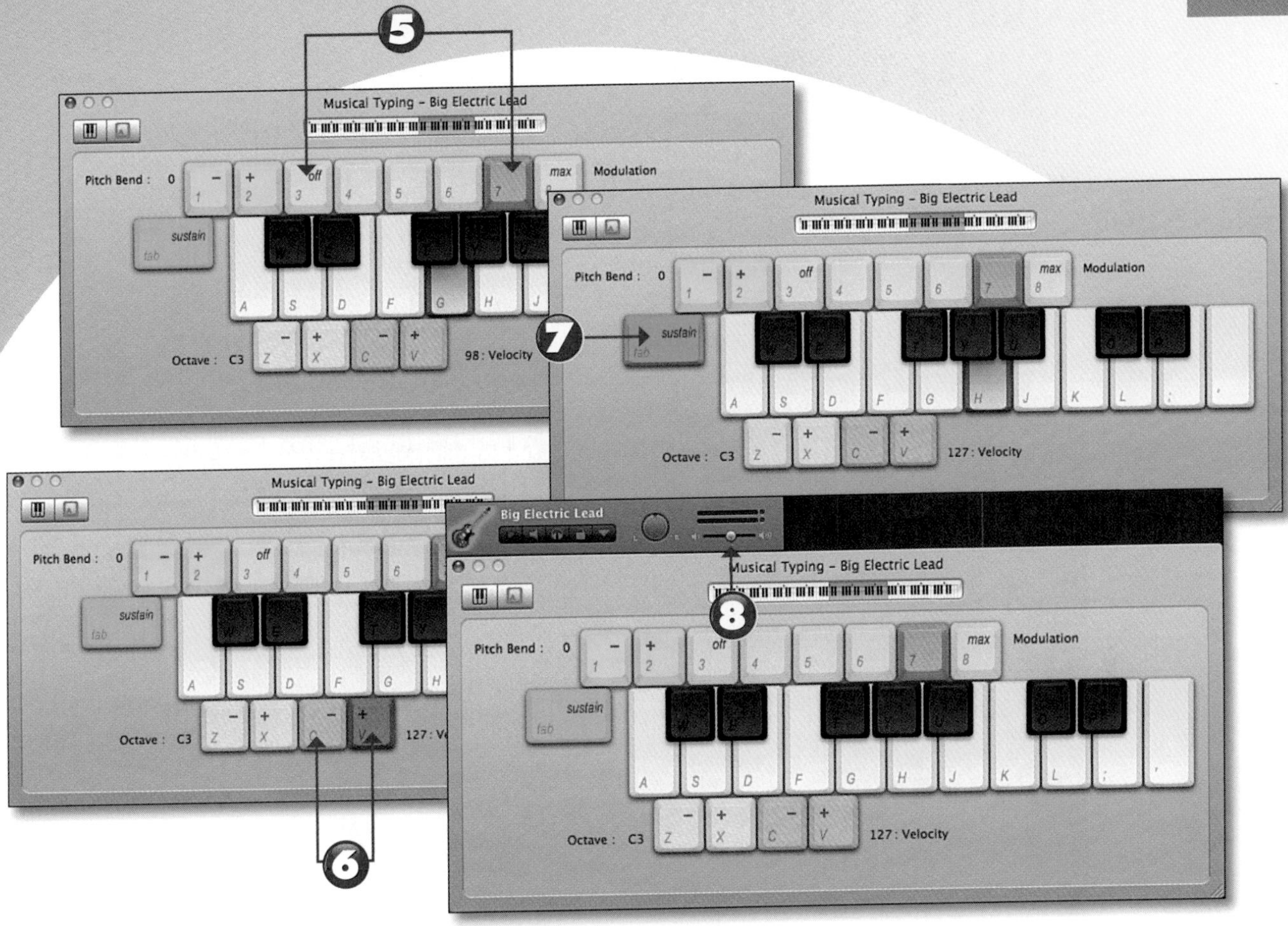

5. Press **3** to turn off modulation or **4** through **8** to set the modulation level.

6. Press **V** to increase the velocity or **C** to decrease it. Each time you press on these keys, the velocity changes by increments of five.

7. Press **Tab** to sustain a note.

8. Drag the instrument's **Volume** slider to the left to make it quieter or to the right to make it louder. When you're done playing, close the Musical Typing window.

End

NOTE

Modulation Modulation changes the sound as you move from one note to another. Higher modulation blends the transition between the notes a bit more. Lower or no modulation makes the differences between the notes sharper. ■

NOTE

Velocity Higher velocity makes notes play "harder." It's difficult to describe, so the best way to understand it is to play an instrument with the velocity set to maximum and then play it with the velocity set to zero. ■

RECORDING A MUSIC TRACK WHILE YOU PLAY AN INSTRUMENT

You can play your instrument while the other tracks in the project play to add a custom track to the project's music. You can play the instrument with either the keyboard or with musical typing. You can play along with all the other instruments, just some of them, or none of them. After you record a track, it becomes part of the project.

1. Click the **Play** button to hear the project until you hear the part you want to add music.
2. Click the **Play** button again to stop playback.
3. Drag the playhead to a point just before where you want to start recording your instrument.
4. Make sure your instrument's track is selected and enabled for recording; the Enabled button should be red.
5. Click the **Mute** button for any instruments you don't want to hear while you record.

Continued

NOTE

Muted Tracks When an instrument is muted, its track in the GarageBand window is darkened; unmuted tracks appear in blue. ■

TIP

Record in Segments You can use these steps to record a track in segments. You don't have to record the whole track in one session. ■

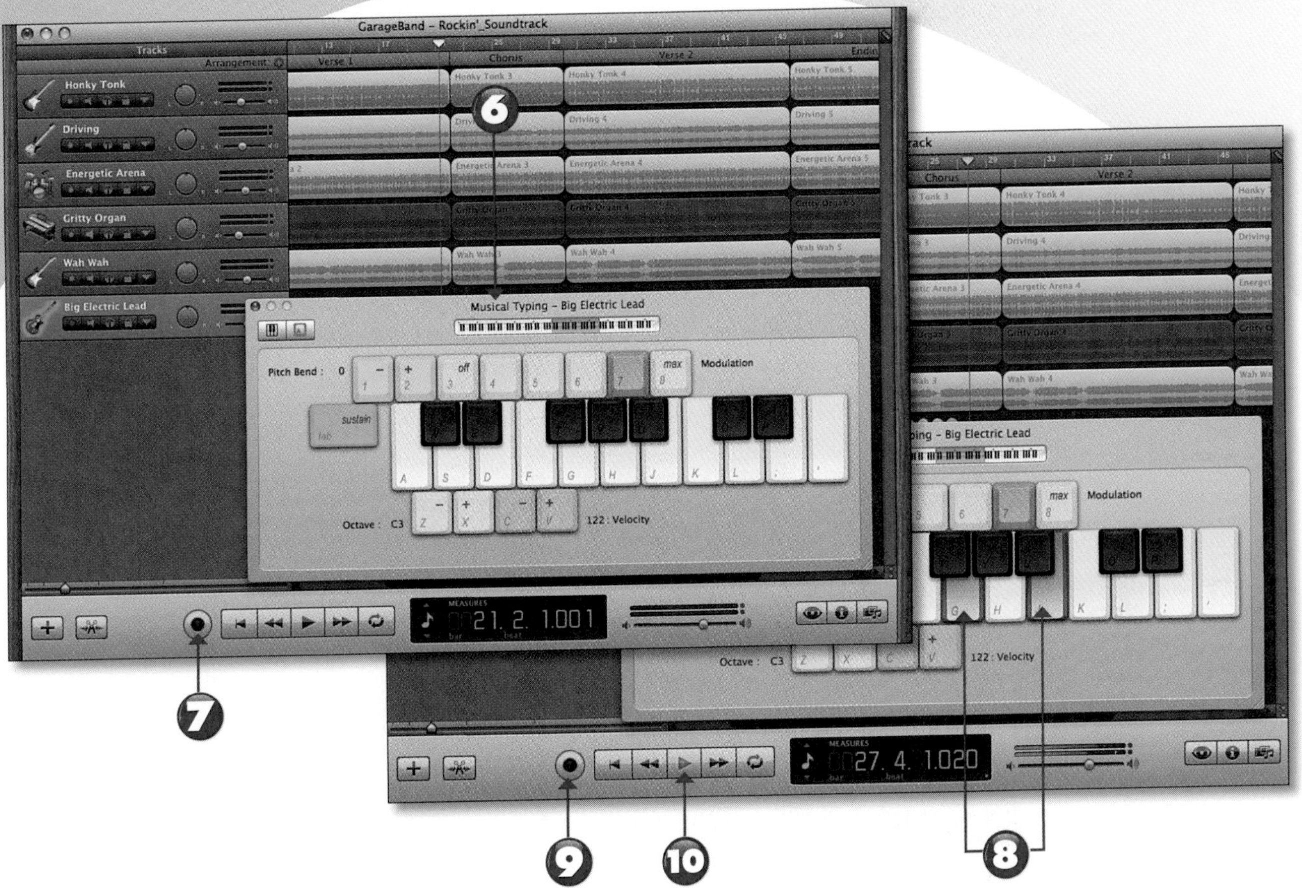

6. Open the Keyboard or Musical Typing window.

7. Click the **Record** button.

8. Start playing the instrument.

9. When you're done recording, click the **Record** button again.

10. Click the **Play** button to stop music playback.

End

NOTE

Laying Down a Track Before you record your instrument, its track is empty. After you record, you see the music you've recorded in a green track. ■

NOTE

Real Instruments In this task GarageBand simulates the sounds of the various instruments. You can also connect real instruments to your Mac and record their output. ■

ADDING A LOOP TO A PROJECT

Loops are relatively short segments of music you can add to your projects. There are a large variety of loops and you can add as many as you want to one project.

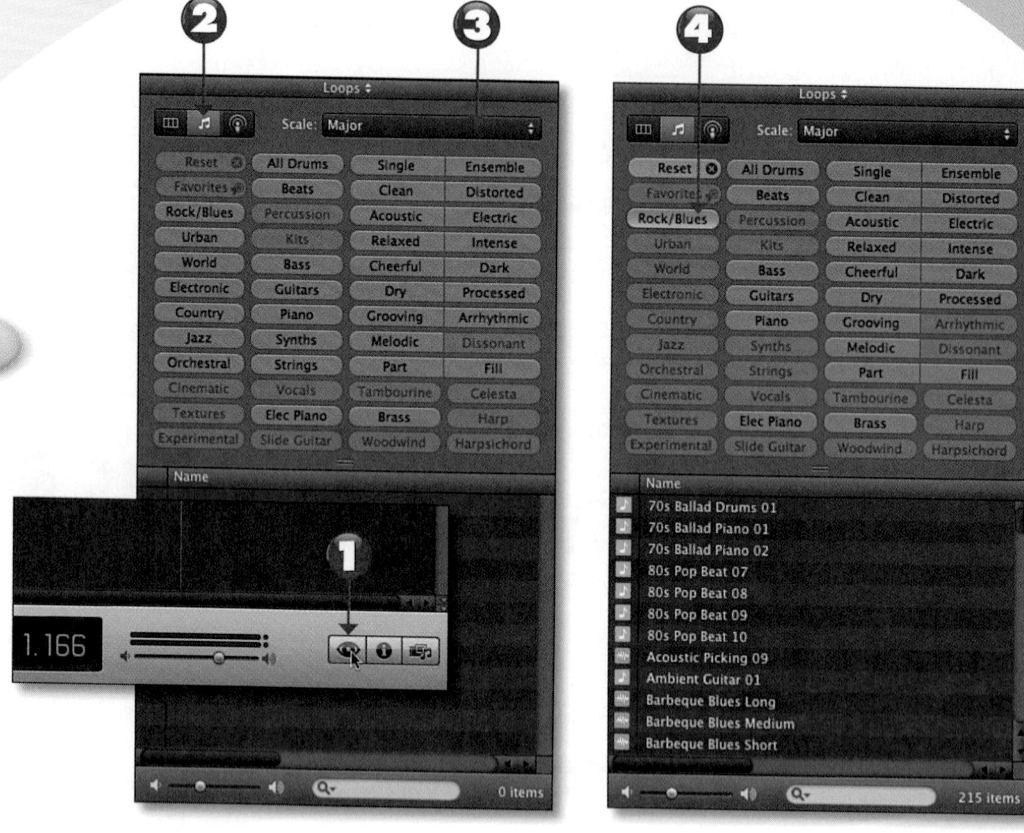

Start

1. Click the **Loop Browser** button.

2. Click the **Musical Button view** button.

3. Use the Scale pop-up menu to limit the available loops to the appropriate scale. (For example, choose **Major** to limit loops to the major scale.)

4. Click the button for the genre you want to use.

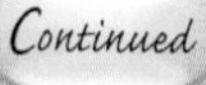
Continued

TIP

Musical Browser The first button at the top of the Loop Browser is the Music Browser button. Use this option to browse for loops by various categories. ■

TIP

Podcast Sounds If you click the **Podcast Sounds** button (the third one from the left at the top of the Loops Browser), you can choose from a variety of sound loops, including jingles and sound effects. You can work with these just as you work with music loops. ■

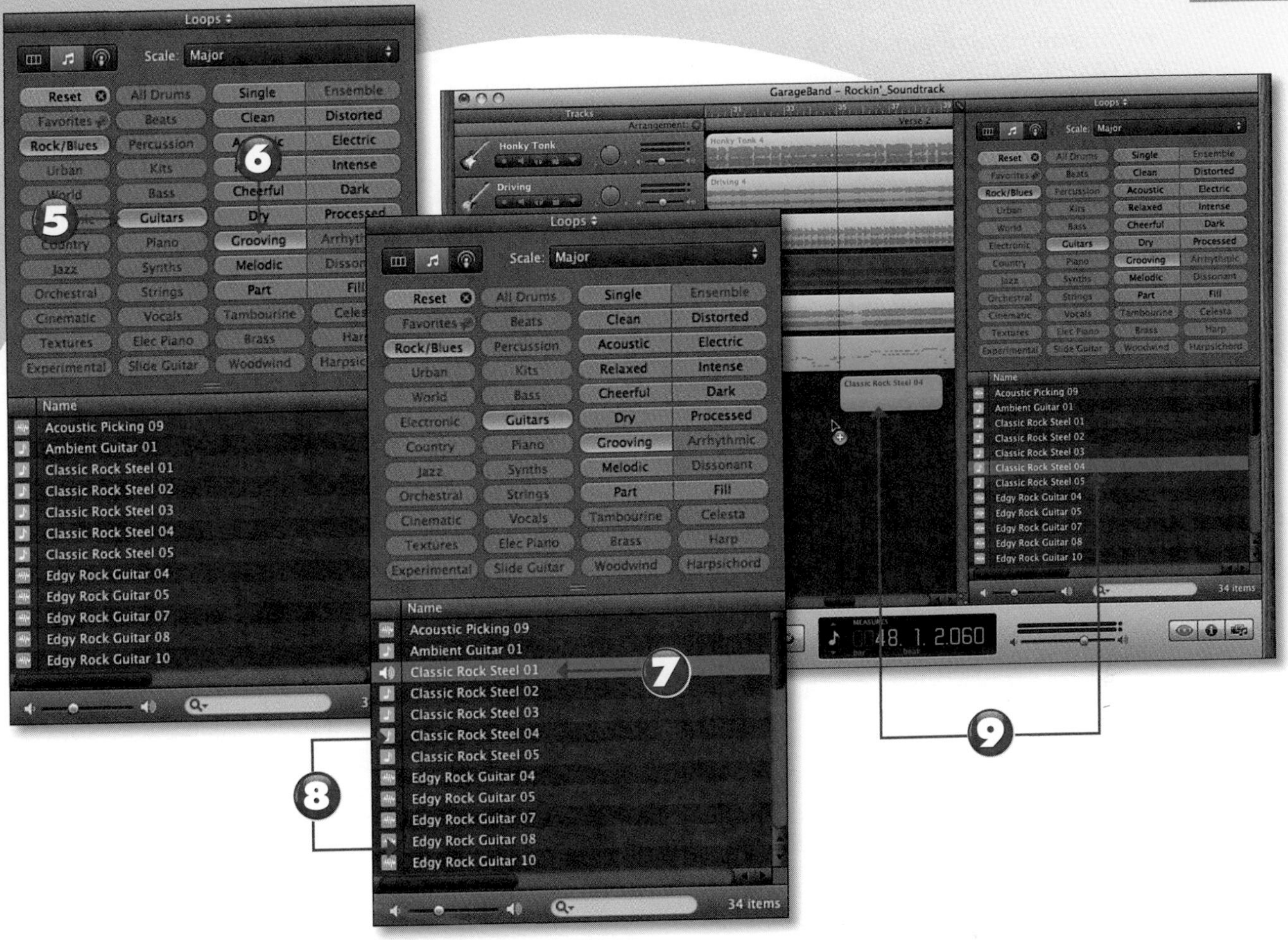

5. Click an instrument button to focus on loops featuring that instrument.

6. Click a mood or type button to focus on loops in the categories in which you are interested.

7. Double-click a loop to hear it; click it once to stop it.

8. Continue previewing loops until you find one you want to use.

9. Drag the loop onto the project where you want it to play.

TIP

Adding Multiple Loops You can add multiple versions of the same loop or other kinds of loops to the same loop track. ■

NOTE

Blue Versus Green Blue loops are recorded real-instrument loops; green loops are software instruments. You can't mix the two kinds of loops in one loop track. ■

MIXING AUDIO TRACKS

After you've configured and added tracks to a project, you should mix those tracks together so that they form a cohesive sound that meets your artistic vision.

Start

1. Play the project by clicking the **Play** button or pressing the **spacebar**.
2. To increase the relative volume level of a track, drag its **Volume** slider to the right; to decrease it, drag it to the left.
3. To have more of the sound play on the left channel, rotate the **Balance** wheel to the left; to have more play on the right, rotate the wheel to the right.
4. Continue setting the parameters of each track in the project until you are happy with the mixed project.
5. Choose **File**, **Save**.

End

NOTE

Just Getting Started There are a lot more editing changes you can make to tracks than there is room to show you here. For example, select a track and choose **Control**, **Show Track Editor**. ■

TIP

Deleting Tracks To remove a track from a project, select it and choose **Track**, **Delete Track**. ■

USING GARAGEBAND MUSIC IN iLIFE PROJECTS

If you save your GarageBand projects in the GarageBand folder, you can access and use them easily in your other iLife projects through the Media Browser.

Start

1. Open or create a project in an iLife application, such as iPhoto.
2. Open the **Media Browser**.
3. Select the GarageBand source.
4. Select your project.
5. Click **Apply** or drag the GarageBand music into the open project.

End

NOTE

iLife Preview When you quit GarageBand or close a project, you're prompted to save the project with an iLife preview. If you click **Yes**, you can select and play a project in the Media Browser.

Index

A

B

C

D

E

F

G

H

I

J-K-L

M

N-O

P-Q

R

S

T

U-V

W-X-Y-Z

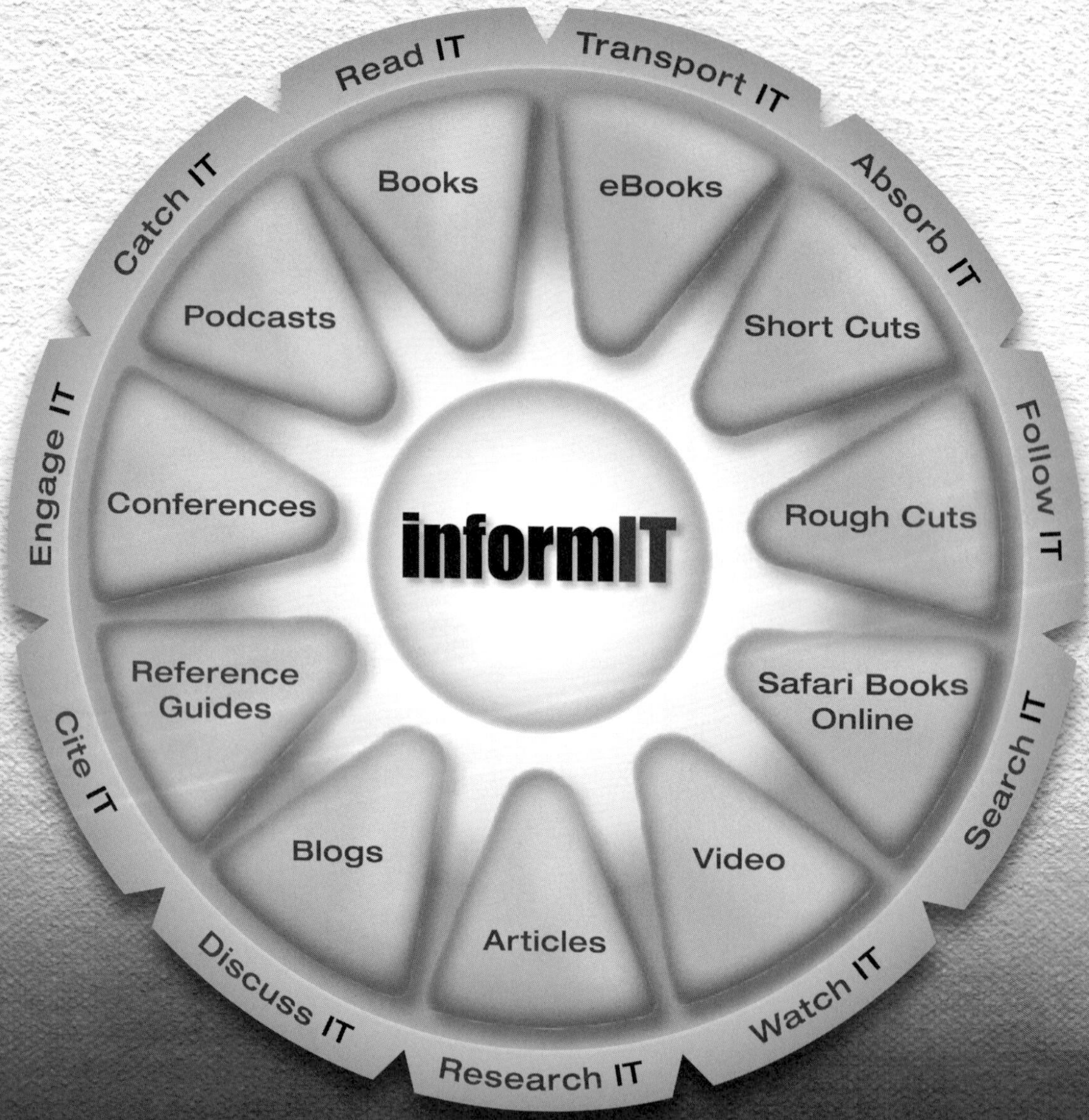